T0314301

THE ECONOMIC INTEGRATION OF EUROPE

The ECONOMIC INTEGRATION of EUROPE

RICHARD POMFRET

Harvard University Press

Cambridge, Massachusetts | London, England   2021

Library of Congress Cataloging-in-Publication Data

Names: Pomfret, Richard W. T., author.
Title: The economic integration of Europe / Richard Pomfret.
Description: Cambridge, Massachusetts : Harvard University Press, 2021. |
Includes bibliographical references and index.
Identifiers: LCCN 2020048892 | ISBN 9780674244139 (hardcover)
Subjects: LCSH: European Union. | Europe—Economic integration. |
European Union countries—Economic conditions. | Europe—
Economic conditions—1945–
Classification: LCC HC241 .P663 2021 | DDC 337.1/42—dc23
LC record available at https://lccn.loc.gov/2020048892

Contents

Preface

THE MODERN STORY of European economic integration started from the postwar rubble of 1945 and passed through two stages. First on a sectoral basis, then economy-wide, a customs union was formed by the most integrationist countries and then expanded to include much of Western Europe by the 1980s. By then, however, removal of tariffs exposed nontariff barriers to trade within the customs union and national currencies made common policies difficult to organize. The response was the Single European Act and monetary integration creating the Single Market and the euro by the end of the 1990s. In the twenty-first century, the European Union (EU) had to address challenges associated with the Single Market including crises of sovereign debt, refugees and Brexit, further deepening of the Single Market and consequences for social inclusion and environmental policy, and widening to include much of Eastern Europe. This book offers an economist's perspective on that road from the nationalism and divisions of World War II to the deep economic and political integration of the EU in the twenty-first century. Although the goal is to understand the EU as it now exists, the perspective is that such understanding is impossible without analysis of the historical evolution and understanding of economic forces.

•   •   •

Since 1945, the nation-states of Europe have pursued a path to integration whose catalyst was political, the quest to avoid another major European war, but whose content has been economic. Starting from the European Coal and Steel Community to the Treaty of Rome and its successor treaties, the process has been toward deeper and wider economic integration (Box 0). This book analyzes that dynamic process, seeking to explain why one step led to another, why some steps were successful and others not, and who gained and who lost at each step.

When Jacob Viner published his seminal work *The Customs Union Issue* in 1950, few people expected discriminatory trading arrangements to be an important feature of the world economy in the second half of the twentieth century. The first article of the General Agreement on Tariffs and Trade (GATT) signed by the major trading nations in 1947 committed contracting parties to treat one another as their most-favored nation—that is, without discrimination. Imperial preferences were grandfathered, but the European empires largely disappeared over the next two decades. Unexpectedly, however, customs unions and free trade areas proliferated between the 1960s and the replacement of the GATT by the World Trade Organization (WTO) in 1995, and regionalism was viewed as a major challenge to the multilateral world trading system— or at least stimulated a debate over whether regionalism was a building block or a stumbling block on the path to global trade liberalization. The EU was the lead actor in the rise of regionalism.

A second classic work in this field was Bela Balassa's 1961 *Theory of Economic Integration* (Box 1), which set out a five-stage linear process from preferential trade agreements through free trade areas (zero tariffs on internal trade) to customs union (a free trade area with common external trade policies) to a common market (customs union with free movement of capital and labor as well as of goods) to economic union (a common market with common macroeconomic and other policies). In Western Europe, the merits of a free trade area versus a customs union were debated in the 1950s and became the basis of bloc competition in the 1960s, between the European Free Trade Area (EFTA) and the customs union of the European Economic Community (EEC); the competition was clearly won by the customs union. The competition illustrated that more than economics was at stake because a customs union challenged national autonomy in two areas: trade policy, because of the common commercial policy, and fiscal policy, because the customs duties had to be a common revenue source.

By the 1980s, it had become clear that Balassa's linear path from less to more economic integration simplified a complex and unstable process. Nontariff barriers to trade could undermine the internal free trade of a customs union and market-determined national exchange rates could make internal prices more volatile than in a national economy with a single currency. The EEC member countries decided to move beyond the simple customs union toward "completing the internal market" between 1986 and 1992 and establishing a single currency between 1993 and 2002. The 1993 Maastricht Treaty institutionalized the Single Market and set out a vision of ever-closer economic and political union. The EEC became part of the EU.

The dynamic process did not end at Maastricht or with introduction of the euro. In the twenty-first century, the EU continued to deepen and widen. However, the integration process lay behind three crises of the 2010s: the sovereign debt crises in the eurozone, disagreement over migration policy when faced with a large influx of refugees after 2011, and the decision to leave the union taken in the British referendum of 2016. At the same time as the EU was addressing these crises, it was also strengthening its internal structures, widening to include Eastern European countries, and coming to terms with its role as a major player in the global economy.

*   *   *

The European integration process has been driven since the 1960s by economics, but political decisions were required, and both the politics and economics played out against a backdrop of changing international relations and an evolving global economy. A good summary of the complexity of the main institution is in the very short introduction to the EU by Simon Usherwood and John Pinder (2018, 1):

> In the simplest of terms, the European Union is an international organization founded on treaties between European states. But such a description does not do justice to a body that has grown and developed since the 1950s to cover many areas of public policy and to reach deep into the political, economic and social lives of its peoples. That change has led some to see it as a proto-state or a new form of political organization altogether. . . . The EU has been driven by and reflected the wider context in which

it operates. . . . If we are to understand why the EU is where it is
now, then we have to begin with [its] birth.

The first part of this book sets the scene by providing a narrative history of European integration, focusing on key dates associated with
deeper or wider integration. Although it is possible to construct a narrative of increasingly deep political and economic union, the path was
not smooth. Some dates represent important markers in the integration
process, such as 1957 (Treaty of Rome establishing the customs union),
1986 (the Single European Act embarking on deeper economic integration), 1993 (Maastricht Treaty creating the EU), and 2007 (Lisbon
Treaty updating the Rome Treaty for the new reality of wider and deeper
integration).

The remaining parts of the book address different aspects of economic
integration. The order in which topics are covered is approximately
chronological, but unlike political decisions that can be precisely dated,
economic consequences accrue over time and often include unintended
and unforeseen twists. Chapter 2 covers the establishment of the customs
union by six countries, a common agricultural policy and a competition
policy, enlargement to twelve countries, treatment of nonmembers in
the common commercial policy, and pressures for deeper integration.
Chapter 3 takes up the story of deeper integration, with establishment
of the Single Market and recognition of the new situation by changing
the institutional name to European Union. Chapter 4 covers currency
union and enlargement to include Central and Eastern European countries; this period also included reform of two original components,
the common agricultural and external trade policies, in response to
changing external conditions. Chapter 5 analyzes three challenges that
arose in the 2010s; although the roots of the financial, migration, and
exit crises lay in the previous stages of integration, the EU appeared
poorly prepared to meet the challenges, which raised questions about
necessary further reforms. All of these developments have occurred
against the backdrop of a changing global economy and world politics,
and Chapter 6 addresses likely developments in the 2020s.

Some topics will be given short shrift. Employment policy and labor
law have received attention at the Community level but remain largely

national competences, apart from some antidiscrimination policies and when practices contravene principles of the Single Market. This is an area studied more by lawyers than by economists, especially when the Court has ruled on economic rights—for example, of workers posted to jobs in another member country. Similarly, issues of justice, crime, or citizenship are ignored as legal rather than economic areas, apart from in Section 5.2 on the refugee crisis. Foreign and security policies will be mentioned in passing but not treated on their own merits. In sum, the book focuses on the first pillar of the Maastricht Treaty and largely ignores the other two pillars, even though the pillars were reintegrated in the Treaty of Lisbon.

♦   ♦   ♦

The book does not assume prior knowledge of economics. More technical economic analysis is in the Appendices rather than the main text. The Appendices to Chapters 2–6 provide a commentary on the evolution of international trade theory and measurement of integration effects, which parallels the evolution of European economic integration. I have tried to make the Appendices accessible and self-contained; Pomfret (2016a) provides fuller treatment and more extensive references.

I am grateful to many people for helpful advice on content and presentations, including several generations of students, anonymous reviewers, and others who may not have realized that I was absorbing their ideas. In particular, I thank Jacques Pelkmans for advice based on his detailed knowledge of the Single Market. I apologize to others who see their ideas in this book, especially if they are inadvertently unacknowledged.

BOX 0 Major Institutional Developments from Rome to Lisbon

The Treaty of Rome (signed 1957, in force 1958) founded the European Economic Community (EEC) and Euratom. The Merger Treaty (signed 1965, in force 1967) brought the EEC, Euratom, and the European Coal and Steel Community (ECSC) together as the European Communities (EC), under a single administration centered on the Commission and the Council of Ministers.

The 1974 Paris Summit established the practice of heads of government meeting three times a year as the European Council and of direct elections to the European Parliament.

The Maastricht Treaty (agreed December 1991, signed 1992, in force 1993) created Three Pillars of European Union: the European Communities, Justice and Home Affairs, and a Common Foreign and Security Policy.

The Lisbon Treaty (signed 2007, in force 2009) merged the Three Pillars into the reformed European Union.

The three treaties are often referred to as the EEC Treaty, the Treaty on European Union, and the Treaty on the Functioning of the European Union (TFEU), emphasizing the continuity as the previous treaty was incorporated and items renumbered.

The Commission, the Council (of member nations), the Assembly / Parliament, and the Court have remained the four main bodies since 1957 although competences, especially of the Parliament, have changed. Since 1974, a distinction is made between the European Council (consisting of member states' heads of government plus the President of the Commission and since 2009, the President of the Council and the High Representative of the Union for Foreign Affairs and Security Policy) and the Council of Ministers, whose composition changes depending on the policy area under discussion.

In this book, to emphasize the continuity of the institution created by the Treaty of Rome, the acronym EU may be used to signify the EEC, European Communities, or European Union. Because the book's focus is economic rather than legal, the catch-all "Court" will refer to the Court of Justice of the European Union (CJEU) in Luxembourg and its predecessors, without distinguishing between the CJEU's component courts, the Court of Justice and the General Court (previously the Court of First Instance).

BOX 1 Typology of Economic Integration

Free Trade Area	Classic definition = no tariffs or quotas on intra-FTA trade
	FTA members determine their national policies vis-à-vis nonmembers.
Customs Union	Classic definition = FTA + common trade policies toward nonmembers
	CU members determine the common trade policy and share tariff revenue.
WTO+	An FTA or CU that goes beyond WTO commitments—e.g., on services, intellectual property, trade-related investment rules
	A Deep and Comprehensive FTA is more radically WTO+.
Common Market	Free intra-CM access in goods, services, capital, and labor.
	Typically involves a combination of negative and positive integration, which determines the extent to which access is free in practice
Single Market	A CM characterized by general intolerance of exceptions to market access obligations (including poor implementation and indirect barriers)

Balassa (1961) envisaged a progression from less to more integration, from the top of the above table to the bottom. However, EU experience did not follow such a path. The Treaty of Rome envisaged creation of a common market without first establishing an FTA. The following decade saw the establishment of a customs union with some common policies. The distinction between the deeper integration of a common market and the EU concept of a single market is a matter of degree that explains the slow and potentially unending process of "completing the single market." In the 1990s, the EU adopted a common currency (and hence a common monetary policy) while many elements of the single market were still being established in the twenty-first century.

The distinction between "negative" and "positive" integration (often ascribed to Tinbergen, 1965) is between measures increasing market integration by eliminating restraints on trade and policies to shape the conditions under which integrated markets operate. Although the classic FTA is entirely about negative integration, the other stages of economic integration involve an increasing amount of positive integration requiring joint decision making or a supranational body.

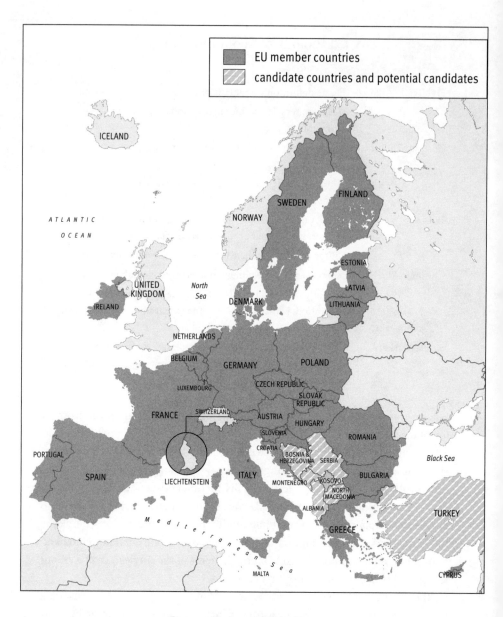

Figure 0.1 The European Union in 2020
Note: For more detail on the status of the western Balkan nonmember countries, see Section 5.5 and Figure 5.4.

THE ECONOMIC INTEGRATION OF EUROPE

CHAPTER ONE

A Brief History of European Union

THE ORIGINS OF European union can only be understood in the context of two highly destructive European wars fought between 1914 and 1945. In 1919, after the first war, the peacemakers tried to prevent renewed war by placing heavy burdens on defeated Germany.[1] The policy failed. After the second war, there were again calls to deindustrialize Germany (spelled out in the 1944 Morgenthau Plan) so that it could not revive as a military power. Others, including Britain's wartime leader, Winston Churchill, called on Europeans to "build a kind of United States of Europe."[2] The debate shifted in 1947 and 1948, when it became clear that the Soviet Union's answer to the challenge was to create Communist regimes in its zone of Germany and in countries east of Germany. The United States responded by offering financial assistance to European countries that would cooperate in economic reconstruction, and over the next two decades, the United States played a role in promoting European integration that included an economically strong Germany.

Within this context, Europeans debated whether cooperation should be intergovernmental among independent states or through supranational institutions. Nationalist politicians have had their successes in shaping Europe. The European Union (EU) reflects how far the supranationalists have come. European integration began as a series of separate European communities: for coal and steel (1952), nuclear energy (1958), and the common market (1958), with some bodies (the assembly and Court of Justice) in common. The 1957 Treaties of Rome established the European Atomic Energy Community (EAEC or Euratom) and the European Economic Community (EEC). In 1967, all the institutions became common (including the Commission and Council of Ministers) in the European Community. The 1993 Treaty of Maastricht made the economic community institutions into one of three pillars of the EU.

Maastricht was a significant milepost in institutionalizing the deeper integration that had taken place in the 1980s and early 1990s. The Maastricht Treaty ratified creation of the single European market and provided a pathway to establishment of the euro as a common currency. A new challenge in the 1990s followed from the end of Communism in Eastern Europe and the evident desire of Eastern European countries to be part of the EU integration project. The constitution for a larger union of twenty-eight countries was established in the 2007 Treaty of Lisbon.

Chapter 1 provides a brief history of European integration.[3] This part contains a narrative of the political evolution which is an essential framework for understanding the economics of European integration. At the same time, it will quickly become clear that the chosen path to European integration focused on economic modalities (from customs union to deeper integration to economic union) and that economic processes could develop their own momentum and path dependence. The remainder of the book will examine the evolution of economic integration, which was slower moving and without dramatic turning points but had a powerful internal logic. The direction of change was not inevitable, as was highlighted by the collapse of monetary union in the 1970s and by Brexit in the 2010s, but the dynamics of economic change and its impact on political choices cannot be ignored.

1.1 From the European Coal and Steel Community to the Treaties of Rome

In 1948, the rift between the West and the Soviet Union became the Cold War. Following the February Prague coup in which the Communists, with Soviet support, seized power in Czechoslovakia, Britain, France, and the Benelux countries (Belgium, the Netherlands, and Luxembourg) signed the Treaty of Brussels establishing the Western European Union in which the five countries pledged to mutual armed assistance against the Soviet Union or Germany.[4] The political counterpart to the military pact was the Council of Europe, although this soon degenerated into a talking shop without influence. In April 1948, the US Congress approved the Marshall Plan to give financial assistance to European countries that would agree on a joint program for economic reconstruction. The institutions for cooperation were the Organisation for European Economic Co-operation (OEEC) and the European Payments Union, which were designed to liberalize intra-European trade by removing quantitative restrictions on trade flows and reducing payments difficulties, while Marshall Plan funds addressed Europe's dollar deficit.

None of this resolved the German problem for the West. The end of the postwar occupation of Germany was foreshadowed in the second half of 1949 by the establishment of the US-sponsored Federal Republic (West Germany) and the Soviet-backed Democratic Republic (East Germany). The United States pressed French foreign minister Robert Schuman to propose a German policy at the May 1950 meeting of the Western occupying powers' foreign ministers. Schuman came up with a proposal from Jean Monnet (head of the French Planning Commission) to combine all French and German coal and steel production under a supranational commission serving pooled markets for coal and steel. For Monnet, internationalization of the key industries would make renewed war between France and Germany inconceivable.

The new West German chancellor Konrad Adenauer embraced the idea, having already stated that Germany wanted to contribute to a new Europe, as long as Germans were treated as equals. Other countries willing to accept the supranational High Authority were invited to join. Belgium, the Netherlands, Luxembourg, and Italy did so. Britain refused to contemplate giving up sovereignty over key industries. The United States was strongly supportive because it saw Western European integration that included West Germany as crucial to resisting Soviet advance.

The treaty conference opened in June 1950, and negotiations took ten months. Although the German and Italian delegations embraced federalism as a route back into a peaceful Europe, Belgium and Luxembourg, in both of which coal and steel were major parts of the national economy, were more concerned about the specifics of how demand and supply would be managed and allocated. The negotiators also had to balance the intrinsic conditions of scale economies and market power in steel against concerns about revival of prewar coal and steel cartels. The United States, in the background but the crucial matchmaker, emphasized three conditions: freedom from restrictive practices in the iron and steel market, effective powers of the High Authority to enforce its decisions, and that the iron and steel community be open to foreign trade.

The treaty establishing the European Coal and Steel Community (ECSC) was signed in April 1951. Ratification by the six governments was completed in June 1952. In July, the six foreign ministers met to allocate posts in the ECSC and to decide its location. In August 1952, the High Authority of the ECSC opened its headquarters in Luxembourg with Jean Monnet as president.

The significance of the ECSC for European integration was highlighted at the inaugural ceremony in Luxembourg on 10 August 1952. Jean Monnet stressed that the six governments had established "the first European Community, merging part of its members' national sovereignty and subordinating it to the common interest." He also made clear that the ECSC was not going to manage coal and steel production: "It is not our task to direct the production of coal and steel: that is the role of firms." Indeed, many firms and representatives of Belgium and Luxembourg complained that Monnet was "far too involved in the politics of Europe . . . and far too little involved in coal and steel."[5] The common market for the raw materials (coal, iron ore, and scrap) opened on 10 February and that for steel on 1 May 1953. Despite many disagreements and mini-crises, the common markets functioned well enough in the expansive conditions of the long economic boom that was already under way.[6] Disputes were settled by discussions that engendered trust or, if the court ruled on a matter, its decisions were never challenged or ignored. The main contribution of the ECSC was that its supranationality provided a setting in which former enemies could accept the revival of German heavy industry without imposing output limits or other constraints (Gillingham 1995, 152).

Meanwhile, the federalists were facing a major defeat as opposition in France mounted against a proposed European Defence Community (EDC) and European Political Community (EPC). An EPC assembly would be elected by universal suffrage and would have authority over the ECSC and EDC. Although five ECSC countries ratified the EDC, the French Parliament rejected the EDC treaty in August 1954 amid scenes of patriotic fervor. The setback encouraged federalists to tread more carefully; no future move would include a powerful high authority with a strong president. The ECSC success and EDC setback also established a precedent for economic rather than political paths toward European integration.

In the first step, the ECSC was seen as an economic institution for peace. However, the EDC setback could have left the ECSC as an isolated and, eventually, archaic symbol of idealistic alternatives to European reality. Instead, the EDC setback stimulated ideas of adopting the ECSC model to further integration, while political and military integration were left on the backburner.[7]

Failure to broaden the European integration agenda to defense led proponents of integration to look to new areas for sectoral integration. At the June 1955 Messina meeting, the foreign ministers of the six ECSC countries found peaceful use of nuclear energy and made a more general commitment to a European common market. The March 1957 Rome Treaties established Euratom and the EEC, which came into existence in January 1958. The treaties could be seen as extensions of the ECSC. Euratom, like the ECSC, focused on sectoral integration, although the commercial nuclear sector remained fairly minor in practice, while the EEC broadened the ECSC vision of integrated markets to include all manufactured and agricultural goods in a customs union.[8] For the most politically sensitive economic sector, a common agricultural policy was to be agreed upon by the end of 1961.[9] Although the Rome treaties envisioned a common market with free movement of capital and labor as well as goods and future political integration, the principal consequence in the next decade was the customs union.

1.2 The European Communities

The EEC customs union was completed in a decade after the Rome treaties. The two typical problems in establishment of customs unions (setting the common external tariff and sharing the revenue) were quickly resolved. For each product, the external tariff would be the average of the Benelux, French, German, and Italian tariff, which would mostly have increased Benelux tariffs and reduced French and Italian tariffs. In fact, circumstances helped, as implementation of the common external tariff in the years up to 1968 coincided with an international step toward global trade liberalization; the Six negotiated as a single unit in the 1964–1967 Kennedy Round of multilateral trade negotiations in which the major trading nations all cut tariffs substantially. Avoiding significant tariff increases was important; although the United States was a strong backer of Western European integration, this position may have met opposition from US domestic interests if the customs union had been established as an area of free internal trade behind high external tariffs. The revenue problem was resolved by allocating tariff revenues to the community budget.[10]

The United Kingdom (UK) had been lukewarm toward the ECSC, in part because of the supranational High Authority, and opposed the principle behind the EEC's common external tariff and shared revenue. In response to the EEC, the UK brought together like-minded European countries (Austria, Denmark, Norway, Portugal, Sweden, and Switzerland) in the European Free Trade Association (EFTA). The January 1960 Stockholm Convention committed the seven members to form a free trade area in which trade among the seven members would be tariff-free and each member would set its own national tariff on imports from outside EFTA.[11] Sapir (2011, 1204) highlights the difference in goals by quoting from the Treaty of Rome whose signatories "determined to lay the foundations of an ever closer union among the peoples of Europe" and the Stockholm Convention in which EFTA members "determined to facilitate . . . the removal of trade barriers and the promotion of closer economic cooperation."

In a brief episode of interbloc competition, the EEC accepted two associate members. Greece applied for associate status in 1961, with a twenty-two-year transition to full membership envisaged. Two years later, a similar application from Turkey was greeted less enthusiastically; associate status was granted but without a timeline to full membership. Finland became an associate member of EFTA in 1963.

The UK quickly realized that the EEC was the main game in Europe and in July 1961, together with Denmark and Ireland, applied to join the

EEC. Norway followed in April 1962. At a press conference in January 1963, French president Charles de Gaulle announced that he would veto British membership, and the four applications were allowed to lapse.[12] One lesson from the aborted applications was that, although Britain thought that it would be entering into negotiations on a more or less equal basis, any application would in fact involve the new member's acceptance of the existing EEC rules, the *acquis communautaire*. The painstakingly negotiated rules would not be unpicked to facilitate expansion. When the four countries reactivated their applications in 1967, the principle was recognized. Once again, de Gaulle vetoed the applications.

The European economies boomed during the 1960s. The customs union in manufactured goods was completed in 1968, and agreement was reached on the features of the common agricultural policy. Nevertheless, the vision of the Treaty of Rome was challenged not only by the rejection of applications for membership. Two key decisions, largely under the influence of France's President de Gaulle, reduced the supranational and democratic elements of the integration process and left the Council of Ministers as the source of authority.

According to the Treaty of Rome, decisions in the EEC had to be unanimous during a transition period, but after 1 January 1966, majority voting in the Council of Ministers would take effect. In 1965, de Gaulle preemptively initiated an "empty chair" policy whereby French representatives were withdrawn from the European institutions until the French veto was reinstated. Under the January 1966 Luxembourg Compromise, members were permitted to use a veto on matters of important national interest, without precisely defining those areas. The national veto remained for two decades.

The July 1967 Merger Treaty combined the ECSC and Euratom with the EEC into the European Communities (EC). Although the communities had a shared parliamentary assembly that, according to the Rome treaties, should be directly elected, the Council of Ministers procrastinated on deciding the voting system and the parliament remained an appointed body. President de Gaulle was particularly active in blocking the parliament's development. The parliament was only granted powers after de Gaulle's resignation as French president in April 1969. The first elections to the European Parliament were not held until 1979, and the voting systems varied by nation (as they still do).

Despite the setbacks, the EC was by 1970 a success. The aftermath of the May 1968 events in France provided a catalyst for further change.[13] In 1969, largely driven by the wage settlements that had terminated French workers' support for change in 1968, major currency realignments took place; devaluation of the French franc by 11 percent and revaluation of the German mark by 9 percent caused large relative price movements in the common market.

Monetary arrangements were not covered by the Rome treaty, which had been signed at a time of International Monetary Fund–mediated fixed exchange rates. A committee set up to advise on monetary change recommended in the 1970 Werner Report that the EC should follow a path to economic and monetary union by 1980. The strategy was to start with narrower bands around the fixed bilateral exchange rates between EC currencies and then to permit no exchange rate changes until the national currencies would be replaced by a European currency.

The vision of a single currency by 1980 reflected the optimism as the EC entered the 1970s. In 1972, Denmark, Ireland, Norway, and the UK applied again for membership. Norway held a referendum in which the voters rejected EC membership. The applications of Denmark, Ireland, and the UK were accepted in 1972 and became effective in January 1973.[14] The remaining EFTA members became part of an EEC-EFTA free trade area in manufactures. The 1974 Paris summit established the practice of the European Council (i.e., the heads of state of all member countries plus the president of the Commission) meeting three times a year and the direct election of members of the European Parliament by the people.[15] A UK referendum in 1975 confirmed popular support for EC membership.

1.3 The Road to Monetary Union, Disrupted and Resumed, 1971–1979

European monetary union was accepted as a goal in June 1971 and launched in April 1972 with the Snake. The basic idea, following the Werner Report, was to reduce margins of exchange rate fluctuation among EC members' currencies, even if the value of third country currencies such as the US dollar were volatile. In May 1972, in anticipation of their EC accession, the UK, Denmark, and Ireland joined the Snake. The economic environment was, however, much less favorable than it had been when the customs union was formed in the 1960s. The Bretton Woods system of fixed exchange rates broke down in 1971–1973, and commodity price increases started to generate inflation and the unanticipated (and inexplicable within existing Keynesian macroeconomics) phenomenon of stagflation—that is, simultaneously increasing unemployment and inflation.

Within six weeks of joining, the UK, Ireland, and Denmark left the Snake in June 1972. Denmark rejoined in October 1972. Italy left the Snake in February 1973. France left the Snake in January 1974, rejoined in July 1975, and left again in March 1976, by which time the Snake had effectively collapsed into a deutsche mark zone of Germany and the smaller EC members (Belgium, Luxembourg, the Netherlands, and Denmark). What had started as a move toward exchange rate stability within the EC had become an unpredictable mixture of sudden and gradual exchange rate changes. The reason was simple; in the face of stagflation and massive external economic shocks such as the first oil crisis in 1973–1974, the large countries wanted monetary policy independence (all the defections occurred when governments faced a choice between implementing contractionary macroeconomic policies or quitting the Snake). Differing monetary policies led to differing national rates of inflation that were inconsistent with fixed exchange rates.

By mid-1976, monetary union appeared dead. However, the idea was quickly and successfully resurrected by the head of the EC Commission, Roy Jenkins, in October 1977. At the EC Council summit in Bremen in July 1978, Jenkins's proposal was supported by German chancellor Helmut Schmidt and endorsed by French president Valéry Giscard d'Estaing. The European Monetary System (EMS) began operation in March 1979 in eight of the nine EC countries; the UK remained outside.

The new features of the EMS included an accounting unit, the "ecu" which had the potential to eventually become a European currency unit, and a divergence indicator to warn if a currency was getting out of line. Otherwise, the EMS seemed little different from the Snake; with the divergence indicator as a novelty, it was jokingly called the rattlesnake.

However, the history of the EMS was quite different from that of the Snake. Between March 1979 and March 1983, many alignments occurred; between March 1983 and January 1987, realignments were less frequent and smaller; and from January 1987 to September 1992, there were no currency realignments. This was exactly the progression envisaged in the Werner Report, although not the precise time frame.

Why did the EMS not follow the Snake to extinction? The external policy environment was better, and more importantly, all members accepted inflation reduction as the principal macroeconomic goal in the 1980s; member countries were now more willing to subsume domestic macroeconomic policy to maintenance of the EMS. The key episode occurred in France in 1981–1983. The newly elected Socialist president, François Mitterrand, was initially tempted to introduce an expansionary fiscal policy in order to reduce unemployment. However, after several devaluations of the French franc, Mitterrand recalibrated macroeconomic policies to focus on exchange rate stability.

The underlying economic reason why Schmidt, d'Estaing, Mitterrand, and other EC leaders were keen to reestablish exchange rate stability so soon after the collapse of the Snake was the threat to the common market and, in particular, the common agricultural policy (CAP). The CAP was based on free trade within the common market, at fixed prices that would be supported by restrictions on imports of agricultural products or EC purchase of surpluses. Setting the common price for an agricultural good involved detailed negotiation between countries concerned about producers' revenues and other countries concerned about the price for consumers. Any variation in exchange rates would upset the balancing act that had been established by negotiators.

The Snake / EMS episode in the 1970s and early 1980s was important in highlighting indirect consequences of common policies and the potential difficulties of partial integration. Thus, as the EC adopted common policies that required decisions over implementation and expenditure that would be affected by internal exchange rates, there was pressure to have a common currency. The pressures would strengthen further in the 1990s and 2000s as the reach of common policies expanded.

For the six original members, some further loss of sovereignty was an acceptable price for maintaining the EC, a decision most clearly reflected in Italy's 1979 decision, after a domestic debate, to be in the EMS and France's decision in 1981–1983 to prioritize EMS obligations over domestic fiscal stimulus. The UK in contrast prioritized macroeconomic policy independence and enjoyed lower inflation with a floating currency and tight monetary policies. The period was also characterized by UK prime minister Margaret Thatcher demanding rebates from the EC because the UK was contributing more money than it received from the EC. Such a contractual view of EC membership was at odds with a more idealistic commitment to integration in the Six, and the episode foreshadowed further disputes in which the UK would resist deeper integration. Meanwhile, Ireland by joining the EMS in 1979 severed its long-standing currency union with the UK and adopted a national currency, the punt.

1.4 The Program to Complete the Single Market and the 1993 Maastricht Treaty

The early 1980s were a challenging period for the EC. In 1981–1983, most EC economies had slow growth and rising unemployment as governments adopted tight money policies to defeat inflation. The future of the EMS was not yet certain. The UK was bargaining over a country-specific recalculation of its membership dues, largely on the basis that the CAP favored more agrarian countries and dominated the EC budget. At the June 1984 Fontainebleau summit, the European Council agreed on a rebate to reduce UK's net contribution to the EC budget by about one-third. In southern Europe, Greece, Portugal, and Spain had overthrown their dictatorships and had returned to democracy; in its 1961 association agreement, Greece already had a blueprint for EC accession, and Portugal and Spain also applied for membership. The existing members worried about the impact of a southward expansion to include poorer countries with differing economic structures and, perhaps, culture. Nevertheless, Greece joined the EC in 1981, and Portugal and Spain joined in 1986.

Although members enjoyed duty-free access to the entire common market, nontariff barriers restricted intra-EC trade. In 1979, a German liquor importer that had been refused permission to import Cassis de Dijon from France because it violated a German law requiring fruit liquors to have a minimum alcohol content of 25 percent took its complaint to the EU court, which found that the German policy breached the Rome treaty's article that "Quantitative restrictions on imports and all measures having equivalent effect shall be prohibited between Member States." This set an important precedent of mutual recognition of technical and other standards.

Nevertheless, over the decade after 1973, poor economic conditions encouraged EC members to adopt a variety of regulations, controls, and other measures to protect employment. The most notorious were nationally determined "voluntary" export restraints on car imports from Japan, but many other measures targeted imports from the new industrialized economies of Asia. Because they were national, such measures required border checks to detect any trade deflection (i.e., importing a good through an unrestricted EC market and then reexporting the good to the country with the restriction). Other national regulations reflecting growing concerns about environmental, health, and other issues, even if not introduced for primarily economic reasons, had the effect of segmenting the internal market.

In 1985, the president of the Commission, Jacques Delors, pushed for completion of the Single Market. The legislation to achieve the goal, the 1986 Single European Act (SEA), emphasized the four freedoms promised in the Treaty of Rome but not yet achieved: free movement of goods, services, people, and capital. Key instruments were mutual recognition and harmonization so that technical standards, regulations or qualifications, different value-added tax rates, and so forth could not impede cross-border trade and factor movements. The SEA also extended EC competence into areas of the environment, research and development, social policies, and cohesion, as well as strengthening the parliament's role and reducing the scope for national vetoes. An important institutional change was reinstatement of qualified majority voting on issues related to the Single Market. Passage of the act was delayed by concerns in Denmark that the European Parliament would be given too much power and in Italy that the parliament would have too little power. However, it was passed and came into force in 1987.[16]

The SEA with its vision of a single market being established by 1992 was a major step toward closer integration. It also had wider consequences. The removal of restrictions on capital movements sharpened governments' choice between monetary independence and stable exchange rates, and for countries valuing exchange rate stability, there was little reason to retain a national currency. The EMS would move rapidly toward currency union in the 1990s. For countries outside the EEC, the Single Market heightened the discrimination between insiders and outsiders. Delors preempted EFTA members' decisions by proposing a European Economic Area (EEA) in which EFTA countries would have equal access to the internal market with free movement of goods, services, labor, and capital if they accepted the Single Market legislation (except with regard to the CAP and the common fisheries policy). However, the EFTA members of the EEA would not be represented in the Commission or the European Parliament nor attend Council meetings— that is, they would have to accept Single Market regulations without having a seat at the negotiating table. The eventual outcome was mixed as Austria, Finland, and Sweden joined the EU in 1995, but Norwegian voters rejected EU membership (for a second time) in a referendum in November 1994. Norway, Liechtenstein, and Iceland accepted EEA status.[17] Swiss voters rejected the EEA in a referendum, and subsequent EU-Swiss relations have been governed by bilateral agreements.

Separately from the SEA, five members (Belgium, France, West Germany, Luxembourg, and the Netherlands) signed the Schengen Agreement on the gradual abolition of common border controls in June 1985.[18] In 1990, the agreement was supplemented by the Schengen Convention, which created the Schengen Area with complete abolition of border controls between Schengen member states, common rules on visas, and police and judicial cooperation. By 1997, all member states except the UK and Ireland had signed the agreement, which was included in the 1999 Amsterdam treaty, with opt-outs for the UK and Ireland, and hence became part of the *acquis communautaire.*

In 1989, as Communist regimes crumbled in Eastern Europe, the Berlin Wall fell, and the German question reemerged. German chancellor

Helmut Kohl pushed for reunification, which raised issues of a resurgent Germany becoming substantially the largest European nation, an outcome viewed with horror by UK Prime Minister Thatcher and with trepidation by other leaders. For European integration, the key element was agreement between French President Mitterrand and German Chancellor Kohl; France would acquiesce in German reunification if Germany would agree to deeper European integration through currency union within a decade.[19]

The year 1991 involved critical negotiations leading to a new treaty being agreed at the December Maastricht summit. The need was clear with the deeper integration of the Single Market, the commitment by France and Germany to currency union, and the anticipated widening of the community. The agreed treaty established a European Union with three pillars: the European Community based on the Treaty of Rome plus monetary union, a common foreign and security policy, and cooperation on internal policing matters and immigration. The second and third pillars had different structures that gave greater powers to the member states, including national vetoes, and less to the EU Commission. This was seen by the more federalist members such as Belgium as a return to the intergovernmentalism of de Gaulle, while the added economic elements (economic and political union and a social chapter) were opposed by the UK and Denmark.

The Maastricht Treaty had to be ratified by every member state, and the process proved more difficult than expected. The treaty was rejected by Danish voters in a 1992 referendum; it passed on a second referendum in 1993 after Denmark was given an opt-out on the currency and on defense matters. Britain insisted on an opt-out from the common currency and from the Social Charter of the Fundamental Social Rights of Workers (Lourie 2004); although no referendum was held, opposition to closer European union and establishment of the UK Independence Party foreshadowed the rise of Euroscepticism that would lead to the Brexit vote in 2016. The formal opt-outs negotiated by the UK and Denmark were a challenge to federalists because it was the first time that members were exempted from observing all of the treaty obligations, raising specters of "variable geometry" or "two-speed European integration."[20] However, all countries joining the EU after Maastricht must accept the *acquis communautaire* in total, with any accession negotiations limited to the transition period.

The Maastricht Treaty, formally known as the Treaty on European Union, finally entered into force in November 1993.[21] The treaty formalized completion of the Single Market and included a commitment to a single currency, as well as adopting the name European Union in place of European Communities. The Maastricht Treaty created EU citizenship (as opposed to a simple right to work throughout the EC), enshrined the principle of subsidiarity and strengthened the Parliament's power over EU legislation, and introduced a Social Charter with policies on workplace health and safety, equal pay, and consultation of employees. The principle of subsidiarity, as defined in Article 5 of the Treaty on European Union, aimed to ensure that decisions are taken as closely as possible to the citizen and that constant checks are made to verify that action at EU level is justified in light of the possibilities available at national, regional, or local level. The treaty also sought to strengthen EU cooperation in areas such as security and defense, immigration and refugees, and criminal justice and law enforcement. However, foreign policy challenges during 1991—Iraq's invasion of Kuwait in January, disintegration of Yugoslavia and wars in the Balkans, and dissolution of the Soviet Union two weeks after the Maastricht summit—all highlighted deep divisions on foreign policy and the impossibility of a coordinated military response.

Faced with expansion to fifteen members in 1995 when Austria, Finland, and Sweden joined and further enlargements as the Eastern European countries' expressed goal was membership, the EU sought to formalize and reform institutional arrangements that had been devised for six members but would be less well-suited to over twenty members. This led to a sequence of poorly drafted treaties that had problems of ratification, starting with the 1997 Amsterdam treaty, the Nice treaty (signed in 2000 and ratified in 2003), and the Constitutional Treaty signed in Rome in 2004 but rejected in Dutch and French referenda. The treaty-amending process was finally completed in 2007 with the Lisbon treaty, which was ratified in 2009.

1.5 Monetary Union Achieved

The EMS worked well in the 1980s. Monetary policies converged as governments adopted similar inflation goals. Exchange rate realignments became less frequent and smaller between March 1983 and January 1987 and ceased for five years after that. The Delors committee, established in 1988 and reporting in 1989, set out a timetable for monetary union that was ratified in the 1993 Maastricht Treaty. All EU members committed to adopting the exchange rate mechanism (ERM); Spain did so in June 1989, the UK in January 1990, and Portugal in 1992. The December 1991 Maastricht summit set targets for policy convergence (i.e., limits on fiscal deficits and public debt / GDP ratios), but the important point was political will.

German economic and monetary union in 1990 clarified some issues. Technically, monetary union was not difficult, although the choice of exchange rate between East and West German currencies created increased unemployment in East Germany. More important for the European economy was the method of financing German economic union. Facing increased expenditures associated with reunification and unwilling to fund the spending by money creation, the German government resorted to borrowing, driving up interest rates. With free movement of capital within the EU, this led to higher interest rates EU-wide.

A major European currency crisis erupted in 1992. Unwilling to accept increased interest rates and running out of foreign currency reserves, Italy devalued the lira on 13 September and left the ERM four days later. The UK delayed for a few more days, during which it lost large amounts of money to speculators, before leaving the ERM on 16 September. Spain and Portugal introduced capital controls; their currencies were devalued, and then the controls were removed.[22] Sweden, whose currency had been shadowing the ecu since 1991, abandoned the fixed exchange rate link in November 1992, after raising interest rates to 500 percent.

The uncertainty continued in 1993. To restore stability and discourage speculation, the ERM margins were temporarily widened to +/ –15 percent in August 1993, although Germany and the Netherlands agreed bilaterally to keep their currencies within the +/−2.25 percent margins. The lesson was that, following the abolition of controls on capital mobility within the Single Market, fixed but adjustable exchange rates were no longer an option; speculators knew in which direction the exchange rate would be adjusted and they had a one-way bet that would be self-fulfilling if enough people chose to bet. Countries with irrevocably fixed exchange rates might just as well have a common currency and effectively commit to no future exchange rate realignments.

Most EU members accepted the Maastricht commitment to currency union but failed to meet the policy convergence targets during the 1990s. Nevertheless, the Kohl-Mitterrand agreement underpinned political commitment to a common currency, which other countries shared because, unlike in the 1970s, there was little disagreement that monetary policy should prioritize low inflation. Creation of the European Monetary Institute in January 1994 to coordinate monetary policy was an important institutional step, signaling renunciation of national monetary policies. A potential currency crisis in 1995 following depreciation of the US dollar was far less significant for the EMS than the 1992 crisis. Austria and Finland joined the ERM in 1995 and 1996, and Italy rejoined in November 1996.

In June 1998, the European Central Bank replaced the European Monetary Institute. In 1999, the euro was adopted as a common currency by all EU members except for the UK, Greece, and Sweden. In a September 2000 referendum, Danish voters rejected eurozone membership.[23] In January 2001, Greece reversed its decision and became the twelfth member of the eurozone. Euro coins and banknotes were issued in January 2002, replacing the national currencies.

Since the Maastricht Treaty, new EU members are committed to adopting the euro as part of the *acquis communautaire,* but they have been slow to do so. Slovenia adopted the euro in 2007, Malta and Cyprus in 2008, Slovakia in 2009, Estonia in 2011, Latvia in 2014, and Lithuania in 2015. Only the UK and Denmark had a formal opt-out; the other seven EU members (Bulgaria, Croatia, Czech Republic, Hungary, Poland, Romania, and Sweden) are formally committed to adopt the euro.[24]

1.6 Enlargement from Twelve to
Twenty-Eight, 1995–2013

The decade 1985–1995 was a tumultuous one in Europe as the EC became wider and deeper through significant institutional change, reflected in renaming as the European Union. The EC10 of 1985 became EC12 in 1986 and the EU15 in 1995. The Single Market had been completed, and the creation of Schengenland and the eurozone was under way. The EU budget had been substantially reoriented by Delors to include a large element of regional development funding aimed at reducing the economic gap between richer and poorer (i.e., Greece, Ireland, Portugal, and parts of Spain and Italy) areas. In 1988, a fourth resource was added to the EC's revenues; in addition to customs duties, variable levies on agricultural imports and a share of value-added tax receipts that had been agreed upon in 1970 after completion of the customs union, members agreed to contribute a percentage of GDP. The fourth resource quickly came to dominate the revenue side of the EU budget. Apart from Delors, the key figure was German chancellor Helmut Kohl, who as the largest contributor to the EU budget accepted increased spending and in the face of substantial domestic opposition reached agreement with Mitterrand on German reunification and EU monetary union.

This was not achieved without serious disagreements. Most clearly, the UK under Margaret Thatcher, and to a lesser extent Denmark, did not share the enthusiasm for ever closer union. From 1988 onward, Thatcher's opposition to greater supranationalism, removal of internal EU border controls, and EU spending on social policies became more fanatical, to the point that her colleagues in the UK government staged a revolt and she was replaced by the more emollient John Major.[25] Attempts toward political union with common defense and foreign policies were set back by failure to maintain a strong common front following Iraq's invasion of Kuwait in 1990 and even more by complete breakdown of coordination in response to the dissolution of Yugoslavia in 1991–1992.

The other big issue that was clearly on the horizon but still in the too-hard basket was how to deal with eastern neighbors. At the June 1993 Copenhagen summit, the EU12 set out three key criteria for successful accession: stable democratic institutions that promoted respect for the rule of law, a functioning market economy able to survive the economic pressures of membership, and capability to eventually take on all obligations of membership including adherence to the aims of political, economic, and monetary union. These went beyond simple acceptance of the *acquis communautaire* at the time of application to include future commitments to economic stability and political structure (to be defined more precisely in the 1997 Amsterdam treaty).

Enlargement to include Austria, Finland, and Sweden in 1995 was relatively easy because their economic and political systems had long been similar to those of the existing members. However, Austria foreshadowed future issues when accession led to resentment in parts of the population about the assimilation process, and in the 2000 election the Freedom Party (FPÖ) made large gains and entered into a coalition with the Christian Democrats (ÖVP). The issue of whether the Nazi-apologist views of FPÖ leader Jörg Haider were consistent with EU principles was settled by confirming that the democratically elected government posed no threats to human rights in Austria, but it would recur with respect to Eastern European countries where such rights might be perceived as more precarious.

Despite the hurdles imposed by the Copenhagen conditions, the new democracies of Central and Eastern Europe were keen to join. Hungary applied for membership in March 1994 and Poland in April 1994. In June and July 1995, Romania, the Slovak Republic, and Latvia applied, followed by Estonia, Lithuania, Bulgaria, the Czech Republic, and Slovenia over the next twelve months. They joined a queue that already included Turkey (applied in 1987) and Malta and Cyprus, who had both applied in 1990. The Commission recommended staggered accession negotiations, which began with the Czech Republic, Estonia, Hungary, Poland, Slovenia, and Cyprus in March 1998, with Bulgaria, Latvia, Lithuania, Malta, Romania, and the Slovak Republic in February 2000 and with Turkey in October 2005. At the December 2002 Copenhagen summit, the EU Council decided that Cyprus, the Czech Republic, Estonia, Hungary, Latvia, Lithuania, Malta, Poland, Slovakia, and Slovenia would be ready to join in 2004. Bulgaria and Romania joined in 2007. In 2013, Croatia became the twenty-eighth member.

Meanwhile, various treaties struggled to define the EU's range of activities, to address issues associated with the perceived "democratic deficit" by strengthening the European Parliament, and to avoid deadlock by extending qualified majority voting to an increasing number of areas. The 1997 Amsterdam treaty made liberty, democracy, and respect for human rights a condition of EU membership and allowed for suspension of membership if the other member states agreed unanimously that a country was in breach of these conditions. Among a variety of other innovations, the Schengen Treaty was absorbed into the EU *acquis.* The 2001 Nice treaty tinkered with the size and future composition of parliament and foreshadowed a convention on the EU's institutional future. Among other reforms, the convention reduced the size of the Commission and created the positions of president and foreign minister, although details were amended before acceptance by the EU Council in 2004. More significantly, after the constitution was ratified by several members' parliaments and in a Spanish referendum, it was resoundingly defeated in referenda in France and the Netherlands in May and June 2005, respectively.

The policy makers' response was to repackage measures agreed in Maastricht and subsequent treaties, while suppressing reference to a constitution and other supranational flourishes such as the flag, the anthem, and the title of foreign minister.[26] The Lisbon treaty (the Treaty on the Functioning of the European Union) was signed in December 2007 and took effect in December 2009. The EU's competence in justice and home affairs was extended, and the areas in which decisions would be by qualified majority were increased; taxation, social security, and foreign and defense policies were the main areas still requiring unanimity. The Commission's powers were constrained by slight increases in the Parliament's powers and by a strong statement of the principle of subsidiarity.[27] The positions of permanent President of the Council and High Representative for Foreign Affairs were confirmed and in December 2009 were filled by Herman van Rompuy and Catherine Ashton. These relatively lackluster appointments highlighted the unwillingness of members to cede authority to the EU in noneconomic areas, especially in defense and foreign policy.[28] Nevertheless, the Lisbon treaty was a major landmark in codifying institutions for the deeper and wider EU that had been created over the previous three decades.

1.7 Finding a Global Role

As a customs union, the EEC participated in General Agreement on Tariffs and Trade (GATT) multilateral trade negotiations as a single unit. In the 1964–1967 Kennedy Round, the EEC agreed to substantial reductions in tariffs on manufactured goods. At the same time, the EEC acquiesced in excluding agriculture and textiles and clothing from the GATT. The EEC was also cavalier in application of unconditional most-favored nation treatment, which was supposed to outlaw discrimination among trading partners who signed the GATT. During the 1960s and 1970s, the EEC used preferential tariff treatment as a foreign policy tool, establishing a complex pyramid of preferences. The policy was not very successful because partners worried about their place in the pyramid rather than being grateful for preferential treatment, but once in place, the structure was hard to dismantle. During the 1980s, the EEC came under increasing external pressure to reform its trade policies.

In the Uruguay Round of GATT trade negotiations that started in 1986, there was pressure from the United States and the Cairns Group of agricultural exporters to bring agriculture into the normal trade regime in which export subsidies are outlawed and the complex CAP regulations should be simplified into their tariff equivalents.[29] At the 1990 GATT ministerial meeting in Montréal, the EU (and the other major trading nations) faced collapse of the world trade system based on multilateralism. As its contribution to successful completion of the Uruguay Round in 1994 and creation of the World Trade Organization, the EC agreed to reduce the CAP's trade-distorting elements and to terminate one-way preferential treatment for favored trade partners.

The MacSharry reform in 1992 began the decoupling of farm support from output. Intervention prices for cereals were cut by one-third, and farmers were compensated by a subsidy related to their land area, not output. Other CAP regimes (e.g., for beef and sheep meat) were also changed, and subsidies were switched to environmental targets rather than output. However, abolition of export subsidies and serious decoupling of assistance as a share of CAP spending only followed the Fischler reforms of 2003–2004.

Reform of external trade policies was slow, perhaps because the EU had other preoccupations (monetary union and enlargement) during the 1990s and 2000s. By 2005, the features of the CAP that caused most distress to other countries had been reformed, although some tariffs on farm products remained high, and quantitative restrictions on textile and clothing imports from low-wage countries had been eliminated. Dismantling or simplifying the pyramid of preferences proved to be more contentious because some trading partners would prefer no change and are reluctant to replace one-way preferences by reciprocal freer trade.

The cumulative change in external trade policies between the 1980s and 2010s was substantial. In 2015, the EU promulgated its "Trade for All" strategy, based on embracing globalization and pursuing ethical trade goals. Tariffs and other protection against imports have been greatly reduced as EU producers are expected to compete in world markets and to have access to globally best inputs in order to do so. In the 2010s, the EU negotiated deep integration agreements with a number of trading partners, including Canada and Japan, which established a WTO+ trade environment among six of the G7 countries. Negotiations toward similar agreement with the United States were abandoned in 2017 by President Donald Trump, whose threats to the global order challenged the EU, Canada, and the leading Asian economies to take a stand on supporting the global economic framework.

1.8 Assessing the EU's Past and Future

Has the European integration project been a success or failure? The answer depends on the criteria for success and, perhaps, on the time period. If the raison d'être for the EU, as for its precursors the ECSC and EEC, was to prevent renewed war between France and Germany, then the project succeeded. Seventy years after the ECSC negotiations, the part of Europe covered by the EU has seen peace; war between France and Germany seems inconceivable. That is a major achievement.

In the twenty-first century, however, the goalposts have been moved, peace in Western Europe is taken for granted and the goal of integration is itself less clear (Hare and Stoneman 2017). Although the treaties refer to a goal of deeper integration, this has not been universally accepted within member countries. Many see the project in narrowly economic terms and assess success in terms of an economic balance sheet; the transactions approach was especially strong in the UK, explicitly since Margaret Thatcher's demand for a rebate in the early 1980s. Other critics are concerned about loss of sovereignty in important areas and perhaps weigh any economic advantages against loss of control over legislation, immigration, or cultural distinctiveness; such people dismiss the ever deeper integration goal as impractical and undesirable. For many in Eastern Europe, EU accession offered economic prosperity and guarantees of independence from Russian hegemony, but once inside the EU, it became clearer that the goals set out in the Copenhagen criteria were not universally accepted.

In the second decade of the twenty-first century, three challenges stood out. A series of financial crises hit EU members between 2007 and 2010 of which the most fundamental for the EU was the sovereign debt of countries using the euro, notably Greece. Dismantling of internal borders under the Schengen arrangement has been one of the most popular EU achievements, but it raised issues of managing the EU's external frontiers which were highlighted after 2011 by a large increase in demands for refugee status. Third, in 2016, the British government held a referendum on whether the UK should remain in the EU, and the voters decided to leave the EU, setting the stage for contentious exit negotiations.

As the EU struggled to address these challenges, the external economic environment was changing. International trade was increasingly conducted along ever more fragmented global value chains. New technologies were reducing the costs of trade and changing its nature as e-commerce flourished and as trade in services and cross-border transfer of data increased. As the WTO proved incapable of addressing new issues, the EU turned to signing deep trade agreements. The 2016 US presidential election added further challenges as the United States abdicated from global leadership in supporting multilateral organizations such as the WTO and embarked on a trade war with China.

In December 2019, a new Commission led by Ursula von der Leyen took office, and other senior EU positions had new faces with Charles Michel as President of the European Council, Josep Borrell as High Representative of the Union for Foreign Affairs and Security Policy, and Christine Lagarde as president of the European Central Bank. The Commission promised a strategic focus on environmental issues in a Green Deal, but in the early months of 2020, the problems of the 2010s reemerged, forcing the Commission to concentrate on short-run management. The COVID-19 pandemic dominated the news as national governments sought to manage the health and economic consequences, reviving demands for EU solidarity from the countries most affected by the crisis and seeing European Central Bank head Lagarde echoing her predecessor's 2012 commitment to do all that it takes to support the eurozone economies. Meanwhile, concerns about immigration were revived when Turkey opened its western border to allow people to move from its refugee camps into Europe and the Brexit saga, apparently ended when the UK left the EU on 31 January 2020, smoldered on as the UK and EU27 hardened their positions in negotiating future relations.

Despite these challenges and setbacks, the extent of European economic integration since 1945 has been remarkable. After slow beginnings in the face of lingering postwar distrust and still-strong nationalism, the customs union was established and expanded through the benevolent external economic conditions of the 1960s and the economic turmoil of the 1970s. The second stage of deeper integration through the Single Market program and monetary union was essentially completed by 2000. In the twenty-first century, the EU is a novel arrangement with deeper economic integration than among any other group of independent countries, although not yet comparable to federal political unions such as the United States, Canada, or Australia. The present will not be the end point because economic integration is a dynamic process, but further change in any direction will be contested.

CHAPTER TWO

The Customs Union

Setting European Integration in Motion

THE FIRST STAGE to European economic integration after 1945 was establishment of a customs union, initially among six countries and by the 1980s among twelve countries spanning much of Western Europe. The road was not easy given the high levels of distrust between former combatants in the 1939–1945 war. The context of the Cold War between the United States and the Soviet Union ensured US support for Western European integration, but the European countries were divided over the form of integration, in particular whether it would involve any supranational authority or whether national governments would retain full control. The long economic boom of the 1950s and 1960s provided a positive economic background, but at the same time, rapid structural change raised concerns in many countries about how to manage the decline of agricultural employment.

This chapter analyzes the origins of the customs union and the specifics of its implementation as the members reached agreement on the common commercial policy toward nonmembers and on a common agricultural policy. I will analyze the consequences of forming the customs union and of its expansion to include new members in 1973 and in the 1980s. The biggest failure was the attempt to complement free internal trade with a common currency, which failed ignominiously in the 1970s. The final section discusses whether the customs union was an equilibrium situation or whether it was inherently unstable, inevitably leading to either deeper integration or eventual collapse.

2.1 The Road to the Customs Union

The decision to create a customs union in Western Europe took a decade from the announcement of the Marshall Plan by the United States in June 1947 to the signing of the Treaty of Rome in 1957. The Organisation for European Economic Co-operation (OEEC) was established in April 1948 with the purpose of administering the Marshall Plan and promoting economic cooperation and trade liberalization among the European recipients of Marshall Plan assistance. The European Payments Union contributed to the reintegration of Western Europe through removal of payments restrictions. The European Payments Union became redundant after controls over access to foreign exchange were generally lifted and it was dissolved in 1958. The OEEC was renamed the Organisation for Economic Co-operation and Development (OECD) in 1960 and became an intergovernmental think tank for the richer market economies. Thus, the initial institutions for European postwar reconstruction and reintegration turned out to be temporary, and modalities for freer intra-European trade moved to debates over the relative merits of a customs union versus a free trade area.

The European Coal and Steel Community (ECSC) was proposed by France in 1950 to ensure that German recovery would not be a prelude to another war. The French foreign minister, Robert Schuman, declared that war would be "not merely unthinkable, but materially impossible," and the ECSC would be "the first step in the federation of Europe." France was joined by Belgium, the German Federal Republic (West Germany), Italy, Luxembourg, and the Netherlands. Membership was open to other European countries, but they opposed the supranational power vested to the High Authority in the ECSC treaty (signed 1951), foreshadowing a divide that would haunt the future process of European integration—especially with respect to the United Kingdom (UK).

The UK, the Scandinavian countries, and others preferred the trade liberalization model of the OEEC—that is, easing intra-European transactions while leaving national governments' authority over trade policy—and they disliked the inconsistency of the explicitly discriminatory ECSC with the General Agreement on Tariffs and Trade (GATT). Meanwhile, among the six ECSC members, federalists pushed for closer European integration. However, after the French assembly rejected a proposal for European defense cooperation in 1954, military and political unification were postponed. At the 1955 Messina meeting, the six countries decided to move forward on a customs union and cooperation in transport and energy, forming the European Economic Community (EEC).

The 1957 Treaty of Rome established a customs union among the six signatories. The customs union was GATT consistent under Article XXIV that permitted customs unions as long as they covered almost all trade and did not raise external trade barriers. The customs union was supported by the United States, and acceptance by nonmembers was facilitated by EEC participation in the Kennedy Round of multilateral trade negotiations, which led to substantial cuts to the common external tariff during the 1960s.[1] The main areas of GATT noncompliance were sector-specific measures in agriculture, textiles and clothing, steel, and cars and preferential treatment of former colonies.[2] The customs union was completed in 1968.

In response, seven countries (Austria, Denmark, Norway, Portugal, Sweden, Switzerland, and the UK) formed the European Free Trade Association (EFTA) in 1959. Their vision was of a free trade area, excluding agriculture and fisheries, without supranational institutions or a common external trade policy. This ushered in a brief period of bloc competition when the EEC signed association agreements with Greece (1961) and Turkey (1963), and Finland became an associate member of EFTA in 1961.

The main difference between a customs union and a free trade area is that, although both feature tariff-free trade among member countries, in a customs union there is a common external tariff (CET), whereas in a free trade area (FTA) national governments set their own tariffs on trade with nonmembers. A customs union was harder to negotiate because it required agreement on the CET and a common negotiating position in GATT. It also required agreement on an EEC budget to the extent that tariff revenues were a union resource rather than national revenues accruing to the nation controlling the port of entry. These two areas, commercial and fiscal policy, have long been considered key competences of the nation-state, and hence raised the supranational specter.

Establishing an FTA appears easier because members retain their own trade policies toward nonmembers and keep their tariff revenue. There is, however, a problem of trade deflection. If Norway and Sweden form an FTA with different tariffs on goods imported from nonmembers, the temptation will be for those goods to be routed via the low-tariff point of entry into the FTA; in that case, the low-tariff country receives all of the tariff revenue and the high-tariff country fails to achieve its presumed goal of protecting domestic producers. This leads to a race to the bottom as each member seeks to be the low-tariff country until the tariff rates drop to zero and no country has an independent trade policy nor receives any tariff revenue. The answer is to impose rules of origin to determine that any good passing across an internal border was genuinely produced in the FTA member and not produced in a third country and falsely labeled.[3] Goods must be checked at the internal border to ensure that any declaration of origin is genuine, and such procedures will interfere with free internal trade by adding complexity.

The battle of the blocs was won by the EEC. Before the end of the twentieth century, five of the seven founder members of EFTA, and associate member Finland, had joined the EEC. The UK already split ranks with EFTA in the early 1960s and after two unsuccessful applications joined the EEC in 1973. This had little to do with the relative merits of a customs union versus a free trade area and everything to do with the economic dynamism of the six signatories of the Treaty of Rome. Recovery from wartime devastation was faster and more thorough than had been anticipated. Cities lay in ruins, but the human capital of the survivors (i.e., skills and attitudes) remained intact and may even have been enhanced by wartime challenges. Physical capital (i.e., factories, infrastructure, and machinery and equipment) could be rebuilt or more likely replaced by newer state-of-the-art facilities. Meanwhile in the UK and Scandinavia, there was less pressure to replace still-functioning factories or to change prewar practices and attitudes that had survived intact.

2.2 Economic Consequences of the Customs Union in Manufactures

The customs union established between 1958 and 1968 benefited from the exceptionally favorable external environment of the global long boom that would last until the early 1970s. The freeing up of internal trade and reduced tariffs on external trade added to the economic prosperity of the Six.

In principle, formation of a custom union could have positive or negative economic impact. The paradox is explained by the coexistence of trade creation and trade diversion (Viner 1950). Removing tariffs on internal trade improves resource allocation by replacing inefficient domestic producers with more efficient partner producers and by allowing consumers to purchase more goods at a lower price; both of these effects involve trade creation. Maintaining tariffs on imports from nonmembers creates a new distortion in that duty-free imports from a fellow member could displace imports from a third country whose pretariff price is lower but whose goods are more expensive than the partner's goods after the tariff is imposed; this diverts trade from a more efficient to a less efficient partner, reducing well-being of the importing country and of the world.

The trade-creating and trade-diverting impact of a preferential tariff can be illustrated by analysis of an import-competing good for which the partner's price is above the world price but below the pre-integration domestic price. The argument is set out with the help of Figure 2A1 in the Appendix to Chapter 2. A key conclusion is that the balance between trade creation and trade diversion is likely to depend on the degree to which the partner's price is close to the world price or to the tariff-inclusive domestic price.

In the customs union in manufactured goods established by the Six in the 1960s, it was highly likely that for any good imported by one of the Six, an EEC partner country would be able to supply that good at close to the world price—that is, trade creation would dominate. This presumption was reinforced by the Kennedy Round reductions in the common external tariff, which left less scope for a partner import to be far above the world price. There may also have been a terms of trade effect (as the Six reduced their demand for imports from third countries, the price of those goods would drop), but the reduced scope for trade diversion diminished the importance of this channel.

A surprising feature of the trade created in the customs union was that rather than the expected inter-industry trade (e.g., Italian shoes for

German cars), much of the new trade was intra-industry trade (e.g., Italian cars for German cars). The most popular explanation of the phenomenon was based on economies of scale combined with diversity of tastes, which meant that minority tastes might be met by imports—for example, Germany imported small cars from Italy and Italy imported large cars from Germany (Balassa 1966; Grubel and Lloyd 1975). The idea was taken up in the "new trade theory" of the late 1970s and 1980s that highlighted increased product choice and reduced costs through realization of scale economies as added gains from trade.

The success of the customs union encouraged many imitators outside Europe, such as the East African Community (EAC) or the Central American Common Market (CACM). The failure of these arrangements among developing countries illustrated the potential ambiguity of customs union. The participants hoped that a larger internal market would help them to industrialize. This partially came true, but industrial development tended to be geographically concentrated—for example, in Kenya in the EAC, and the EAC partners Uganda and Tanzania found that their manufactured imports were coming from Kenya rather than as generally lower-priced and better-quality imports from the established industrial powers. Triggers for dissolution of the customs unions were idiosyncratic (the overthrow of Ugandan dictator Idi Amin by Tanzanian forces and the Honduras-Salvador soccer war in Central America), but the underlying source of customs union failure in both cases was the dominance of trade diversion.

In sum, the customs union contributed to the success of European integration in the 1960s, not because customs unions are inherently good but because the EEC included enough of the world's leading producers of manufactured goods and because the customs union was not constructed behind a high common external tariff. The customs union was incomplete insofar as some sectors received special treatment, notably agriculture for which a common agricultural policy was under construction in the 1960s, textiles and clothing, for which a complex array of quotas on imports from low-wage countries was being established by the high-income countries (including the Six), and cars for which there were some restrictions on imports from outside the EEC. These were of little significance in the 1960s, but agriculture would assume greater salience in the 1970s as the common agricultural policy was implemented.

2.3 Including Agriculture in the Customs Union

When the Treaty of Rome was signed, agriculture was a major source of employment in the six countries.[4] Agriculture would be included in the common market, but it was agreed that special policies were needed for the sector. The common agricultural policy (CAP) implemented in the 1960s and early 1970s aimed to maintain farmers' incomes by manipulating farm gate prices and supply conditions, while keeping the principle of free trade within the customs union. The CAP took longer to complete than the customs union in manufactures, largely due to the specificity of farm products, and required annual bargaining on the common prices for every product. Hard bargaining was inevitable; for any good, producers and consumers had opposing interests.

The CAP details varied from product to product and in some cases by season (e.g., because of different degrees of perishability) but generally involved protecting the income of the poorest farmers. A common approach, applied to cereals for example, was for the six members to negotiate an intervention price at which crops would be purchased and to maintain this price by a variable import levy—that is, a tax on imports equal to the difference between the intervention price and the world price.

When the CAP was introduced in the 1960s, the EC was a net importer in agricultural markets so that the burden of the CAP fell primarily on consumers, who paid higher prices to support farm incomes. However, as labor productivity and agricultural product self-sufficiency increased, surpluses emerged at the intervention prices and stocks began to accumulate (not only in grains but also as butter mountains and wine lakes). In order to dispose of the surplus, the EEC offered export subsidies.[5] The stockpiles and subsidies were financed from the EC budget, and by the second half of the 1970s, they accounted for the lion's share of EC expenditure. The CAP also included measures intended to promote structural reform and improve efficiency, although farmers and national ministries of agriculture resisted any change other than increases in intervention prices. Perversely, the CAP was of greatest benefit to large-scale farmers or landowners and did not maintain poorer farmers' income sufficiently to keep them in the farm sector.[6] In each of the six countries, less than 5 percent of the workforce was working in agriculture in the 1990s.

When the UK joined the EU in 1973, it suffered substantial economic costs from adopting the CAP. As a major food importer, the UK had to abandon its existing efficient suppliers in favor of less efficient intra-EC suppliers. British residents suffered from higher food prices, while farmers in Australia and New Zealand lost their biggest export market. The CAP was also at the heart of the budget imbalance that lay behind Prime Minister Thatcher's demand for a rebate in the 1980s. France, which was a major beneficiary from the CAP, adamantly opposed any serious reform despite the increasing claim of the CAP on the EC budget.[7]

Although the CAP was complex, and became increasingly so, the essentials of its impact can be analyzed in similar manner to a tariff (i.e., with the partial equilibrium Figure 2A.1). A variable levy targeted to achieve a specific level of imports has equivalent effects to the tariff that would reduce imports to that level; one instrument works on quantity and the other on price, but the short-run impact on producers and consumers and the deadweight losses are identical. Differences arise over time because the gap between world price and domestic price is fixed by a tariff but variable under the CAP. When world agricultural prices were high (as in early to mid-1970s), the gap was small and the policy was relatively inexpensive. When world prices fell but CAP intervention prices did not fall, the variable levies and the net welfare losses increased.

The end of the Bretton Woods fixed exchange rates regime in 1971–1973 caused serious complications for the CAP. Each common agricultural price was the outcome of hard bargaining between importers and exporters of a good with varying degrees of interest in consumers' and producers' welfare. When exchange rates fluctuated, national prices diverged, which was incompatible with maintaining internal free trade and the policy objectives underlying the negotiations. Negotiating new common prices would be arduous (and impractical in conditions of daily exchange rate fluctuations). Common prices were maintained by using artificial "green exchange rates," and monetary compensation amounts (MCAs) from the Community budget were used to compensate member governments for the difference between support at green exchange rates and at market exchange rates. These stop-gap measures added to the complexity of the CAP and encouraged smuggling as green exchange rates differed from market exchange rates. National responses to MCAs were asymmetrical; governments receiving MCAs were slower to adjust the support prices in their national currency than governments with negative MCAs which required payment into the EC budget. By the late 1970s, the CAP ate up three-quarters of the EC budget, but farmer opposition stymied effective reform.

A further dynamic effect of the CAP was the supply-side impact. As agricultural productivity increased, the EC shifted from being a net importer to having a surplus in many agricultural goods at the support price. The Commission maintained the support prices by accumulating stocks in grain or butter mountains and wine lakes. In this situation, the notional variable levy might be high, but with no imports there was no revenue from levies, and the costs of maintaining stocks mounted. Some of the surpluses were disposed of as aid to poor countries or exported. Because the EU price was above the world price, exports involved subsidies, increasing the strain on the Community budget.

2.4 Enlarging the Customs Union in 1973

In January 1973, the UK, Ireland, and Denmark joined the EEC. The new members were obliged to accept existing policies (the *acquis communautaire*), including the CAP. For the UK, the political decision to be part of Europe was economically costly in the short run because the UK had low trade barriers, which meant that there was little scope for trade creation in manufactured goods, and was a food importer so that the CAP ensured substantial trade diversion in agriculture.

Pressure from agricultural ministries led to support prices rising when world prices were high and not falling when world prices were low so that the variable levies on imports became larger over time. The large and increasing variable levies meant that EEC prices were substantially above world prices for many farm products, including grains, meats, and dairy products. For the UK, the situation was exacerbated by the requirement to observe the common commercial policy and abandon Commonwealth Preferences favoring countries such as Australia and New Zealand. The overall result was large short-run losses for the UK due to trade diversion, and loss of a major market for Australian and New Zealand farmers. In sum, the first enlargement had large negative impact on these three countries, while having less effect on other countries. Ireland and Denmark, as agricultural exporters, benefited from the CAP. The remaining EFTA countries formed a free trade area in manufactures with the EC9, establishing more or less tariff-free trade in Western Europe.

One interpretation of the UK's accession debacle focused on the importance of being at the table when rules are being set. The UK's pre-accession agricultural policy was based on subsidies to farmers rather than support prices. For a given level of assistance, this is a superior approach because it does not harm consumers (i.e., it results in only one of the deadweight-loss triangles in Figure 2A.1). If the UK had signed the Treaty of Rome, it could have influenced the CAP design. The general point about a seat at the table is valid, but the CAP design was influenced by the EEC's limited financial resources; a subsidy approach in the 1960s would have required commitment of public funds beyond the EEC's capacity, whereas the variable levy and support prices placed the burden on consumers. Since everybody consumes food, and meat, grains, and dairy products are not a major part of the average European household's budget, the CAP as implemented was a politically astute solution, even though it was economically second best and would lead to long-term problems by encouraging excess supply.

The net economic costs to the UK of EEC accession were a short-term phenomenon. British farmers adjusted to the CAP, and the large landowners became significant recipients of funds. The long-run impact of EU membership is harder to assess, but it was probably positive (see Appendix to Chapter 6). In particular, success stories like the revival of the UK car industry as an assembly hub for Japanese companies and the success of London as a global financial center after the Big Bang reforms of the 1980s would both have been less plausible in the absence of EU membership.

2.5 Enlarging the Customs Union in the 1980s

The accession of Greece in 1981 and of Portugal and Spain in 1986 was made possible by political changes in those countries in the mid-1970s. There was no reason to exclude the newly democratic countries from the EEC, but existing members were concerned about expansion to include poor southern European countries. As with the 1973 enlargement, the new members were obliged to accept existing EEC policies (the *acquis communautaire*).

The challenge for the CAP was that it had been designed to assist northern European farmers who produced grain and animal products. Italy as the only major producer of Mediterranean products was happy with simpler regimes for its farm products that protected farmers from nonmember competition. Accession of Greece and Spain opened up the prospect of greater internal competition in citrus fruit, tomatoes, and olive oil. This involved extension of the CAP and negative effects especially on Morocco and Tunisia (Pomfret 1981).

An unanticipated consequence of the 1980s enlargement was the emergence of Spain as a major car exporter within Europe. In 1973–1976, Ford Motors opened a greenfield facility in Valencia to produce a new European model, the Fiesta, benefiting from the opening of the Spanish economy during the final years of Franco's dictatorship to source components from across the EEC for the assembly line in Valencia.

When the first car rolled off the assembly line in 1976, Spain was a democracy aspiring to EEC membership. The Ford Fiesta quickly became a prime example of a car assembled from components sourced from across the EEC and sold in markets across the EEC.

The Ford example highlights the difficulty of measuring accession benefits when the probability of joining is apparent years before the formal accession date and when membership in the union is contemporary with other major changes such as the end of fascism in Spain and Portugal (or the end of communism in Eastern Europe two decades later). In such circumstances, it is unclear to what extent past parameters can be used to generate estimates of economic outcomes[8] and difficult to establish the counterfactual of nonmembership (see Appendix to Chapter 6).

2.6 Other Economic Consequences of Market Integration

Many supporters of European integration argued that the static resource allocation effects captured in the trade-creation versus trade-diversion framework ignored dynamic effects of the customs union. Integration affects growth via its effect on investment in physical capital, human capital, and knowledge capital. At a minimum, the improved allocation and efficiency reflected in trade creation lead to a better investment climate and more investment in machines, skills, and technology. Increased output per head is not only good in itself; assuming a constant propensity to save out of income, increased output is associated with higher savings and investment, creating a virtuous higher investment and growth circle. With diminishing returns to capital, the rise in output per person eventually stops at a new, higher level (Solow 1956).

The growth effects are difficult to prove because growth and investment are typically driven by multiple causes. Such consequences of the first enlargement are essentially unproven. The Irish economy enjoyed spectacular growth in the decades after joining the EEC for which accession was surely a catalyst, even if it was not the only cause, but changes in long-term economic growth were less obvious in Denmark or the UK.[9] The second enlargement was associated with a dramatic increase in foreign direct investment in Spain, from about one percent of gross domestic product (GDP) in 1986 to almost five percent in 1990, but no discernible change in this ratio in Greece or Portugal. Again, suggesting that economic integration was a catalyst but not the sole cause.

A significant part of globalization since the 1980s is that global value chains (GVCs) have become an important element of the global economy. Historically, international trade was mostly arm's-length trade, selling a good or material for barter or cash. The GVC phenomenon emerged when reductions in the cost of doing international trade led to increasing fragmentation of the production process as tasks were shifted across borders to lower-cost or better-quality suppliers of components and services.[10] Much of the initial relocation of labor-intensive activities in the 1960s and 1970s was to Asia, but where access to final markets in rich countries was restricted (e.g., in clothing or in cars) lower-wage countries with preferential market access might be more attractive. A quarter of Malta's workforce in the 1970s assembled Wrangler jeans for export to the company's European marketing center in Brussels (Grech 1978). Ford's Valencia factory in Spain, which used inputs from other EC member countries, was a striking early example in the European car industry.

Despite the abbreviation GVC, in the early twenty-first century the process was more regional than global. In Europe, the integration of an economically heterogeneous set of countries was the explanation for the expansion of regional value chains. The process started within the Global Mediterranean Policy of the 1970s and the imminent EEC accession of poorer southern countries after the democratic revolutions in Greece, Portugal, and Spain in the mid-1970s. It would gather force with the accession expectations of a larger number of even lower-wage Eastern European countries after 1989.

2.7 Relations with Nonmembers

From the start, the Community rather than the nation-states held exclusive power to set trade policy. There was agreement on tariff cuts in the Kennedy Round. Other early issues included differing national interests on postcolonial relations, and differing attitudes toward other nonmembers, especially as trade policy and foreign policy overlapped (e.g., on relations with Greece and Turkey). These were more controversial than the common external tariff and less satisfactorily resolved. The EEC created a pyramid of preferences, but partners worried about their place in the hierarchy and members worried about the complexity.

With no common foreign policy, the EEC used trade policy to strengthen external ties and in doing so created a hierarchy of preferential treatment. As part of the first enlargement, the EC-EFTA free trade area in manufactures was created in 1972. Special relations with Greece, Turkey, North African and eastern Mediterranean countries, and the islands of Cyprus and Malta were consolidated into a Global Mediterranean Policy in 1972, under which the EEC offered free market access in manufactures plus some privileged treatment for agricultural goods.[11] The Yaoundé Convention granted special treatment to ex-colonies and was extended to include former British colonies and other African, Caribbean, and Pacific (ACP) countries in the 1975 Lomé Convention.[12] The EEC was a promoter and supporter of the Generalized System of Preferences (GSP) as an exception to GATT rules on nondiscrimination; the GSP was legitimized in 1971 as a ten-year waiver to GATT Article I requiring most-favored nation (MFN) treatment, and in 1979, the waiver was replaced by the Enabling Clause that provided a permanent legal basis for granting preferential tariffs on imports from developing countries and special treatment for the least developed countries.[13] The supposedly nondiscriminatory MFN tariff only applied to imports from seven of the EU's trading partners in the 1970s: Australia, Canada, Japan, New Zealand, South Korea, Taiwan, and the United States. The Communist nonmarket economies received worse than MFN treatment.

The pyramid of preferences was inherently unstable. Partner countries tended to focus on their treatment relative to countries that they saw as competitors or rivals, rather than on benefits accruing from preferential treatment. This was an insoluble conundrum for the EEC because any step to encourage warmer relations with a partner through the offer of better preferential trade terms was inevitably associated with relatively worse discrimination against other trade partners. During the 1980s, external trade relations with countries in the pyramid of preferences were pushed into the background by more urgent internal EEC concerns and trade relations with MFN partners (i.e., the United States and Japan). The day of reckoning came at the 1990 GATT ministerial meeting in Montréal when the major trading nations (the United States, EEC, Japan, and Canada) committed to supporting the nondiscriminatory global trading system, that in 1995 would be institutionalized in establishment of the World Trade Organization (WTO). This commitment would leave little scope for preferential tariffs and one-way trade preferences were outlawed.

2.8 Areas of Limited Progress:
Competition Policy and Regional Policy

The Treaty of Rome prohibited any action that prevents, restricts, or dis-torts competition in the common market, and put the Commission in charge of enforcing these strictures. The treaty contained two articles on competition policy: Article 101 dealing with horizontal and vertical agreements and Article 102 dealing with abuse of dominant position.[14] The European Commission has sole power to regulate the EU's compe-tition policy (i.e., its decisions are not subject to approval by the Council or the Parliament, but they can be overturned by the EU Court) and the Commission was granted extensive powers, including the right to

- make on-site inspections without prior warning;
- with a court order, inspect the homes of company personnel;
- impose fines on firms found guilty of anticompetitive conduct, up to a maximum of 10 percent of the firm's worldwide turn-over; and
- force firms to repay subsidies it deems to be illicit.

These surprisingly sweeping powers were considered essential to prevent nation-states' support of domestic firms from distorting competition within the common market. However, implementation was lax, and the first fines were not issued until 1969 when six firms were found guilty of fixing quinine markets. After the 1973–1974 oil crisis, industrial policy took precedence over competition policy and the Commission explic-itly allowed "crisis cartels" in declining industries.

The Treaty of Rome bans state aid (broadly defined) that provides firms with an unfair advantage and thus distorts competition. This was necessary because member governments differ over how much they can or want to subsidize loss-making firms. If only some governments sub-sidize their firms, the outcome may be "unfair" since restructuring may be forced on the firms in nations that do not subsidize. As another example, consider subsidies that prevent restructuring because each government makes annual payments to all firms exactly equal to their losses: all firms break even, no new firms will enter, and taxpayers pay for inefficient firms. Exceptions to the ban on state aid are allowed if assistance is related to social policy, natural disaster aid, and economic development aid to regions. As with other aspects of competition policy, enforcement was weak during the customs union decades.

The Treaty of Rome provided for common policies with respect to trade, transport, and competition but envisaged no supranational role in promoting distributional equity. The CAP may have helped the poorer rural population, although in practice the biggest financial benefits went to large landowners. The only explicitly distributive feature of the Rome treaty was a commitment to the principle of equal pay for equal work by men and women, inserted at French insistence due to fears that members who did not enforce equal pay would undercut French producers by using cheap female labor. Social policies were largely ignored at the Community level between 1958 and the 1970s, even though increased unemployment after 1973 led to calls for social harmonization.

Similarly, with respect to regional policy, although some level of economic solidarity is implicit in the Treaty of Rome, the expectation appears to have been that geographical inequalities would diminish in the customs union as market forces led to economic convergence. The reality of the customs union was less clear, especially for the poorer countries that joined in the 1970s and 1980s—for example, Ireland converged quickly toward the incomes of the original members whereas Greece did not.[15] The Social Fund established in the Rome treaty was small and initially not concentrated on poor regions, although in the 1970s, it became focused on vocational training in problem regions. The Structural Agricultural Fund, introduced in 1968 to promote modernization of agriculture, may have disproportionately gone to poorer rural areas. The Regional Development Fund was introduced in 1975. By the 1980s, these could all have been vehicles to accelerate convergence, but the funding levels were small.

A general feature of the EC during the 1960s, 1970s, and early 1980s was the limited resources available to the Commission. The revenue from trade taxes and a fraction of value-added taxes was largely consumed by the CAP, leaving little funding for other policies. The budgetary constraint would only be loosened in the late 1980s when the EU began levying a common percentage of members' gross national income.

2.9 Monetary Integration: Attempted, Failed, Revived

The Treaty of Rome made no mention of monetary integration. In 1957, the main financial constraint on economic integration was foreign exchange controls, which limited firms' ability to obtain the foreign currency to pay for imported inputs. After the Six removed their foreign exchange controls in 1958, the Bretton Woods system based on fixed exchange rates was expected to last indefinitely. However, in 1969, a large devaluation of the French franc and revaluation of the German mark undermined expectations of exchange rate stability and raised questions of how well the customs union could function if exchange rates were not fixed.

The EEC's response was the 1970 Werner Plan, which proposed gradually increasing the degree of fixedness of bilateral exchange rates between EEC members until permanently fixed rates could be replaced by a common currency in 1980. The prospects for success were assessed against the optimum currency area (OCA) criteria developed by Robert Mundell and Robert McKinnon in the 1960s. There is a trade-off between the microeconomic benefits from a common currency and the loss of a macro policy instrument when a country gives up their national currency.

For a small open economy, the microeconomic benefits of joining a larger currency area are large and the loss of macroeconomic independence is minor; thus, Brunei, Monaco, Timor-Leste, and other small economies use another currency (SGD, EUR, USD in these cases). The microeconomic benefits consist of reduced transactions costs and easier comparability of prices. The benefits include elimination of foreign exchange fees and of exchange rate risk (for transactions and foreign direct investment) which reduces uncertainty. Harder to quantify, price transparency reduces search costs, and facilitates competition as firms are better able to identify best suppliers and customers and as consumers can shop around in a larger market. In labor and capital markets, people can be better matched to jobs and investors can better compare locations across countries when prices are in a common currency. All of the above intensify trade and investment flows and increase economic integration. Exchange rate volatility exacerbates the costs of having separate currencies.

What does the OCA trade-off depend on? Mundell (1961) focused on labor mobility. If labor is mobile between two countries, then macroeconomic imbalances can be resolved by labor movement, as interstate labor mobility does in the United States. Labor mobility is easier within national borders (due to similarities of culture, language, legislation, welfare state, etc.) than across countries, and Mundell's criterion helps to explain the general phenomenon that the number of currencies matches the number of countries, except for microstates.

McKinnon focused on openness. Traded goods' prices are set worldwide; if all goods are traded, domestic prices of goods must be flexible (adjusting to the world price) and the exchange rate does not matter for competitiveness. This criterion helps to explain why smaller EU countries such as Belgium, Luxembourg, the Netherlands, and Denmark were more willing to maintain a fixed exchange rate (to the German mark) during the turmoil of the 1970s.

Following the Werner Plan, the first step toward monetary integration was to manage more limited fluctuations in EEC countries' bilateral exchange rates. This took place against the background of the 1971–1973 collapse of the Bretton Woods fixed exchange rate system. As the US dollar was allowed to float, the movement of the European currencies was conceived as a snake within a tunnel; the wider tunnel represented the potential range of EEC national currencies' exchange rates against the dollar, while the narrower Snake captured the actual range of EEC countries' dollar exchange rates given the constraints on their bilateral exchange rate fluctuations. The Snake broke down almost immediately in 1972–1973 because EEC national governments would not give up their control over monetary policy, and hence of the value of their national currency against other currencies. The arrangement was finally formally abandoned in 1976.

Circumstances were adverse. After twenty-five years of prosperity with generally stable exchange rates and prices, the early 1970s saw large, probably asymmetric, shocks. As well as the end of the Bretton Woods system of fixed exchange rates, prices of many commodities spiked (e.g., beef in 1972, oil in October 1973). The EEC member countries experienced unforeseen stagflation (simultaneous increases in unemployment and in inflation) and had different priorities; low inflation for Germany, low unemployment for Italy and the UK, and France wanted to maintain the Snake and reduce unemployment. Fixed bilateral exchange rates between these four large countries were untenable, although the smaller countries were more willing to prioritize exchange rate stability. After the collapse of the Snake, the German mark rose in value against the US dollar while the UK pound and the Italian lira fell in value (Figure 2.1).

Surprisingly, German chancellor Helmut Schmidt, French president Valéry Giscard d'Estaing, and chair of the EU Commission Roy Jenkins set about introducing a new version of the Snake in 1977–1978. The European Monetary System (EMS) was effectively the same as the Snake with a few cosmetic changes: exchange rates were expressed in terms of a unit of account (the ecu) and a divergence indicator highlighted when an exchange rate was nearing the limit of its range. The intentions resembled the Werner Plan in starting with fixed but adjustable exchange rates in 1979 and, after gradual tightening of the degree of fixedness, replacing national currencies by a common currency. The difference was that the EMS fulfilled these intentions when it was replaced by the euro two decades later. The survival of the EMS cannot be explained by more favorable initial conditions; the second oil shock in 1979–1980 was arguably as severe as the 1973 oil shock (Figure 2.2).

Why did Schmidt, Giscard, and Jenkins revive the Snake? Apart from trade, the main EEC common policy was the CAP, which had been introduced gradually in the 1960s. By the mid-1970s, the CAP accounted for two-thirds of the EEC budget, and the cost was rising as excess supply increased. Operation of the CAP was disrupted by the more volatile exchange rates after the Snake collapse. To smooth out the domestic price changes for agricultural products that would follow exchange rate changes, the EEC introduced artificial "green exchange rates" that changed more slowly than market exchange rates. Monetary compensation amounts (MCAs) were paid to or collected from countries suffering or benefiting from the gap between green and market exchange rates. The system was designed to stabilize prices, but there was a bias as countries adjusted their green exchange rates quickly if the gap

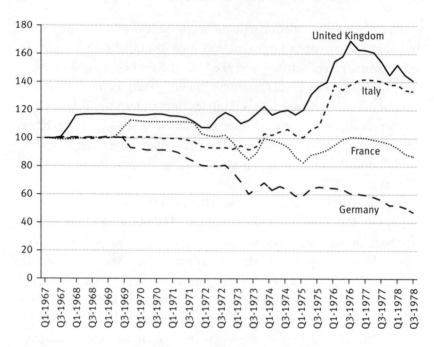

Figure 2.1 **Exchange Rates against the US Dollar, 1967–1978**
Notes: Exchange rates defined as amount of national currency to buy one US dollar,
indexed to January 1967 = 100; increases indicate a weakening currency.

Source: OECD.

involved making payments and closed the gap between green and
market exchange rates at a more leisurely pace if they were receiving
MCAs. In short, the CAP was becoming more complex and expensive
in the presence of exchange rate changes.[16]

During the 1970s, much of the academic debate on monetary integration was conducted within the framework of optimal currency area
theory and the trade-off between the microeconomic benefits of a supranational currency in the form of reduced transactions costs and the
macroeconomic benefits of a national currency in terms of monetary
policy independence. The benefits of a supranational currency are greater
for a small economy which has little monetary policy independence and
whose currency has little international use. Large countries are less concerned about the transactions benefits and have more monetary inde-

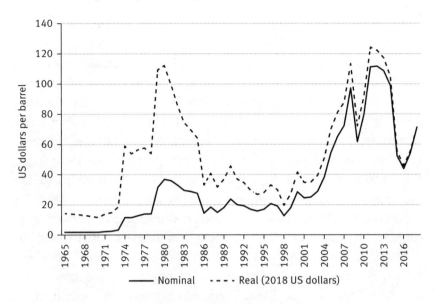

Figure 2.2 Oil Prices, 1965–2018
Source: BP Statistical Review of World Energy 2019.

pendence to lose, which is why the UK, Italy, and France were the most eager to leave the Snake.

By the late 1970s, both the macroeconomic and microeconomic sides of the OCA calculus were being reassessed by policy makers. The capacity to fine-tune the macroeconomy by fiscal and monetary policies to achieve a preferred balance between unemployment and inflation was being questioned, with the conclusion being to prioritize inflation and then tackle unemployment.[17] As all EEC governments adopted this perspective, the benefits of an independent monetary policy rather than a shared European monetary policy diminished. On the microeconomic side, the experience with the CAP and MCAs showed that beyond the reduced private transactions costs that accompany a common currency, there are reduced public sector bargaining costs. Although the CAP was the trigger, the more general argument is that floating exchange rates in a federation with common policies leads to higher public sector transactions costs (i.e., political bargains become undone and need to be revised) and this helps to explain why almost all countries have a single national currency as legal tender rather than a set of subnational currencies.

The experiences of the 1970s and early 1980s involved a learning process in which most EEC leaders came to recognize the role of exchange rate fluctuations in increasing private and public transactions costs. Acknowledgment of the costs of exchange rate fluctuations is evident from the chronology of EMS realignments (Table 2.1).[18] Between 1979 and 1986, realignments were frequent and included the two major French realignments after François Mitterrand became president in 1981. Between 13 January 1987 and the currency crisis of 13 September 1992, there was a single realignment. After September 1992, the only changes were to the exchange rates of the Spanish peseta and Portuguese escudo.

Application of OCA theory is limited, because the general rule is *one country, one currency* (Pomfret 2005). Nevertheless, OCA theory is useful in explaining the road to the euro because over time labor became more mobile in the EEC, members' economies became more open, and the EU became more like a federation after 1993. Thus, sacrificing a macroeconomic policy tool became less costly and the microeconomic benefits of a common currency became larger. Equally important was the painful lesson from the 1970s' stagflation that the idea of a long-term trade-off between inflation and unemployment was illusory. The Western European countries all drew the conclusion in the 1980s that inflation was the appropriate target for monetary policy. Agreement on the conduct of monetary policy is the essential prerequisite for voluntary currency union.[19]

2.10 The Limits to Customs Union as an Integration Instrument

By the 1980s, the pathway to European integration via establishment of a customs union had clearly been successful—up to a point. The customs union, including the controversial agricultural policy, yielded economic benefits from integration, although as with any major economic change there were gainers and losers along the way. The twentieth-century enlargements, including the 1995 extension to Austria, Finland, and Sweden, had teething problems but were relatively easy because they involved more or less similar economies to the original Six.

Table 2.1   Exchange Rate Realignments within the EMS, 1979–1995

Date	24/9/79	30/11/79	22/3/81	5/10/81	22/2/82	14/6/82	21/3/83	18/5/83	22/7/85
Number	2	1	1	2	2	4	7*	7*	7*

Date	7/4/86	4/8/86	12/1/87	8/1/90	14/9/92	23/11/92	1/2/93	14/5/93	6/3/95
Number	5	1	3	1	3#	2	1	2	2

Note: * complete realignment; # on 14/9/92 the British pound and Italian lira left the ERM, subsequent realignments involved only the Spanish peseta and Portuguese escudo.

External trade policy in the 1960s had been positive and imaginative in engaging in multilateral trade negotiations to reduce tariffs on an MFN basis. Attempts to use tariff preferences as foreign policy tools were less successful, and that policy was looking threadbare by the 1980s, but it was not an existential issue for the EEC. The Ford Fiesta was a harbinger of the need to adapt to a changing global economy based on fragmentation of production along global value chains, but that challenge was still on the horizon in the 1980s.

More fundamental were the pressures for deeper integration suggesting that the customs union was not a stable equilibrium. The failed monetary integration of the early 1970s and speedy readoption of the target in 1977–1978 was the strongest sign. The common competition and state aid policies, not yet actively pursued in the 1970s, were an indicator that the Commission should shift gears in enforcing a level playing field—a position reinforced by growing concerns over the implications of mergers and acquisitions during the 1980s. Most striking was a 1979 decision of the European Court showing that, once internal tariffs had been eliminated, nontariff barriers became more significant and needed to be addressed.

The 1979 *Cassis de Dijon* case was the first step toward deeper integration of goods markets.[20] Completion of the customs union and increased internal trade exposed nontariff barriers that impeded trade among EEC member countries. The European Court found against the German government's ban on the sale of cassis, which was permitted in Germany neither as a wine (the alcohol content was too high) nor as a spirit (the alcohol content was too low). The Court concluded that since the alcoholic beverage could be sold in France, there was no basis in health or other reasons for banning sale in Germany. This assertion of the mutual recognition principle, given the force of law by the EU Court, immediately threatened many nontariff barriers to internal trade. If a member objected to mutual recognition, as did many producers (e.g., German brewers wanting to protect their centuries-old traditional ingredients for beer), then they would have to harmonize rules to incorporate, or to ban, such exceptions. The balance between mutual recognition or harmonization would be central to the Single Market program adopted in the 1980s to "complete" the internal market by 1992.

Measuring Economic Impacts of a Customs Union

In the original customs union in manufactured goods between the six signatories of the Treaty of Rome, tariffs on trade among members were eliminated by 1968 and a common external tariff was applied to imports from third countries. In principle, the economic impact on the Six could have been ambiguous, depending on the balance between new trade being created and existing trade being diverted from more efficient external suppliers to less efficient internal suppliers (Viner 1950). The simplest way of illustrating this ambiguity, and resolving it under specific circumstances, is to use a partial equilibrium demand and supply diagram for an import-competing industry in one of the member countries (Figure 2A1).

The EEC Customs Union, 1958–1968

In Figure 2A1, the domestic price of a good (P_d) before the customs union is determined by the world price, P_w, plus the tariff. The customs union has an impact if the duty-free price from the preferred partner, P_b, is lower than P_d, in which case preexisting imports Q_1Q_2 are diverted from third countries to the preferred partner. The lower price, $P_b < P_d$, encourages greater consumption, by an amount Q_2Q_3, and displaces some domestic production by imports, quantity Q_0Q_1, both of which create more international trade (Q_0Q_3 instead of Q_1Q_2). The trade-creating effects $(Q_0Q_1 + Q_2Q_3)$ are positive resource allocation effects, while the trade

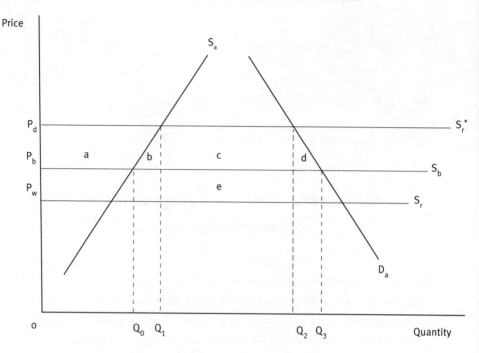

Figure 2A1 Effect of a Zero-Value Preferential Tariff
Note: The zero-valued tariff is granted by importing country A on imports from partner B,
assuming no impact on prices from the rest of the world, r.

diversion ($Q_1 Q_2$) is a negative resource allocation effect because imports
come from a less efficient supplier.

The welfare impacts consist of benefits to consumers (consumer surplus increases by area $a + b + c + d$), losses to domestic producers (producer surplus decreases by area a), and lost tariff revenue (area $c + e$). The
net welfare effect ($b + d - e$) is ambiguous, depending on the relative
magnitude of created and diverted trade, the slopes of S_a and D_a, and
where P_b lies in the range between P_w and P_d.

A tariff reduces the potential gains from trade, because units produced domestically at price P_d could be imported at lower cost and
units that would be consumed at P_w are not consumed. The first-best
policy would be to remove the tariff on all imports, maximizing the size
of the two triangles and eliminating area e. Preferential trade reduction
is a second-best policy and removing one distortion ($P_d - P_w$) while introducing a new distortion ($P_b - P_w$) may or may not be net welfare improving. With either a preferential or a non-preferential tariff reduction,

there are distributional effects: consumers gain and import-competing producers lose from tariff reduction, and the producers may lobby against change (or be considered deserving of protection, as in the case of European farmers).

In the customs union in manufactured goods formed between 1958 and 1968, the welfare gains from trade creation swamped the welfare costs due to trade diversion, because for most manufactured goods a producer somewhere in the Six would have been producing at close to the world price. If P_b is close to P_w, then $b + d - e$ will be positive. Thus, the trade diversion costs should not have been great, whereas the trade creation gains from removing the high pre-1958 tariffs on intra-European trade would have been more substantial.

Figure 2A1 is based on strong simplifying assumptions. With perfectly elastic supply curves, transfer of $Q_1 Q_2$ units from outsider suppliers to insiders is complete, and there is no cost to outsiders who can sell all they want on the world market at P_w irrespective of demand in this country. Incorporating more realistic upward-sloping supply curves is not difficult, although it makes the figure more complex and less clear (Pomfret 2001, 198). Exporters in country b still benefit from the preferential tariff treatment, and exporters in the rest of the world lose; there is little evidence that for the EC6 the other adjustments would change the principal conclusions based on Figure 2A1.[21] The analysis is partial equilibrium, meaning that it ignores impacts on labor markets (the workers who are displaced by the fall in domestic production find new jobs in the perfectly competitive labor markets) and the increased imports are paid for without affecting the exchange rate (and hence P_w, measured in domestic currency units, is unchanged).

Many studies have estimated the trade and welfare effects of the customs union. Mayes (1978) and Pomfret (2001, 264–275) review this literature, which generally confirms the presumption of net economic benefits to the Six from the customs union in manufactured goods due to trade creation. Trade diversion did occur, suggested by the share of intra-EEC trade increasing from around 30 percent of member countries' total trade in 1958 to around 45 percent in 1970 (Baldwin and Wyplosz 2015, 126–127). However, although third countries lost market share, their exports to the customs union increased rapidly; in 1970, the EEC6 imported $90 billion worth of goods from nonmembers, compared to

$25 billion in 1958. Some of this may have been due to integration-induced growth in the EEC and some would have been a result of the reduction of the EEC common external tariff negotiated in the Kennedy Round, and some had nothing to do with formation of the customs union. The world economy looked very different in 1970 from 1958; trade liberalization within the customs union and reduction of its external trade barriers were part of the transformation, but how great a part?

The dominance of trade creation was not an inevitable outcome for all customs unions or free trade areas. The evidence for EFTA was mixed, and the many customs unions among poor countries that aimed to mimic the EEC collapsed primarily as a result of trade diversion dominating trade creation.[22]

The CAP and Accession

When the UK joined the EEC in 1973, external tariffs on trade in manufactured goods were already low. Meanwhile, the EEC had agreed on a CAP that strongly favored producers over consumers. As a large net food importer, the UK suffered from costly trade diversion (Winters 1987). Although the UK reaped some trade creation benefits in manufactured goods trade and British (and Irish and Danish) farmers enjoyed large windfall gains, the net impact on Britain was dominated by trade diversion in agricultural goods. In terms of Figure 2A1, the CAP price P_b was typically above the British price for a farm product P_d, and by joining the customs union the UK suffered from trade destruction as well as trade diversion; the former may not have been large, because the demand for agricultural goods is inelastic, but there was a substantial welfare transfer from British food consumers to EEC farmers (and lost markets for efficient third-country suppliers in the Americas and Australasia).

When Greece, Portugal, and Spain joined the EEC in the 1980s, the economic impact was less drastic. Again, however, there was trade diversion in agricultural products as the adoption of the CAP by Greece and Spain led to tighter restrictions on third-country exports of Mediterranean products such as citrus fruit or olive oil to the EEC, mainly to the disadvantage of North African countries (Pomfret 1981).

Beyond Trade Creation and Trade Diversion

The Vinerian framework is useful for understanding the short- to medium-term impact of customs unions in the 1960s. Nevertheless, the framework of Figure 2A1 came under some criticism. It is a partial equilibrium analysis ignoring how the labor market adjusts to the fall in output (by Q_0Q_1) or how the balance of payments and exchange rates are affected by the changes in the level and origin of imports. Some studies found that the terms of trade effect—that is, changes in the relative price of exports and imports—could be substantial.[23] The intra-industry trade literature suggested that perfect competition, as in Figure 2A1, may be an inappropriate framework (see the Appendix to Chapter 3).

A second line of criticism was that the Vinerian framework underestimated impacts by ignoring long-term effects through investment and growth. Britain's decision to abandon EFTA in favor of the EEC was largely driven by beliefs in the beneficial growth effects of being in the larger market despite reservations about the institutional arrangements of the customs union. The influential book by Balassa (1961) emphasized the "dynamic" effects of economic integration, but the analytical tools of that era were inadequate to analyze growth or investment effects convincingly.[24] Many empirical studies paid lip service to these effects.[25] However, they entered mainstream empirical assessment only after the development of new trade theories in the 1980s (Appendix to Chapter 3) and recognition of the global value chain phenomenon in the 2000s (Appendix to Chapter 4).[26]

In sum, initial empirical work on European integration was largely confined to analyzing trade effects. Although potential investment and growth effects were acknowledged, measurement of productivity and growth effects would become more sophisticated after the EEC moved from a customs union to deeper integration. For the simpler customs union introduced in the 1960s and then extended to agriculture and for the enlargements of the 1970s and, to a lesser extent, of the 1980s, Figure 2A1 captures the essential economic impacts that were driven by the adjustment of trade flows to new relative prices.

CHAPTER THREE

Deep Integration

Creation of the European Union

THE CUSTOMS UNION and the common agricultural policy had been established by the early 1970s, but aspects of the functioning of internal free trade suggested a need for further integration. The collapse of the Bretton Woods system of fixed exchange rates in 1971–1973 introduced a new source of price volatility in the internal market that was especially disruptive for the agricultural policy based on common support prices. The *Cassis de Dijon* case highlighted the importance of nontariff barriers (NTBs) to trade that protected national markets from competition within the customs union in much the same way as national tariffs would have done but with less transparency. The challenge of volatile bilateral exchange rates would be taken up in the European Monetary System established in 1979, and the challenge of NTBs and other obstacles to free internal trade would be taken up in the 1980s with the program to establish a Single Market by 1992.

Apart from the dynamics of integration pointing toward deeper integration measures, the European Communities (EC) faced two specific challenges in the early 1980s. The EC budget was dominated by the common agricultural policy (CAP), but the upcoming enlargement to include Greece, Portugal, and Spain, none of whom would be major net benefits from a CAP designed with northern farmers in mind, was adding pressure for more spending on assistance to poorer regions. The second challenge came from the world trading system where Japan and new industrializing East Asian economies (Hong Kong, Singapore, South Korea, and Taiwan) were gaining global market share in areas of manufacturing previously dominated by the old industrialized economies.

The sense of crisis was heightened by United Kingdom (UK) demands for revision of its budget contributions. Britain complained that the existing system meant that it made large net payments. There was no immediate prospect of this changing; the UK did not benefit from the CAP, and if spending were reoriented toward support for poorer regions, the UK would not benefit from that either. The Commission's receipts (tariff revenues and a share of value-added taxes) were related to national income, which was relatively high in the UK. The solution was a special package deal negotiated in 1984 between the UK and the other nine members.

This solution resolved the immediate budget crisis but also highlighted divergent approaches to the integration project. For the UK, the European Economic Community (EEC) was a transactional arrangement; the UK wanted to be in a European free trade area, and anything beyond that should leave each member with a nonnegative net contribution. For the signatories of the Treaty of Rome with federal aspirations, common policies were not about balancing national financial contributions; they were intrinsic to the concept of a European "community."[1] Starting in 1985, the member countries used qualified majority voting to overcome resistance to deeper integration from the UK, sometimes supported by Denmark and Greece.

Meanwhile, the world trading system was under challenge in the 1980s, as the United States responded to the new Asian competition by imposing trade barriers that were against the spirit of world trade law embodied in the General Agreement on Tariffs and Trade (GATT). The US response was aggressive unilateralism and the main instrument was voluntary export restraint (VER) agreements, which were voluntary insofar as exporters agreed to limit the quantity exported, but they did so under threat that if they refused, import quotas would be imposed. When in 1981 Japan agreed to restrict its annual car exports to the United States to 1.68 million, the EEC faced the prospect of Japanese cars being redirected to European markets. For many EEC members, doing nothing was not an option, although the members disagreed about what "doing something" involved. France negotiated a VER agreement under which Japan would limit its car exports to a maximum of 3 percent of the French market, whereas Italy continued to enforce an annual limit of 2,500 cars imported from Japan.[2] These measures required border officials to check that Japanese cars were not being smuggled into France or Italy from customs union member countries without restrictions; such border checks were contrary to the spirit of free internal trade.[3]

A second challenge to the world trading system based on multilateralism (i.e., nondiscrimination among GATT signatories) was the rise of regionalism in the 1980s. The United States broke its post-1945 opposition to discriminatory trade policies by negotiating preferential trade agreements with Caribbean countries and with Israel, and the Canada-US free trade agreement negotiated in 1986–1987 covered the world's largest bilateral trade flow. Elsewhere, Australia and New Zealand signed the Closer Economic Relations agreement in 1983. The response of the GATT signatories in 1986 was to launch a new set of multilateral trade negotiations, the Uruguay Round, but by the end of the decade, the Uruguay Round appeared to be on the verge of collapse. The EC would be forced to reassess the market-distorting agricultural policy and the approach to nonmembers if it wished to reaffirm its place in the global trading system.

Against this background, the EC embarked on a program of deeper integration aimed at creation of a Single Market by 1992. Despite the dangers of exacerbating the divergence between transactionists and federalists and adding to global fears about regionalism displacing multilateralism, the program was successful. The success was codified in the Maastricht Treaty and reflected in rebranding the EC as the European Union. The transition from customs union to Single Market was accompanied by strengthening of two policy areas from the 1970s. Competition policy became tougher in terms of number of cases and size of fines after the 1979 case against Pioneer Hi-Fi Company. The European Monetary System after a low-key start in 1979 gradually became a fixed exchange rate system during the 1980s (Table 2.1).

3.1 The Single Market Program

By the 1970s, the customs union was in place, covering both manufactured and agricultural goods, but many restrictions on trade within Europe remained. The *Cassis de Dijon* case highlighted the existence of indefensible nontariff barriers to trade. Moreover, faced by the stagflation of the 1970s, many technical regulations were being introduced by national governments. The new regulations were partly because countries were becoming richer and more environmentally conscious, but they were often also technical barriers to trade (TBTs).[4] Moreover, differences in national taxes, transport regulations, and so forth led to border-crossing delays that added to the cost of international trade within the customs union. Although the Treaty of Rome had foreseen integration beyond trade in goods within a common market, movement of services, capital, or labor was restricted in practice

A 1985 intergovernmental conference recommended a Single European Act that would complete the internal market and tidy up the institutional structures. Initially, this was a disappointment for European federalists who thought that the conference had succumbed to the minimalist view of UK prime minister Margaret Thatcher, who wanted freer trade within Europe but no increase in the Commission's authority or in moves toward greater political union. At the June 1985 Milan summit, the Italian hosts outmaneuvered the UK by delegating the decision to the intergovernmental conference which could revise the Treaty of Rome to allow qualified majority voting (QMV). The UK opposed this sleight of hand, but when the Italian interpretation was put to a vote—the first time that the Council had ever had a formal vote—the UK was supported by only Denmark and Greece, which was not enough to defeat the proposition.

Under the forceful leadership of Jacques Delors, who became president of the European Commission in 1985, the Single Market project became a vehicle for deep integration.[5] The Council decision, formalized in late 1985 to allow QMV on all Single Market issues was crucial. Restraints of trade are typically introduced in response to a powerful domestic lobby and change will be resisted by that lobby's national government, as happened in the *Cassis de Dijon* case and was likely to happen more forcefully if, for example, Germany's beer laws were challenged. QMV meant that no single country could resist a challenge to its TBTs unless it could find support from other members; in practice, resistance was rare as national governments understood that such support would not be forthcoming. In consequence, the Commission, which had the power to propose changes, became far more important during the era of Delors's presidency (1985–1994).

Just before the June 1985 Milan summit, the Commission unveiled a white paper, *Completing the Internal Market,* which contained three chapters. Chapter 1 described the removal of physical barriers at internal borders, with controls on plants, animals, and foodstuff to be carried out at the point of dispatch. Chapter 2 covered the elimination of TBTs by mutual recognition in both goods and services, including a single "passport" for most financial services, and mutual recognition would also be applied to diplomas and professional qualifications. Common rules would apply to public procurement and natural monopoly areas such as transport, energy, water, and telecoms. Chapter 3 addressed fiscal barriers, calling for some harmonization of value-added and excise taxes. The most controversial were the value-added tax proposals, based on replacing the destination principle by the origin principle, with a "clearinghouse" to rebalance revenues so that no country lost out. The white paper went beyond generalities to list almost three hundred specific proposals that would need to be implemented to complete the internal market before the target date of the end of 1992. The enabling legislation was the 1986 Single European Act (SEA), and all the major proposals, except those concerning the value-added tax had become law by 1993.

The SEA aimed to create "an area without internal frontiers in which the free movement of goods, persons, services and capital is ensured" (i.e., reinforcing the four freedoms promised by the Treaty of Rome) by 1992. It also implemented important institutional changes, including QMV on issues related to the Single Market. By 1988, Delors was pushing the reforms further to include monetary union, and he insisted that the Single Market had to be complemented by integration of social policies and by structural funds for poorer regions. Delors was clear about the goal: "Just as the Customs Union had to precede Economic Integration,

Economic Integration has to precede European Unity." The hostility of Margaret Thatcher and from the UK tabloid press became equally clear, especially as monetary union and social policies became more prominent.

In 1993, the Commission announced the "completion" of the Single Market, although this clearly referred only to removal of many barriers to trade in goods. Goods trade liberalization was promoted by harmonization and mutual recognition of technical standards in production, packaging, and marketing, and by harmonization of value-added tax rates within wide bands. Removal of barriers to trade in services and to movement of labor and capital was far from complete. In crucial areas such as capital markets, the digital economy, and energy, the process is still ongoing thirty years later. Nevertheless, the depth of the Single Market and its continuous further deepening are impressive. The Single Market created a much stronger economic union than the simple customs union of the 1970s.[6]

Establishment of the customs union was an example of negative integration—that is, removing obstacles to economic integration—but the Single Market inevitably required positive integration. The *Cassis de Dijon* case highlighted the need to include NTBs to trade in this process. To address the NTB issue, positive integration in the form of common policies and common regulations would be required because many NTBs have a public policy purpose—for example, protecting health, safety, or the environment. By defining the area without national borders to include regulatory or fiscal borders, the architects of the SEA set out an ambitious agenda that challenged national authority to set regulations or to use fiscal policies to assist domestic firms in the Single Market. Common policies already existed with respect to agriculture, external trade, and in other less comprehensively regulated areas such as transport, but they were specific actions rather than evidence of Commission competence to regulate.[7] Although it evolved more slowly, stronger implementation of competition policy would limit market segmentation, state aid, and other discriminatory policies, as well as abuse of market power. Streamlining or elimination of border formalities was reinforced by adoption of the Schengen Agreement (see Section 3.2). Government procurement was liberalized.

Beyond the specifics, a more general approach to standardizing and in the process reducing regulatory burdens without undermining the fundamental objectives of regulations became apparent. This was most obvious in the process of standardizing food regulations in which risk assessment to minimize restriction of intra-EU trade while maintaining health objectives was the guideline. About 160 of the directives under the EC92 program consisted of sanitary and phytosanitary (SPS) measures concerning health and safety in food, animal feed, and plants. By 1993, a principal competence of the EU Commission was risk regulation in the Single Market—that is, all regulation to satisfy safety, health, environmental, investor / saver, and consumer (sometimes referred to as SHEIC) protection was a Commission rather than a national function.[8] The important transformation was from voluntary national standards to SHEIC-based risk regulation whose acceptance was mandatory.[9]

The EC92 program influenced attitudes toward market liberalization. This was part of a wider philosophical shift toward more market-friendly policies, which was associated with US President Reagan and UK Prime Minister Thatcher, but also became apparent in center-left or socialist governments' policies in the 1980s.[10] The contemporary adoption of the Schengen Agreement and removal of border controls on many road frontiers illustrated the winds of change. Whatever the underlying process, reforms such as the removal of all foreign exchange controls among the EU12 countries, which would have been considered drastic in 1980, had become acceptable by 1990. In the late 1980s, the Commission began to address the difficult question of mutual recognition of professional qualifications, an area in which powerful vested interests fought to maintain market segmentation. Establishment of a single aviation market in the 1990s transformed what had been a highly regulated industry dominated by state-owned airports and national airlines into a market in which all commercial restrictions for EU-owned airlines flying within the EU had been terminated; prices fell dramatically, choice of routes and quality of service improved in many respects, and the number of passengers increased rapidly.

Creation of the Single Market did not end in 1993 with the Maastricht Treaty but has been an ongoing process. The long road (Mariniello et al. 2015) is in part a consequence of reaching more difficult areas such as services, and especially professional or financial services, or fiscal harmonization (e.g., the highly distortionary variations in corporate tax rates) and encountering new areas such as the digital economy. Progress since 1993 has been substantial but uneven, with important landmarks such as the 2006 services directive, the 2008 goods package (including improved conformity assessment), establishment of regulatory agencies for medicines, chemicals, and food, and safety agencies for rail, air, and maritime transport. Other steps include the Emissions Trading System established in 2003, addressing barriers to integrating stock exchanges, progress in the difficult area of intellectual property rights which remains fragmented in many respects and the 2010 Digital Agenda (followed by the 2015 announcement of a Digital Single Market).

The process has encouraged examination of the subsidiarity principle: what should be addressed at the EU level and what at the national or regional or local level? There has also been increased attention to enforcement (Pelkmans and Correia de Brito 2012), recognizing that resort to the Court is an expensive last resort. Especially since the 2007 Single Market Review, EU members have sought more cooperative approaches to implementation of Single Market directives.

The overall economic impact of the Single Market program has surely been positive, but the size of the benefits is disputed. The Cecchini Report (Cecchini et al. 1988) used macroeconomic models to estimate the effect of the 1992 program with various supporting policies and institutional reforms and found that improved resource allocation added between 4.25 percent and 6.5 percent to income levels in the EU. Baldwin (1989) introduced a variety of dynamic effects based on endogenous growth theory; he concluded that in addition to the Cecchini one-off effect, future EU economic growth rates would be 0.2 percent to 0.9 percent higher, giving a substantially larger total impact.

Subsequent empirical estimates based on ex post analysis were less positive. The Single Market program appears to have been trade-creating over the period 1985–1995 (Allen et al. 1998), but despite introduction of the common currency, this trend lost momentum in the 2000s (Ilzkovitz et al. 2007). In their literature survey, Boltho and Eichengreen (2008) settle on a consensus view of increased income by five percentage points due to the Single Market, less optimistic than the Cecchini / Baldwin combined estimates but still a substantial bonus accruing every year. Mariniello et al. (2015, figure 2) try to capture the productivity gains from the Single Market by comparing gross domestic product (GDP) per hour worked in the EU and United States; the productivity gap narrowed considerably from 1950, when the EU level was 40 percent of the US level, to 1995 when it was over 85 percent, and then widened slowly but steadily over the next two decades to below 80 percent.[11]

Ex post estimates using actual data may appear superficially more plausible than model-based ex ante estimates, but in both cases the comparison should be between the situation with the Single Market and the situation without the Single Market; both approaches need to identify the counterfactual. Thus, ex post estimates have to take into account all things that would have determined the EU's performance in the absence of the Single Market program. One way to address the problem of the counterfactual is the synthetic control method (see the Appendix to Chapter 6 for more details). Lehtimäki and Sondermann (2020) find that the performance of the EU12 members between 1964 and 1992 is mimicked by a weighted average of other Organisation for Economic Cooperation and Development (OECD) countries' performance, but after 1993, the synthetic country's performance is poorer than that of the EU12, and by 2014, the gap between the two is over 20 percent. The divergence was initially slow and then accelerated, which is consistent with the slow implementation of Single Market directives in the mid-1990s, and that the positive impact of the Single Market was largest for Ireland, Spain, the Netherlands, and Portugal. These results are plausible and closer to Baldwin's projections than to those of the Cecchini Report.

A subplot of the EC92 program was the changing perceptions in the UK, personified by Prime Minister Thatcher. Following Britain's successful lobbying for a recalculation of its contribution to the Community budget, Margaret Thatcher became a supporter of Jacques Delors's forceful pursuit of the European Single Market, which seemed to fit with Thatcher's goal of deregulating the UK national economy. In 1988, however, she realized that the Single Market would be accompanied by political integration, and her nationalism was stronger than her commitment to free markets. In a September 1988 speech in Bruges, Prime Minister Thatcher warned against "a European super-state exercising a new dominance from Brussels"—fears that were realized in the Maastricht Treaty's reassertion of the Rome treaty's aspiration to ever closer union. Her increasingly strident opposition to the EU, and fear of German domination after reunification in 1990, put her out of step with her cabinet, and she was replaced in 1990 by the more emollient John Major.[12] This was the start of the split over Europe that would tear apart Britain's Conservative Party over the next thirty years and see the party challenged from the right by the UK Independence Party.

3.2 The Schengen Agreement

In 1985, separately from the SEA, five EEC members (Belgium, France, West Germany, Luxembourg, and the Netherlands) signed the Schengen Agreement on the gradual abolition of common border controls. The Schengen Agreement was signed independently of the SEA due to lack of consensus over the pace of removal of border controls and over whether the EEC had the jurisdiction to abolish border controls. In 1990, the agreement was supplemented by the Schengen Convention, which created the Schengen Area with complete abolition of border controls between Schengen member states, common rules on visas, and police and judicial cooperation.[13] It was implemented between 1995 and 1997.

By 1997, all member states except the UK and Ireland had signed the agreement. It was included in the 1999 Amsterdam treaty, with opt-outs for the UK and Ireland, and hence became part of the *acquis communautaire*.[14] Thus, any new member would be required to join the Schengen zone. By 2019, the Schengen zone included almost all of Europe apart from the British Isles and the Balkans (Figure 3.1). As EU members, Cyprus, Bulgaria, Romania, and Croatia were committed to join Schengen.[15] The European Free Trade Association members (Iceland, Liechtenstein, Norway, and Switzerland) have also signed the Schengen Agreement.[16]

The Schengen Agreement reinforces free movement of labor because there are no checks of labor market status at internal borders. A corollary is that citizens of nonmember countries require a common Schengen visa, which implies a common policy toward immigration and refugees

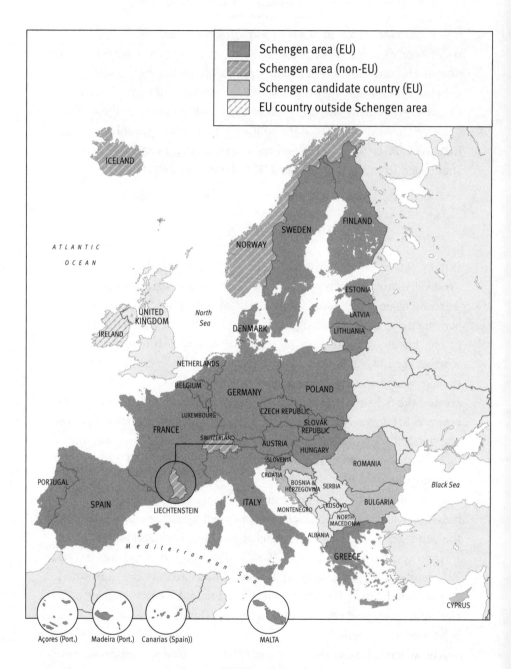

Figure 3.1 The Schengen Zone in 2020

(Ademmer et al. 2015). Although not initially an important element, the granting of exemption from Schengen visas became an instrument of EU policy toward eastern neighbors (Section 4.2), and refugee policy became a major issue after the 2011 Arab Spring (Section 5.2).

The manner in which the Schengen Agreement was brought into the *acquis communautaire* also had consequences. The concept of "enhanced cooperation" has been adopted to cover areas where some members oppose common policies. For example, with increased integration and mobility, more marriages involve people of different nationalities, and in contested divorces it may be desirable to have common principles to avoid jurisdiction shopping, but Malta and Sweden could not accept the divorce principles agreed on by the majority of EU members.

3.3 Social Harmonization and Cohesion

The SEA included two articles on social policy, and in 1988, the Commission published a report on *The Social Dimension of the Internal Market*. In 1989, Delors proposed a Social Charter that was approved by all members except the UK, whose government opposed social harmonization and insisted on an opt-out from the Social Charter. The timing of the introduction of social harmonization was associated with the SEA and also with the southern enlargement of the 1980s. The fear in richer member countries was of "social dumping" as producers in poorer members of the Single Market would have a competitive advantage due to fewer protections for workers in terms of minimum wages, occupational health and safety requirements, and so forth. Although the UK accepted some of the Social Charter's provisions—for example, free movement for workers and the right to join (or not) a trade union—it contested others—for example, the right for workers to participate in companies' decision taking and a maximum number of working hours per week.

The Social Charter was attached to the Maastricht Treaty and was designed to protect workers' rights throughout the EU. In 1992, Britain secured an opt-out from the provisions on social policy in the Maastricht Treaty. It was only after Labour's victory in the 1997 UK election that there was unanimous agreement to convert the protocol into a chapter in the Amsterdam treaty. After the Social Charter was included in the 2007 Lisbon treaty, it became binding on all EU members, except the UK which retained its formal opt-out from 1992.

It is unclear how much impact the Social Charter (or EEC requirements of equal pay for men and women dating back to the Rome treaty) has had in practice, but social dumping remains a contentious issue. The "Polish plumber" (i.e., mobile Eastern European workers who undercut the wages of Western European workers) was seen as a reason for French voters rejecting the EU constitution in 2005 after the expansion of membership to eight Eastern European countries and was a contributor to Brexit sentiment in the UK. Concerns about certification standards inhibit creation of a Single Market in services and the movement of professional workers.

The SEA introduced the concept of "social and economic cohesion," which has become jargon for reducing regional disparities within the EU. After 1988, it became explicit that the structural funds described in Section 2.8 (the Social Fund, Structural Agricultural Fund, and Regional Development Fund) were intended to reduce regional disparities, and funding doubled between 1988 and 1993. In 1993, as a component of the package leading to monetary union, a Cohesion Fund was introduced, and in 1994 a small Fisheries Fund was added.[17] Despite the blossoming structures and increased financing, the funds for social and economic cohesion appear to have had little impact in the 1990s.[18] The convergence issue and role of structural funds would assume greater salience in the 2000s with the accession of poorer Eastern European countries (see Sections 4.4 and 5.7).

3.4 Environmental Policy

Before the Maastricht Treaty, the EC sought to harmonize environmental regulation to avoid distortions within the common market. International obligations were met through multilateral agreements, although the attitude toward international protection of the environment was not especially strong before Maastricht).[19] Little attention was paid to bilateral relations with neighboring countries—for example, related to transmission of acid rain.

The SEA affirmed that the EC's objective was to "preserve, protect and improve the quality of the environment" and provided for an EC environmental policy. The Maastricht Treaty identified sustainable development and environmental protection as goals of the EU. Several hundred environmental measures were enacted to deal with air and water pollution, waste disposal, noise limits for aircraft and motor vehicles, wildlife habitats, and quality standards for drinking and bathing water. The Sixth Environmental Action Programme, approved in 2002, contained a ten-year framework for promoting sustainable development in the fields of climate change, nature and biodiversity, environment and health, and natural resources and waste. Later in 2002, the EU played a leading role in the World Summit on Sustainable Development in South Africa. By 2004, the "polluter pays" principle had been incorporated in EU law.

The Lisbon treaty confirmed EU competence in these areas (de Sadeleer 2014). Sustainable development strategy has become an EU priority, with climate change the most prominent element, explicitly mentioned in the Lisbon treaty. In 1996, the EU became the first major political body to put a number on the 1992 Rio de Janeiro Earth Summit's goal of preventing "dangerous anthropogenic interference in the climate" when it set a target of keeping the increase in global warming below 2^0C. In 1998, the EU signed the Kyoto Protocol, with its target of cutting greenhouse gas emissions by 2012 to 8 percent below their 1990 level.

To keep the EU's emissions within the Kyoto target, quotas were allocated to the member states for their emissions. In 2005, the EU introduced its Emissions Trading Scheme (ETS), allowing those industrial producers that emit less than their quotas to sell the unused rights to those that pollute more and creating a "carbon market," which determines the cost of carbon within the EU. Initially, the rights were issued too generously, and the price was too low. The EU responded by auctioning ETS pollution rights, helping to raise the carbon price to a high enough level to discourage greenhouse gas emissions.

3.5 A Single Market for Services

Services trade was scarcely mentioned in the Treaty of Rome, perhaps because there were few traded services in 1957, and received little attention before the mid-1980s. Even though explicitly mentioned in the Single Market program and accounting for an increasing share of EU GDP, services market integration has proceeded much more slowly than goods market integration.

In part, this reflects the heterogeneity of services. Many personal services, including much retail activity, schools, and health, are inherently local and largely nontraded. Perhaps the largest internationally traded service sector is tourism, which is characterized by free trade within Europe apart from local certification of hotels and other suppliers and local taxes. By contrast, networked services (e.g., broadcasting, gas and electricity, postal and telecoms, rail and air transport) are regulated everywhere, and although they could be traded, disputes over competences often separate the national markets. The fastest growing service subsectors in recent years have included business services and finance, which could be provided in an integrated EU market, but national regulations supported by entry barriers imposed by professional associations have often prevented market integration. Other rapidly growing subsectors include internet-based activities, which did not even exist in the 1980s, and entertainment, including professional sports.[20]

Financial services market integration began with a simple right of establishment throughout the EEC in the 1970s. The EC92 extension was similar to the principle of mutual recognition; the prudential control of financial institutions exercised by the home country authorities had to be recognized by financial sector supervisors in all member countries—that is, the license issued by the home country served as a "passport" to enter all EU markets. However, the impact was disappointing as governments found loopholes to frustrate the operation of the passports and because cross-border money transfers remained expensive until the adoption of the euro at the turn of the century (Pelkmans 2006, 138–142). Technology has probably had a greater impact than policy in integrating European financial markets since the 1980s and its impact has been selective, in banking rather than insurance and in wholesale rather than retail banking services.

The sectors known as public utilities or network services were largely left out of integration in the twentieth century. Before the 1980s, gas and electricity, rail and air transport, postal services and telecommunications, and to a lesser extent, broadcasting were considered to be natural monopolies, and were largely state-owned.[21] The Rome treaty was silent on ownership but did not allow state-owned enterprises to distort markets; this was tacitly ignored. Distortions caused by network services can be important because such services are frequently inputs into practically all other economic activities.

The Single Market program included attempts to integrate the EU network services markets within a more competitive environment, but incumbent firms resisted change and progress was slow until technology broadened the options. A 1996 electricity directive, 1998 gas directive, and the first railway package in 2001 were first steps rather than effective changes. Air transport was deregulated in 1992, but British Airways' entry into the Frankfurt-Munich market in 1997 was repulsed within six months by Lufthansa's predatory price cutting. Ireland's Ryanair was a more effective opener of European skies, increasing its number of revenue passengers from 2.25 million in 1995 to 139.2 million in 2018; a crucial feature of Ryanair's business model was the introduction of online ticket purchase in 2000 and the abolition of airport check-in counters in 2009. Most dramatically, state-owned monopolies in telecommunications and broadcasting were unable to withstand the impact of new technologies.

A comprehensive attempt to establish a single market in services was not made until 2004. The services directive, commonly known as the Bolkestein Directive after the then-commissioner for the internal market, came under intense criticism and was watered down by the national governments before being agreed to in 2006. The services directive that finally came into force on 28 December 2009 contained many exemptions, which reduced its effectiveness. Jensen and Nedergaard (2012) ascribe the disappointing outcome to the increased role of the European Parliament, which initiated many of the deletions from the initial draft of the directive, largely in response to lobbying from domestic businesses concerned about the impact of increased intra-EU competition.[22]

The view from EU Commission staff (Monteagudo et al. 2012) was more positive.[23] The directive should make it easier for EU service providers to operate in any other EU member state—for example, it requires all member states to establish web portals so that anyone who provides a service will have a "point of single contact" where they can find the legal requirements they need to meet to operate in the country, and service providers can also use the web portals to apply for any license or permit they need. Moreover, the directive did ban some of the most restrictive practices with respect to services trade and investment in services. Pelkmans (2019) focuses on these successes, while acknowledging the lingering problems that segment the EU market in services.

3.6 Capital and Labor Markets

As with services, the Treaty of Rome mentioned free movement of capital and of people, but implementation was neither clearly specified nor actively pursued in the 1960s and 1970s. Free movement of factors was related to means of payment across borders, which was restricted by foreign exchange controls in 1957, and even though such controls were loosened, they continued to exist. In 1974, the Court prohibited exchange controls affecting the free movement of goods, but such a partial prohibition is difficult to implement. Only in 1988 did the members accept a directive to fully remove exchange controls, and this was incorporated into the Maastricht Treaty.

The microeconomic argument for allowing capital mobility is clear; movement of capital from an area with low marginal productivity of capital to a location with high marginal productivity of capital increases joint output. The relevant price is the interest rate; high risk-adjusted interest rates signal that capital is scarce and are the mechanism to attract capital flows from a low-interest-rate location. However, interest rates are also an instrument of macroeconomic policy, and with mobile capital, the interest rate can only be a useful macroeconomic policy tool if the exchange rate is flexible, which was problematic for the common market.

The impossible trinity helps to explain the reluctance to promote capital mobility in the 1960s and 1970s (Section 2.9) and the consequence of doing so in the 1990s (Section 4.1).

Well-functioning capital markets linking savers to investors in physical capital require banks and other financial intermediaries. Banks take deposits from customers who want easy access to their cash and make large loans that are illiquid over their term. Regulators address the asymmetric information problem (depositors do not know whether the banks' loans are sound) with prudential regulations to guard against over-risky bank lending and with deposit insurance to reassure small depositors. In the extreme case of a run on a bank when customers seek to withdraw their cash, creating a liquidity problem even if the bank's long-term position is secure, regulators act as a lender of last resort, providing the necessary liquidity albeit at a penalty interest rate. When nonbank financial intermediaries take on some of the functions of banks or develop new financial services, the grounds for financial regulation are likely to increase. In practice, the need for opening up and regulating the internal financial market was neglected in the EU until after the financial crises of 2008 and 2010 (Section 5.1).[24]

The lack of EU action did not mean that integration was absent. Financial innovations were lowering barriers to integration in many branches of finance. A first step, in the 1960s, was the emergence of Eurodollar markets, in which USD-denominated assets were traded in London to avoid US restrictions on interest rates. Eurodollar markets soon expanded to include offshore asset trading in other currencies and beyond Europe in centers such as Hong Kong. London's preeminence as an international financial center was reinforced by the Big Bang reforms of the 1980s, which deregulated many areas leading to reduced fees and other costs and encouraging international banks, including banks from other European countries, to open branches in London. The integrating effect was most pronounced in investment banking and other wholesale financial activities, while areas where contact with many individual clients was important, such as retail banking, mortgage lending, or insurance, remained in separate national markets.

A distinct category of cross-border financial flows is foreign direct investment (FDI) in which the investor retains control over the use of the assets and receives profits rather than contractual interest payments. FDI, whether by acquisition, merger, or greenfield investment, has been liberalized in principle across Western Europe since the 1960s and any regulation is a national rather than an EU competence. Once the foreign firm, whether owned within the EU or outside, is operational, it receives national treatment similar to that received by any domestic firm. The EU Commission did become involved to maintain a level playing field—for example, with the 1997 EU Code on Harmful Tax Competition, and when a merger or acquisition ran up against the competition policy (Section 2.8).[25]

Freedom of movement of labor is enshrined in the Rome treaty but was even less evident in the Single Market than capital mobility. Even the Maastricht Treaty limits its coverage of labor to the right to work anywhere in the EU without discrimination on the basis of nationality, apart from in some reserved public service jobs. No attention was paid to the reasons why few workers actually moved. Some determinants stem from national policies—for example, minimum wages that forestall unskilled migrants from competing on price, or social security or tax provisions that may be hard for migrants to access or to resolve disputes in host-country courts. In many professions, accreditation has been an obstacle to crossing boundaries.[26] Housing markets, and especially access to low-cost rental accommodation, can also be an obstacle to migration. Beyond all of these economic considerations, differences in language or culture and the strength of family ties are important. In sum, integrating EU labor markets may be simple with respect to daily commutes across the Luxembourg border but is much more difficult when it comes to migration over longer distances to a new place of residence.

3.7 Competition Policy

In the 1980s, the Commission became more active in pursuing competition policy and levying serious fines. The transformation may be explained by increased experience of the Commission staff and by a political climate more conducive to promoting competition. An important turning point in anticartel policy was the leniency program introduced in 1996 and clarified in 2002 that gave some immunity to the first firm to provide evidence of anticompetitive behavior by a cartel. Between 1998, when the first leniency notice was issued, and 2014, eighty-nine out of ninety-five cartel cases pursued by the Commission followed a leniency application. Convictions and fines increased, with 90 percent of all fines, adjusted for inflation, resulting from application of the leniency program (Ordóñez-De-Haro et al. 2018, 1092).

Following growth of acquisitions and mergers in the 1980s, the Commission sought to block mergers that create firms that would dominate the market, leading to a long debate over whose authority should apply. Since adoption of Regulation 4064 in 1989, EU merger regulation has addressed any concentration that would significantly impede effective competition in the common market. However, three conditions have to be met before a merger must be referred to the Commission; joint turnover must exceed €5 billion, at least two of the parties must have annual turnover over €250 million, and the parties must conduct less than two-thirds of their business in a single member state. Unless all three conditions are met, the national competition authority has jurisdiction.

The competition policy provisions apply to trade within the EU, irrespective of the parties' domicile and whether the cartel is permitted in their home country. Similarly, mergers can be investigated even if the companies involved have their headquarters outside Europe. On the other hand, European companies forming a cartel to cover trade outside the EU are not subject to EU competition policy.[27] All applicant countries have been required to align national competition laws with EU competition policy before accession.

Enforcement of competition policy and restrictions on state aid strengthened in the 1990s and 2000s under strong commissioners. The European Commissioner for Competition from 1993 to 1999, Karel van Miert, enraged French president Jacques Chirac by forcing the French government to sell assets of its failing bank Crédit Lyonnais before approving a bailout, incensed Washington by obtaining concessions over Boeing's planned purchase of McDonnell Douglas, and, ignoring threats by German chancellor Helmut Kohl, he vetoed a digital television joint venture between the Kirch Group and Bertelsmann. Mario Monti, Commissioner for Competition 1999–2004, like van Miert showed intent to challenge competition-restricting mergers even when supported by powerful national governments—for example, Scania and Volvo in 1999, WorldCom and Sprint in 2000, General Electric and Honeywell in 2001, Schneider Electric and Legrand in 2001, and Carnival and P&O Ferries in 2002. Monti was also responsible for levying the EU's largest ever fine at the time (€497 million) against Microsoft for abusing its dominant market position in 2004. Neelie Kroes's appointment as Monti's successor was criticized for her supposed pro-business bias, but she oversaw a major expansion of cases against consumer goods cartels.

In the early 2000s, beer markets were the scene for several investigations ending in small fines or warnings. In December 2001, InBev (owner of Stella Artois) and three smaller brewers were fined €91 million for operating a cartel in Belgium, and four companies were fined €448,000 for operating a cartel in Luxembourg. Subsequently, an inquiry into an alleged Italian cartel was closed without proceedings, the British and German beer markets were specifically excluded, and in France Heineken and Kronenbourg were fined €2.5 million, with the penalty reduced for cooperating. The biggest case was investigated between 2005 and 2007 and concluded when the Commission imposed a €219 million fine on Heineken for operating a price-fixing cartel in the Netherlands between 1996 and 1999 with three other companies; Grolsch was fined €31.65 million and Bavaria €22.85 million, whereas InBev escaped without a penalty because it provided evidence of the cartel's operation. Neelie Kroes said, "This is simply unacceptable: that major beer suppliers colluded to up prices and to carve up markets among themselves" and urged consumers to launch actions for damages in national courts.[28]

A stark example of tougher prohibition on state aid was the airline industry. Loss-making national airlines such as Sabena, Iberia, TAP, Olympic, and Alitalia received repeated subsidies from their governments in the late twentieth century. However, when in 2001 members sought to ease restructuring of their national airlines after passenger demand declined following the 9/11 terrorist attacks, the Commission insisted that subsidies could cover only the "exceptional losses" due to the attacks.[29] The position was justified because, although Belgian airline Sabena was liquidated in November 2001, more efficient airlines (e.g., Ryanair and EasyJet) performed well without subsidies.[30]

Another example of the stricter EU position is that professional sports teams must fund their own facilities without state aid, unlike in the United States or Australia where taxpayers contribute to stadium funding.[31] Self-financed stadiums were shown to be feasible and long-term profitable by Arsenal's stadium, built in London in 2002–2006, and Bayern's stadium, built in Munich in 2002–2005. Both were designed to maximize match-day revenues and have been followed by many other self-financed stadiums.

3.8 Committing to the Multilateral Trading System

During the 1970s and 1980s, the EU was preoccupied with the Snake and monetary union, absorbing new members, implementing the Single Market program, and by 1989 reacting to the end of Communism in Eastern Europe. What to do about trade relations with nonmembers was reactive at best. The use of preferential treatment as a foreign policy tool to favor some countries was clearly flawed, as partners worried about their place in the hierarchy, and with low tariffs and limited flexibility on agriculture the EEC had little room to maneuver (Section 2.7). The CAP was itself under increasing threat as leading agricultural exporters joined forces in the Cairns Group to lobby for bringing agriculture into the GATT.

The EEC and other GATT signatories had launched the Uruguay Round of trade negotiations in 1986 to bolster the multilateral trading system in the face of challenges from regionalism and new protectionism. However, by the time of the 1990 meeting of trade ministers in Montréal, the GATT faced existential threats. The proliferation of preferential trading arrangements threatened the core principle of nondiscrimination, embodied in Article I of GATT that requires unconditional most-favored-nation treatment of all signatories' trade.[32] The major GATT contracting parties, the United States and EEC, were circumventing the spirit of their market-opening commitments through nontariff barriers to trade or by imposing measures like VERs and "orderly marketing arrangements" on exporters. The response in Montréal of the United States, EEC, Japan, and Canada was to reassert GATT principles and push over the next four years for a more thoroughgoing overhaul of trade rules to outlaw new protectionist measures like VERs, to take firmer treatment against GATT-inconsistent discriminatory policies, to bring previously excluded sectors (agriculture, services, and textiles and clothing) under world trade law, and to set up a dispute resolution mechanism. All of these and more were included in the Final Act of the Uruguay Round in 1994, and the GATT was succeeded by the World Trade Organization in January 1995.

The renewed and strengthened commitment to the multilateral trading system implied that key reforms would need to be implemented in Europe. The first steps to CAP reform were undertaken in 1993–1994, but it would take a decade before substantial change was in place. Replacing discriminatory trade regimes like the Lomé Convention would take even longer. Both of these topics will be analyzed in Chapter 4.

An important background to the renewed commitment to multilateralism was globalization and the emergence of global value chains. The global background was highlighted by the high-profile car industry. Protection through VERs was initially popular as a step toward saving national car producers in North America and Europe, but within a few years the failure of this approach was apparent. Average car prices in the United States went up by around $1,000, which helped local producers but also added profits to the Japanese companies (one reason for acquiescing in the VERs was the opportunity to act as a cartel and increase prices and profits). In the longer term, restricting Japanese car imports was ineffective as substitutes emerged; Korean cars filled car import demand beyond the Japanese quota, and the Japanese producers started exporting light trucks (which they called sport utility vehicles) that were not subject to the VERs. Although the VERs had been less extreme in Europe (outside Italy), similar consequences loomed. Meanwhile, more and more carmakers were following the Ford Fiesta approach of locating assembly in a lower wage location and sourcing inputs over a wide area. In Asia, Japanese manufacturers responded to the rapid appreciation of the yen after 1985 by moving car assembly to Thailand.[33] In the 1980s, European car manufacturers were exploring assembly operations in Eastern Europe (e.g., Fiat in Poland); this would turn into a stampede after 1989, as all major EU carmakers established assembly operation in Czechoslovakia, Hungary, or Poland.[34]

The change would be slow, but 1990 marked the start of a transition from sheltering European producers from global competition to recognizing that globally competitive firms often produce along international value chains in which access to world-class suppliers at every stage is essential. The Single Market and more proactive response to anticompetitive behavior helped to provide the internal platform for EU competitiveness, which would be reinforced before the end of the century by a common currency. In the twenty-first century, the EU would formally embrace global value chain participation as a cornerstone of its external trade policy. The CAP would be reformed and the Multifibre Arrangement restricting textile and clothing imports from low-wage countries would disappear without a whimper.

Shifting Trade Theory from Nations to Firms

International trade theory from Adam Smith (1776) and David Ricardo (1817) to the twentieth-century extension and formalization by Heckscher, Ohlin, Samuelson, and Meade was based on the nation as the unit of analysis. Goods, labor, and capital move freely within countries but not across national borders. Domestic prices could diverge from world prices, but within countries, prices were equalized by competition. These assumptions proved useful in explaining international trade patterns and the welfare effects of trade, and they underlie the analysis in the Appendix to Chapter 2.

Monopolistic Competition with Similar Firms

The presumption that national comparative advantage determines trade patterns (e.g., Britain exported cloth to Portugal in return for wine) was challenged by the evidence of intra-industry trade in the European customs union, which suggested that the majority of trade within Europe in manufactured goods did not follow the assumed inter-industry pattern.[35] The "new trade theory" of the late 1970s and 1980s extended the standard analysis by allowing for monopolistic competition in some industries, leading to potential trade in varieties of the same good and realization of scale economies (Krugman 1979, 1980).

Monopolistic competition describes an industry in which each firm can differentiate its product from the product of competitors. Firms have

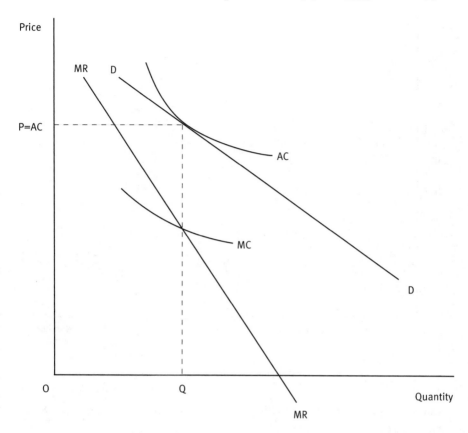

Figure 3A1 Price Determination for the Representative Firm under Monopolistic Competition

some monopoly power, but free entry and exit prevents monopoly profits (i.e., price equals average costs that include normal profits). A firm producing a differentiated product faces a downward-sloping demand curve (DD in Figure 3A1) and maximizes profits when marginal revenue (MR) equals marginal cost (MC). Because DD is downward sloping, the firm must be producing on the downward-sloping part of its average cost (AC) curve—that is, has increasing returns to scale.

In the simplest monopolistic competition model, symmetric firms are assumed to be equal sized, and each of the many firms ignores the impact of changes in its own price on the prices of competitors. With these assumptions, we can determine the number of firms (n) in the industry

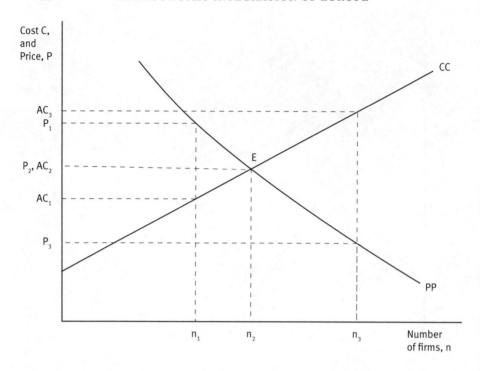

Figure 3A2 **Domestic Equilibrium with Monopolistic Competition**

and the equilibrium price, which must be equal to average cost due to free entry.

In Figure 3A2, the PP line linking the number of firms to prices is downward sloping. Given the externally determined size of the industry, the more firms in the industry, the more they compete, and the lower the price of each differentiated product—that is, larger n is associated with lower price. The CC line relates n to the average cost for each firm and is upward sloping. Given the industry's total sales, the more firms in the industry, the smaller is each firm's market share; with increasing returns to scale, larger n is associated with higher average costs and fewer firms with lower AC. Point E with n_2 firms in the industry is a stable equilibrium. With $n < n_2$, price is above average cost (e.g., $P_1 > AC_1$) and new firms are attracted to the industry. With $n > n_2$, price is below average cost (e.g., $P_3 < AC_3$) and firms exit the industry. At n_2, price equals average cost and each firm has zero economic profits; there is no incentive for entry or exit into or out of the industry.

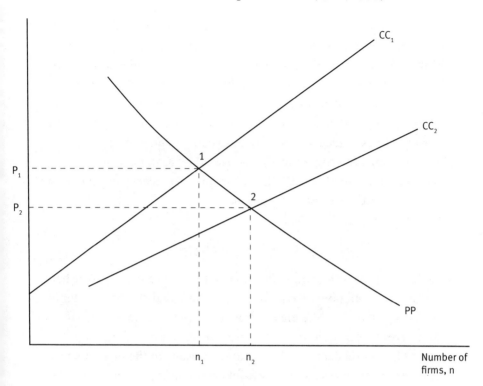

Figure 3A3 Monopolistic Competition and International Trade

Increased market size shifts the demand and marginal revenue curves in Figure 3A1 to the right, so that MR = MC at a higher output level and lower AC. Trade increases the market size, shifting the CC line to the right (from CC_1 to CC_2) in Figure 3A3. Each firm has lower average costs, and because average cost is equal to price, consumers benefit from a lower price. The number of firms in the international industry is larger than the pretrade number in each national market; with every firm producing a different variety of the product, consumers benefit from greater choice because n_2 varieties are now available. However, the total number of varieties in the trading nations is less than the number before trade (e.g., with two equal-sized partners $n_2 > n_1$ and $n_2 < 2.n_1$) and some producers go out of business.

In sum, monopolistic competition introduces additional gains from integration as consumers enjoy greater choice and efficient producers realize economies of scale. Countries with similar relative factor endowments may engage in intraindustry trade, as their firms produce differing varieties. Not all firms survive, and the simple model says nothing about which firms will survive. It is unclear if firms will locate in the domestic country or in foreign countries, although this may be of interest to policy makers, as well as to firm owners and workers in the industry. Issues of location of competitive firms came to the fore after the new economic geography was pioneered by Krugman (1991). Brülhart (2011) concludes that there is little empirical evidence in support of a location effect due to EU integration.

Heterogeneous Firms

In practice, firms producing differentiated products are likely to be heterogeneous. Monopolistic competition is more realistic but harder to model if we allow for differences across firms—for example, carmakers that differentiate by quality have higher average costs and prices.

Large firm-level data sets that became available in the 1990s allowed researchers to analyze characteristics of firms that export and those that do not. Analysis of firm-level data identified a positive relationship between exports and productivity, although the direction of causality is controversial: are more productive firms more likely to export, or are firms that export likely to be more productive? A second major challenge from firm-level studies was the empirical evidence that in "export" industries, many firms did not export (Bernard and Jensen 1995; Bernard et al. 2006). The theoretical solution was to assume exogenous productivity variance across firms (Melitz 2003).

With heterogeneous firms, trade liberalization increases the potential gains from trade. The most efficient firms become exporters and become more productive, where "most efficient" may be determined by price or quality or a mix of the two. The least efficient firms may go out of business or maintain niches in the domestic market.[36] Firm-level data are now available for many countries, and they reveal that firms respond to trade opportunities along a variety of dimensions, including price competition, scaling-up to realize scale economies, improved quality, and innovation. All of these are features of monopolistic competition with differentiated products.

The "new" trade theories based on monopolistic competition and the heterogeneous-firms literature both imply that the model used in the Appendix to Chapter 2 may underestimate the gains from trade. That analysis ignored the benefits from increasing the number of available varieties and from economies of scale, as well as the gains from increased within-industry productivity as the more efficient firms export and expand.

However, it is more difficult to predict patterns of trade, which are driven by firm competences as much as by national characteristics. Industry-level policies to stimulate export or import-competing industries will be misdirected because they encourage both high- and low-productivity firms in favored industries, and such policies hinder the sorting process by which efficient firms prosper and inefficient firms decline. Better policies would encourage efficient firms, but policy makers may not be good at identifying such firms.

Growth Effects

The above analysis helps to explain why the growth in European trade in the 1960s was larger than predicted and much was intra-industry trade. The monopolistic competition model shifted the emphasis from resource allocation efficiency in response to price signals (as in the trade creation and trade diversion in the Appendix to Chapter 2) and identified additional sources of growth (economies of scale) and increased consumer satisfaction (greater product variety). The heterogeneous-firms analysis questions the value of industrial policies that favor all firms in an industry, including both those that are efficient and those that are inefficient. If nations within the EU want to prosper, they must aim to improve the environment in which producers operate in their country so that the more efficient firms thrive.

Empirical studies began to focus on the impact of economic integration on productivity and growth, rather than the narrower analysis of trade effects described in the Appendix to Chapter 2. The richer firm-level analysis of trade has supported the hypothesis that the deeper integration of the Single Market program, which promotes efficient firms that were previously constrained by the size of their home market, has increased economic growth.

CHAPTER FOUR

Deeper and Wider

From Maastricht to Lisbon

THE MAASTRICHT TREATY celebrated the success of the Single Market program and reflected a new sense of confidence in European integration. The "European Communities" became the economic pillar of the "European Union." The treaty set out the framework for a stronger European Parliament, the principle of subsidiarity in relations between the EU and member countries, and a timetable for monetary union by the end of the century. A succession of inadequate treaties tried to tidy up the details; it was not until 2007 that the Lisbon treaty, also known as the Treaty on the Functioning of the European Union, provided a satisfactory successor to the 1957 Treaty of Rome.

The years between Maastricht and Lisbon were a period of consolidation as the consequences of the Single Market and of the Uruguay Round played out against a backdrop of the transition from Communism in Eastern Europe. After the seismic shocks of German reunification in 1990, dissolution of the Soviet Union in 1991, and the onset of civil war in Yugoslavia in 1992, the external environment in which the European Union (EU) was deepened and widened remained remarkably calm until the financial shocks that began in 2007 (Section 5.1). The EU played its part in the completion of the Uruguay Round and establishment of the World Trade Organization (WTO) in 1995, but apart from that, the focus was almost completely internal to Europe.

German reunification and the creation of the euro were major disruptions that, at least at the EU level, were resolved remarkably quickly with currency union achieved before the end of the 1990s. The adoption of a common currency and removal of physical border-crossing points in the Schengen zone, completing processes described in Sections 2.9 and 3.2, were the most visible signs of deeper economic integration across most of Europe—with the United Kingdom (UK) the most prominent nonparticipant. Implementing the WTO commitments of reforming the external trade policy and the common agricultural policy (CAP) took longer as trading partners and farmers resisted change, although the shape of the reformed policies was clear by the early 2000s.

The Commission became more active in promoting competition within the internal market, continuing a development described in Section 3.7. The number and size of penalties imposed by the Directorate-General for Competition increased rapidly in the early 2000s. In 2001, fifty-six companies were fined a total of €1.83 billion, which was more than the sum of all previous fines imposed by the EU, and in the three years 2005–2007, participants in twenty cartels were fined €5.86 billion (Wilks 2015, 145).[1] The Commission took on tech giants for abuse of dominant positions, ruling in 2004 that Microsoft must share software design details and fining the company €497 million. Powers to block mergers that created a dominant position were strengthened in 1989 and led to some high-profile cases in the 2000s—for example, a proposed merger between Ryanair and Aer Lingus was blocked in 2007. However, merger policy was often controversial; decisions were criticized, especially by US and UK economists for failure to understand "dominant position," and the 2002 decision to ban the merger between Air Tours and First Choice was overturned by the EU's General Court, which gave a scathing judgment criticizing the processes and the quality of economic analysis (Wilks 2015, 150–151; Pelkmans 2006, 261). The impact of this critique was reflected in the Commission's choice of cases to pursue rather than legislative changes.[2]

The widening of the EU saw the number of member countries increase from twelve in 1993 to twenty-seven in 2007. Several Eastern European countries were impatient with what they saw as Western European foot-dragging on admission during the 1990s. However, in the longer term, the process was remarkably smooth with the transition from Communism and centrally planned economies to democracy and market-based econ-omies spanning the pre- and postaccession years. Enlargement would slow down after 2007, with Croatia joining in 2013 and a queue of south-western European countries waiting while their applications were slowly processed (Section 5.4).

Meanwhile, the internal dynamics of the EU were shifting as the Single Market became an ever more apparent new reality and as the pro-spective new members added diversity. Concern for Europe's disadvan-taged regions was mentioned in the preamble to the 1957 Treaty of Rome. However, significant EU funding for less-favored regions was introduced only when the first "poor" member, Ireland, joined in 1973. The Regional Development Fund was set up to redistribute money to the poorest re-gions, but its budget was minor. The situation changed in the 1980s after the accession of Greece, Spain, and Portugal who were substantially poorer than existing members and did not benefit much from CAP funding. Since 2004, the largest share of cohesion spending has gone to Eastern Europe. The political difficulty of changing EU spending from 70 percent of the EU budget on the CAP and 11 percent on cohesion in 1980 to over one-third of the budget on cohesion and less than half on the CAP in the 2010s can be imagined.

4.1 Monetary Union

The process of moving from the European Monetary System (EMS) to monetary union began in 1990 with the phasing-out of controls on cap-ital movement and German reunification. Without capital controls, an EU member would face a sharper choice between maintaining a fixed exchange rate with other members' currencies or having an independent monetary policy. With the increased weight of a reunited Germany, other countries feared that they would have to follow German mone-tary policy. The fears were soon realized. To finance reunification, the German government could create money, which it was reluctant to do for fear of inflation, or it could borrow. Increased German borrowing pushed up interest rates, leading in 1992 to an exchange rate crisis within the EMS as other countries resisted having to match German interest rate increases. The 1992 crisis highlighted the impossible trinity or tri-lemma: it is impossible to have free movement of capital, a fixed exchange rate, and an independent monetary policy.

By 1992, all twelve EU members, and some candidate members, were in the EMS. The 1992 exchange rate crisis offered two options, which were starker now that capital could move freely across borders in the single market: maintain the fixed exchange rates and give up monetary policy independence by following Germany's interest rate increases, or maintain monetary policy independence and quit the EMS. The UK, Sweden, and Denmark abandoned their EMS commitments and allowed their exchange rate to change. During the 1992 crisis, Italy floated its cur-rency, whereas Portugal and Spain imposed capital controls and de-valued their currencies (Table 2.1), but Portugal and Spain never formally left the exchange rate mechanism (ERM) and Italy rejoined the ERM in 1996. After the immediate shock, the EU members, apart from Denmark, Sweden, and the UK, agreed to adopt the euro as an accounting unit and coalesced around a timetable to establish a common currency by the end of the decade (Section 1.5 provides the historical background).

The Maastricht Treaty provided a timetable for currency union and described in detail how the system would work, including the statutes of the European Central Bank (ECB).[3] It set the conditions under which monetary union would start and specified entry conditions for using the common currency, including five convergence criteria which were in-tended to determine whether a country was ready to adopt the euro:

1. **Inflation:** not to exceed by more than 1.5 percentage points the average of the three lowest inflation rates among EU countries.

2. **Long-term nominal interest rate:** not to exceed by more than 2 percentage points the average interest rate in the three lowest inflation countries.

3. **ERM membership:** at least two years in the exchange rate mechanism of the EMS without being forced to devalue.

4. **Budget deficit:** deficit less than 3 percent of gross domestic product (GDP).

5. **Public debt:** debt less than 60 percent of GDP.

The first criterion was intended to certify which countries had adopted a "culture of price stability" and the long-term interest rate reflected the markets' assessment of long-term inflation. ERM membership signaled commitment to ceding monetary policy to the ECB. The last two criteria, intended to ensure that national fiscal policies were consistent with a monetary policy targeting low inflation, turned out to be the most difficult for potential adopters of the euro to fulfill during the 1990s.

Concerns about fiscal discipline were addressed by adoption in 1997 of the Stability and Growth Pact (SGP) under which the fiscal restrictions criteria (3% deficit / GDP ratio and 60% debt / GDP ratio) would apply not only to countries seeking admission but also to countries using the euro. Under a "budgetary surveillance" process, eurozone member countries submit economic data and policy statements for periodic review, and an early warning mechanism notifies countries of slippage; peer pressure is to be imposed on member states to honor their commitments. However, some countries concealed their true fiscal situation, which invalidated surveillance—for example, Greece before 2010 manipulated its budget data to minimize the apparent size of the deficit. When commitments are not met, peer pressure has been ineffective. In 2003, the largest eurozone economies, France and Germany, were in violation with no consequences, and in 2009, only Luxembourg and Finland fulfilled both criteria. In sum, the SGP failed to address concerns about fiscal discipline in an effective way.

Fulfillment of the criteria was to be evaluated by late 1997, a year before the euro would replace the national currencies. In practice, the evaluation in 1997 was ignored. All the countries that wanted to adopt the euro qualified, even though over half of the first twelve adopters of the euro had debt ratios above 60 percent.[4] By contrast, all EU countries that joined the eurozone experienced a decrease in inflation before joining and met the first of the five criteria (Figure 4.1).

The priority given to the first three convergence criteria and neglect of the SGP conditions is consistent with the overriding emphasis on price stability in the monetary policy outlined in the Maastricht Treaty:

> *The primary objective of the ESCB shall be to maintain price stability. Without prejudice to that objective, it shall support the*

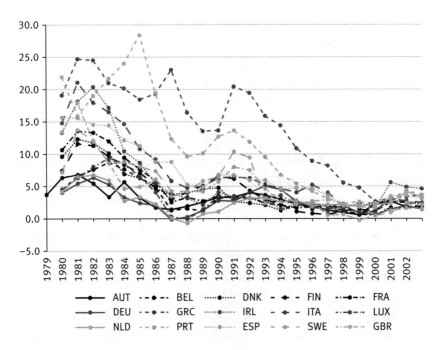

Figure 4.1 **Inflation Rates, 1979–2002**
Source: OECD.

general economic policies in the Union in order to contribute to
the achievement of the latter's objectives. (Article 282–2)

The European System of Central Banks (ESCB) defines price stability as a year-on-year increase in the Harmonised Index of Consumer Prices for the eurozone below, but close to, 2 percent, to be maintained over the medium term, which is commonly understood to refer to a two- to three-year horizon.

The primacy of the first of the convergence criteria was crucial to the euro's successful establishment. By the 1990s, there was agreement among future eurozone members about the need to aim monetary policy at an inflation goal; France's decision in 1981–1983 to prioritize EMS commitments over expansionary macroeconomic policies was a key episode. By contrast, in Yugoslavia, Czechoslovakia, and the former Soviet Union, disagreements over the priority of reducing inflation led to over twenty new currencies being introduced in the early 1990s where three currency areas had existed in 1980s (Pomfret 2016b).

On 4 January 1999, the exchange rates of eleven countries were "irrevocably" frozen, and the power to conduct monetary policy was transferred to the ESCB, under the aegis of the ECB in Frankfurt. The ECB runs monetary policy for all eurozone members and is independent of political control. The euro was introduced for financial transfers in 1999, and euro banknotes and coins circulated from January 2002. The eleven countries were Austria, Belgium, Finland, France, Germany, Ireland, Italy, Luxembourg, the Netherlands, Portugal, and Spain. Greece adopted the euro in 2001.

The third condition in the Maastricht Treaty for joining the monetary union—that is, at least two years of ERM membership—remains in place. In 1999, all of the countries still in the ERM, except Denmark and Greece, adopted the euro and in doing so exited the ERM. Greece followed in 2001. Denmark remains in the ERM but has not adopted the euro; the Danish krone has, however, remained fixed relative to the euro, suggesting that maintenance of a national currency is cosmetic rather than economically useful to Denmark. The UK left the ERM during the 1992 exchange rate crisis and opted to keep its national currency. Both Denmark and the UK obtained formal opt-outs from having to adopt the euro. For countries joining the EU after 1995, adoption of the euro is part of the *acquis communautaire*.

New EU members are required to join the ERM, which has been re-engineered to define parities against the euro rather than as bilateral exchange rates. The new ERM operates as a grid of agreed exchange rates, with mutual support and joint realignment decisions, and is used as a temporary gateway to euro adoption. In practice, there has been a split between the large new member countries, which have retained their national currencies and monetary independence, and the seven smaller economies, which were willing to join the ERM in 2004 or 2005 and after some years' delay (more than the two-year minimum) adopted the euro (Table 4.1).[5] The Czech Republic, Hungary, Poland, and Romania—as well as Sweden—show no urgency about joining the ERM.

The euro has the microeconomic benefits of a common currency: lower transactions costs, easier to make price comparisons, harder for

Table 4.1   ERM Membership

Pre-2000 EU members	Joined ERM	Left ERM	Post-2000 EU members	Joined ERM	Left ERM
Austria	1995	1999	Bulgaria		
Belg/Lux[a]	1979	1999	Croatia		
Denmark	1979		Cyprus	2005	2008
Finland	1979	1999	Czech Rep		
France	1979	1999	Estonia	2004	2011
Germany	1979	1999	Hungary		
Greece	1998	2001	Latvia	2005	2014
Ireland	1979	1999	Lithuania	2004	2015
Italy	1979[b]	1999[b]	Malta	2005	2008
Netherlands	1979	1999	Poland		
Portugal	1992	1999	Romania		
Spain	1989	1999	Slovakia	2005	2009
Sweden			Slovenia	2004	2007
UK	1990	1992			

Notes: a. Belgium and Luxembourg were already in a monetary union before 1979; b. Italy left the ERM in 1992 and rejoined in 1996.

monopolists to segment markets, and so forth. Although critics of the euro can be found, no government of a country in the eurozone has seriously considered exiting, including Greece at the height of its post-2010 financial crisis.[6] Eurozone membership has increased from twelve countries in 2002 to nineteen EU members since 2015, and nonmembers Kosovo and Montenegro use euros. The macroeconomic consequences of the euro will be addressed in Section 5.1.

4.2 Trade Policy toward Nonmembers

As a result of deeper integration and conclusion of the Uruguay Round, the EU had to revisit its trade policy toward nonmembers. In particular, the EU committed to reforming the common agricultural policy so that it was less trade distorting and protectionist and to abandoning one-way preferences for the African, Caribbean, and Pacific (ACP) countries covered by the Lomé Convention. These reforms would leave the EU with an integrated internal market and more open to the global economy, and raised the question of how does the EU perceive its external trade policy in a world where tariffs have diminished importance? For two decades, changes were piecemeal, and only in 2015 did the EU present a clear statement of principles behind its trade policy (Box 5.1).

With deepening of integration within the customs union (the EC92 program), the EC proposed in 1988–1989 to replace the 1972 European Economic Community—European Free Trade Association (EEC-EFTA) free trade area in manufactures by a more comprehensive European Economic Area (EEA). Meanwhile, following the end of the Cold War, Austria applied for full EEC membership in 1989, followed by Finland, Norway, Sweden, and Switzerland between 1991 and 1992. The EEA agreement was signed on 2 May 1992 by the then-seven EFTA and then-twelve EEC members. On 6 December 1992, Switzerland rejected the EEA agreement in a national referendum (and then froze its EEC application). Norway's voters rejected EU accession in a November 1994 referendum. On 1 January 1995, three EFTA members—Austria, Finland, and Sweden—joined the EU.

Thus, since 1995, the EEA consists of the EU member countries and three of the four EFTA members: Iceland, Liechtenstein, and Norway, but not Switzerland. The EEA agreement permits Iceland, Liechtenstein, and Norway to participate in the EU internal market with free movement of goods, services, capital, and labor but not in EU decision making.[7] The EU also has customs unions with Andorra, San Marino, and Turkey. Switzerland's relations with the EU rest on bilateral agreements covering, inter alia, trade in industrial and agricultural and processed agricultural products, public procurement, research, taxation of savings, technical barriers to trade, and free movement of persons. Iceland, Liechtenstein, Norway, and Switzerland are all in the Schengen Area (Section 3.2).[8]

The Lomé Convention with the ACP partners, which had been renewed and extended to 2000, was WTO incompatible because it neither created a free trade area nor was it extended to all developing countries, as required by the Generalized System of Preferences (GSP). The Lomé Convention was replaced in 2000 by the ACP-EU Partnership

Agreement or Cotonou Agreement, which provided a framework for future relations. Negotiation of Economic Partnership Agreements (EPAs) to replace the trade regime of the Lomé Convention began in 2002 between the EU and seven regional configurations—West Africa, Central Africa, Eastern and Southern Africa, the East African Community, the Southern African Development Community, the Caribbean Forum of the ACP Group of States (CARIFORUM),[9] and the Pacific region—although negotiations are often bilateral with individual nations. The aim has been to support trade diversification by shifting ACP countries' reliance on commodities to higher-value products and services. However, negotiations were difficult because the ACP countries wanted to retain preferential access to EU markets and did not want to open their economies to free access to EU goods. Of the five African groups, only the six countries in the southern group had concluded negotiations and implemented the EPA by 2019.[10]

In 2012, the EU reformed its GSP scheme in order to focus support on the developing countries most in need. The "Standard GSP" grants duty reductions for circa 66 percent of all EU tariff lines to countries of low- or lower-middle-income status that do not benefit from other preferential trade access to the EU market.[11] There are thirty Standard GSP beneficiaries. The EU also provides two special arrangements. The Special Incentive Arrangement for Sustainable Development and Good Governance (GSP+) grants complete duty suspension for essentially the same 66 percent of tariff lines as the Standard GSP to countries especially vulnerable in terms of their economies' diversification and import volumes. To qualify for GSP+, beneficiary countries must ratify and effectively implement twenty-seven core international conventions; as of November 2016, there were nine GSP+ beneficiaries (Armenia, Bolivia, Cabo Verde, Georgia, Mongolia, Pakistan, Paraguay, and the Philippines). The Everything But Arms (EBA) special arrangement grants full duty-free, quota-free access for all products except arms and ammunition, for countries classified by the United Nations as least-developed countries; there are forty-nine EBA beneficiaries. Having EBA status helps to explain why many ACP countries were not anxious to negotiate an EPA, as the EBA granted access to EU markets without requiring reciprocity. On the other hand, administrative costs, especially associated with documenting fulfillment of the rules of origin, deter utilization of GSP or EBA preferential tariff rates; Cadot et al. (2006) estimated that such costs averaged 6.8 percent of the value of the goods.

In addition, the EU retains a patchwork of trade agreements with a bewildering array of not-always-consistent names. Association Agreements set up a framework to conduct bilateral relations—for example, leading to Economic Partnership Agreements or Cooperation Agreements. Stabilisation and Association Agreements are used to establish a progressive partnership with Western Balkan countries with the aims of stabilizing the region and establishing a free trade area, eventually leading to EU membership. Deep and Comprehensive Free Trade Agreements (DCFTAs) are supposedly more ambitious than other agreements in this paragraph. The 1994 Barcelona process, also referred to as the Euro-Mediterranean process, aimed to revitalize the EU's relations with North African and eastern Mediterranean countries.

In 2003, the Commission proposed replacing the Euro-Mediterranean process, PHARE and TACIS.[12] In 2007, these programs were incorporated into the European Neighbourhood Policy (ENP).[13] Since 2008, the southern neighborhood has become the more formal Union for the Mediterranean with two fundamental pillars: fostering human development and promoting sustainable development.[14] The economic content has been limited because one-way tariff preferences are off the agenda and few Mediterranean partners share the EU's vision of free bilateral trade. The eastern neighborhood has splintered into the Western Balkan countries seeking EU membership, the six Eastern Partnership countries from the western former Soviet Union, and ad hoc relations with Russia, the Central Asian countries, and Mongolia (see Section 5.5).

The complexity of the arrangements described above illustrates the lasting legacy of using trade policy in lieu of foreign policy to establish a pyramid of preferences. Almost from the start, the pyramid of preferences yielded poor returns in increased influence for the European Community and led to tensions as often as to genuine cooperation. Nevertheless, the arrangements were allowed to continue because no partner wanted to lose their preferential treatment. Even when reform was externally imposed by the WTO charter, change proceeded piecemeal with apparently endless negotiations and acronyms.

4.3 CAP Reform

At the 1990 GATT ministerial meetings in Montréal, the EU had to agree to terminate the trade-distorting elements of CAP or face the breakdown of the Uruguay Round. Although Montréal was the catalyst, internal pressures for CAP reform had been building. Initially, when the CAP mainly consisted of protection for import-competing farm products through the variable levy system, the CAP brought in revenue and the burden was borne by consumers who paid higher prices. As output in many farm products increased and began to exceed domestic demand, variable levy revenues disappeared, and the costs of storage and disposal of the surplus had to be paid out of Commission resources. The budgetary shortfalls were exacerbated by the rebate given to the UK since 1984, and the share of the budget available for the CAP was challenged by the increased pressure for cohesion payments after the Mediterranean enlargements of 1981 and 1986.

The MacSharry reform in 1992 began by reducing market-support measures, including abolition of the variable levy on imports. Intervention prices for cereals were cut by 30 percent over three years and for beef and veal by 15 percent, and farmers were compensated by a subsidy related to their land area, not output (the coupled direct payments in Figure 4.2). CAP regimes for oilseed and sheep meat were also changed. Accompanying measures included support for environmental measures, aid for farmers' early retirement, and other rural development measures.

Since 1995, the EU has adopted preemptive reforms of the CAP to make it WTO compatible. The WTO agricultural agreement required tariffication of nontariff barriers and divided subsidies into more or less trade distorting (the so-called traffic light system). In the 1999 Agenda 2000 package, EU intervention prices were further reduced: by 15 percent on cereals, by 20 percent on beef and veal, and by 15 percent on dairy products. A consequence of lower intervention prices was the declining

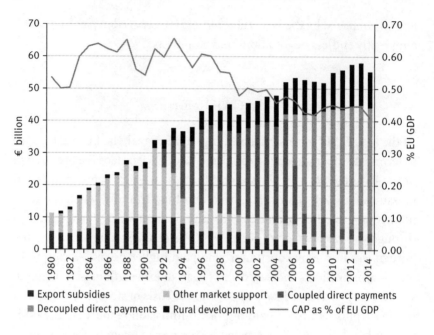

Figure 4.2 **Expenditures on the Common Agricultural Policy, 1980–2014**
Note: Market support since 2010 includes expenditure for wine programs,
producer organizations in the fruit and vegetables sector, school fruit and
milk schemes, promotion, beekeeping, and so forth.

Source: European Commission.

need for export subsidies, which are WTO illegal—a point confirmed
in a dispute brought by Australia, Brazil, and Thailand against the EU's
subsidized sugar exports. Export subsidies have disappeared from the
EU budget since 2010 (Figure 4.2). The Agenda 2000 package had provisions relating payments to environmental goals, although little money
was set aside for this change.

The CAP link with production was largely broken by the Fischler reforms in 2003 and 2004, which extended decoupling from output or
farm size and placed greater emphasis on the multifunctionality of
farms.[15] Farms could provide environmental services such as maintaining country landscapes, payment for which is not trade distorting
and hence is WTO compliant. Since 2006, decoupled payments and rural
development subsidies have dominated the CAP budget. The reforms

have deflected foreign criticism of the CAP structure, although protection for some farm products remained high.[16] CAP spending in euros continued to increase in nominal terms until 2014, but as a share of EU GDP, it has fallen dramatically since 1993 (Figure 4.2). In the twenty-first century, European agricultural policy aims for a competitive agricultural sector that is "greener, more trade-friendly, and more consumer-oriented."

The general protection of agriculture has been much reduced, but tariffs remain on some farm products, often in the form of tariff rate quotas (TRQs). Under a TRQ, certain quantities of imports, often allocated to specific partners, enter the EU at a lower tariff rate, and after the quota limits are reached, a higher tariff rate applies. In some cases, TRQs were a response to the WTO's tariffication requirement; the EU wanted to encourage some imports because domestic output did not meet demand at the support price, while high above-quota tariffs are imposed in order to keep domestic prices high for farmers. TRQs sometimes appear liberal insofar as the within-quota tariffs are low, but the quota is typically reached well before demand at the low tariff rate is exhausted. Foreign suppliers fortunate enough to receive rights to sell within the quota will enjoy rents from selling at the domestic price, and the discriminatory element of allocating quota rights to preferred partners is a throwback to the old pyramid of preferences mentality.[17]

There are many nontariff barriers to internal and external trade in agricultural products. Some EU legislation that may impede internal EU trade as well as acting as a trade barrier against imports from nonmember countries is also potentially welfare improving—for example, plant health and veterinary rules and regulations, bans on use of genetically modified products and other food law. The general rule in the WTO's world trade law is that such technical or sanitary barriers to trade must have a scientific justification and should not interfere unnecessarily with international trade. The EU's geographical indications of origin also interfere with trade, especially when there is doubt whether an indicator that may have been originally geographic has become generic—for example, feta cheese—and will be analyzed in Section 5.6.

CAP spending remains large, even though as a share of EU GDP it has fallen by one-third since the MacSharry reforms. Even after the 2013 "recalibration" of the CAP (before setting the 2014–2020 budget) that was intended to simplify agricultural policy, the CAP remains complex, in part because EU agriculture has become more diverse since the 2004 enlargement and also because consumers demand better information and regulation of food products.[18] Sharing competence over health (especially after the mad cow disease epidemic of the 1990s) and over environment matters between directorates of the Commission and hence between national ministries has eroded the influence of farm lobbies (Roederer-Rynning 2015, 210). Although the shift away from output support is welfare improving, distributional inequities remain as decoupled payments continue to benefit very large holdings. In England, the Duke of Westminster, one of the wealthiest men in the country, has been one of the main recipients of CAP support, and Queen Elizabeth II and Prince Charles were also among the biggest beneficiaries before Brexit.

4.4 Enlargement to the East

At the same time as the EU faced the challenges of revising the CAP and the common external trade policy, it faced the prospect of many applicants for membership after the collapse of Communism in Eastern Europe. At the June 1993 Copenhagen summit, the EU12 set out three key criteria for successful accession:

- Stable democratic institutions that promoted respect for the rule of law

- A functioning market economy able to survive the economic pressures of membership

- Capacity to eventually take on all obligations of membership including adherence to the aims of political, economic, and monetary union

These went beyond simple acceptance of the *acquis communautaire* at the time of application to include future commitments to closer economic and monetary union and to democratic institutions. The Copenhagen criteria guided accessions in 2004 and 2007, but questions arose about backsliding on the first of the three criteria by Hungary and Poland after they had become members. The Copenhagen criteria were also a statement of EU members' core shared beliefs, including that the EU was now more than a simple customs union.[19]

The 1995 enlargement from twelve to fifteen members was easy because Austria, Finland, and Sweden accepted the *acquis communautaire* and were expected to have minimal adjustment problems. The next enlargement would be more difficult because the Central and Eastern European countries were in transition both from central planning to market-based economies and from authoritarian regimes to democracies. The EU members decided that both of these transitions should be firmly cemented before accession. However, progress toward meeting the Copenhagen criteria was uneven, which raised the question of whether the Central and Eastern European countries should be treated as a group or separately. As it turned out, eight of them, together with Cyprus and Malta, joined in 2004, and Bulgaria and Romania in 2007.

The GDP per capita of the ten new members from Central and Eastern Europe was only 40 percent of the EU15 average in 2000 but reached 52 percent in 2008. Their economic growth was not only faster than that of the EU15, but it also exceeded preaccession forecasts. Growth drivers included foreign direct investment and technology transfer, reflecting lower interest rates due to a reduced risk premium (especially before the 2007–2010 financial crises), and incorporation into global value chains (GVCs), most visibly in cars in the Visegrád-Four countries (the Czech Republic, Hungary, Poland, and Slovakia).

None of the centrally planned economies' car factories provided the basis to compete in global car markets after 1989. The first move by a major western producer in the 1990s was Volkswagen's purchase of Škoda. Opel and Suzuki invested in Hungary in 1991, followed by Audi in 1993. Despite these early moves, expansion was slow. In 1998, Opel (GM) opened a greenfield plant in Gliwice, Poland, initially with an annual capacity of seventy thousand cars. Accession to the EU in 2004 and to Schengenland in 2007 reduced intra-EU trade costs for the Eastern European countries and provided a catalyst for development of GVCs, especially in the car industry (Pomfret and Sourdin 2017). In the Czech Republic, the TPCA greenfield factory started production of small cars such as the Toyota Aygo, Peugeot 107, and Citroen C1 in February 2005;

production reached the planned yearly capacity of three hundred thousand cars in 2006. Hyundai started production in November 2008, with a capacity of two hundred thousand cars a year. Slovakia became one of the leading car producers in the world due to the presence of three companies: Volkswagen (since 1991), PSA Peugeot Citroën (since 2003), and Kia Motors (since 2004). By 2006, the three factories had a capacity of over a million cars (PSA 450,000, VW 300,000, and Kia 300,000), the largest in Eastern Europe, all with state-of-the-art technology. When the TPCA and Hyundai factories in the Czech Republic and the PSA and Kia factories in Slovakia reached capacity, these two countries had the highest per capita car output in the world. A contributory factor to the rapid expansion of Slovakia's car industry is that Slovakia has been the only one of these four countries to adopt the euro, removing exchange rate uncertainty in trade with Germany, France, and other eurozone countries.

Private sector restructuring led to increased productivity, maintaining EU competitiveness in both old and new members, with little evidence that shifting tasks to new members created unemployment in EU15 countries. Case studies (e.g., of machinery, furniture, medical instruments, chemicals, and wood products) suggest skill complementarities created win-win outcomes. There was some migration from new to preexisting members; between 2006 and 2009, around 1.6 million people migrated from east to west, joining two million EU10 nationals already in the EU15 countries, but even 3.6 million migrants represented less than 1 percent of the working-age population in the EU15 countries. Ireland was the only country where the share was more than 1 percent. In sum, the 2004–2009 experience of the new members was that the economic benefits of EU accession exceeded expectations, and Campos et al. (2014) argue that this continued into the 2010s.

Part of the positive experience may be explained by EU policies to ease accession. The 1997 Stability and Growth Pact may have helped to deter new members from running excessive budget deficits. Structural and cohesion funds to lower-income regions focused on investment in infrastructure and human capital and improved public spending, which aimed to ease the transition to EU membership and contribute to the sources of growth. However, empirical studies have questioned whether these policy targets were achieved. The European Structural Funds (Section 3.3) increased in value, but Breidenbach et al. (2019) conclude that the contribution of structural funds to regional economic growth between 1997 and 2007 was insignificant or even negative for some regions due to competition over scarce factors; structural funds augmented rather than overcoming fundamental problems of scarcity of crucial resources or poor administrative capacity in low-income regions.

Not all new members benefited equally from accession to the EU, although it is difficult to make appropriate with-and-without comparisons of accession (see Appendix to Chapter 6). As the poorest countries in the 2004 accession group, Estonia, Latvia, and Lithuania were enthusiastic EU members and enjoyed rapid convergence toward EU living standards during the 1990s and early 2000s; they may have been the main beneficiaries of accession among the 2004 cohort, at least during the decade to 2008 (see Table 6A1, from Campos et al. 2019). However, after half a century as republics inside the Soviet Union, they were less well prepared to weather EU-wide shocks, and their relatively fragile economies were hard hit by the global economic downturn in 2008–2009. The Visegrád-Four countries seemed likely to benefit the most due to their relatively well-developed human capital and memories of market economies before the late 1940s, but the Czech Republic, Hungary, and Poland resisted economic integration (e.g., by maintaining national currencies despite commitment to adopting the euro) and in the 2010s expressed resistance to basic EU principles such as judicial independence. By contrast, Slovakia, Slovenia, Malta, and Cyprus embraced opportunities associated with integration.[20] Bulgaria and Romania were the poorest of the non-Baltic 2004–2007 entrants, which explains their accession delay, but even after 2007, they had difficulty taking advantage of EU opportunities.

4.5 The Lisbon Treaty and the EU Budget Process

In 2007, the EU could take stock as the challenges of both deepening and widening had been met. The Single Market will always be a work in progress, but it was operating with borderless trade (the Schengen Area) and a functioning common currency in much of the EU. Fifteen new members had been absorbed between 1995 and 2007, and although there were transition issues, the smaller new members were starting to adopt the euro, the more dynamic Eastern European economies were actively participating in European value chains, and fears of indigestibly large labor migrations appeared to be unfounded. The Treaty for the Functioning of the European Union (the 2007 Lisbon Treaty) ended the messy period of constitution amending that had followed the Maastricht Treaty.

The Lisbon Treaty formalized the EU budget process. Before 1988, budgets were negotiated annually, often with bitter disagreements between members as in the UK's rebate negotiations in the early 1980s. The annual budgets became the focus of power struggles over the role of the Parliament after direct elections were initiated in 1979; the European Parliament rejected the draft budgets in 1980 and 1985. The Delors Commission initiated a process of multiannual budgets in 1988 (for the period of completing the internal market up to 1992) that was repeated in 1992 for the period 1993–1999 and in the Agenda 2000 budget.[21] The system of multiannual financial planning was given treaty status in the Lisbon Treaty. The Financial Perspectives for 2007–2013 and for 2014–2020 allowed consideration of future-oriented policies and enlargements, as well as of long-term patterns in the two main budget items (the CAP and cohesion spending).

The budget negotiations in 2013 for the 2014–2020 Financial Perspective illustrated a new level of involvement in economic policy making with more complex balancing of competing interests. Negotiations in the November 2012 Council meeting were unsuccessful, and agreement was only reached in February 2013 after two days and one night of deliberations (Laffan and Lindner 2015, 236–237). A group of net contributors led by Germany (plus Austria, Denmark, Finland, the Netherlands, and the UK) wanted to limit the size of the budget and shift the content toward newer areas of public goods, competitiveness, citizenship, and global Europe. The emphasis of Eastern European members led by Poland was on traditional areas (CAP and cohesion) and, if possible, a larger overall budget. They were supported in these wishes by France, Greece, Italy, Portugal, and Spain, but patterns of support varied and Belgium and Ireland in particular did not fit easily in any of these three groups. The resulting compromise agreed to reductions in spending on the CAP and cohesion that was greater than the Eastern European or Mediterranean countries would have wished and a smaller spending on, for example, competitiveness than the Commission had proposed.

The Council's decision went through a process of approval by the European Parliament, whose principal revision in 2013 was to introduce flexibility (and increase the Parliament's powers) through a right to review and revise the budget after 2016. Issues of flexibility were highlighted after the 2016 Brexit referendum when it became necessary to calculate the UK's outstanding financial commitments as part of its exit bill. The increasing complexity of the EU budget raised issues of the Commission's managerial competence and increased the status of the independent Court of Auditors that had been created in the 1975 Budgetary Treaty.

The significance of the EU Commission has increased with deeper integration, but the importance of the Commission as a regulation setter is hardly reflected in the size of its budget. For 2014–2020, the long-term budget of €1,082.5 billion equaled 1.02 percent of forecast EU28 gross national income. The Commission staff of around sixty thousand is smaller than that of the city of Vienna or of the French ministry of finance. The budget issues are likely to be ongoing, in particular as debates over macroeconomic policy and financial regulation following the crises of the 2010s (Section 5.1) will lead to new institutions and funding needs. Despite the reservations, the budget process and the content of the Financial Perspective for 2014–2020 reflected how far the EU had already come in deeper integration since the Single Market program was introduced in the 1980s.

Trade Costs and Global Value Chains

Twentieth-century trade theory focused on tariffs as the source of the wedge between domestic and world prices. As tariffs fell in the 1950s and 1960s, the focus shifted to nontariff barriers (NTBs), many of which could be analyzed with the same framework as had been used for tariffs (e.g., the analysis of the CAP variable levies in the Appendix to Chapter 2). However, even after NTBs were cut in trade agreements or gradually reduced in the Tokyo and Uruguay Rounds of multilateral trade negotiations, a wedge between domestic and world prices remained.

Two influential articles published in 1995 highlighted that tariffs and NTBs were not the only obstacles to international trade. John McCallum (1995) showed that even after Canada and the United States had signed a free trade agreement and shared one of the most open borders in the world, a Canadian province was much more likely to trade with another province than with a similar-sized US state that was a similar distance away, and US states were much more likely to trade with other states than with a Canadian province given size and distance. Dan Trefler (1995) used current state-of-the-art models of international trade to predict how much trade should take place in the world, and he found that the estimates were substantially larger than actual world trade.[22]

James Anderson and Eric van Wincoop (2004) estimated that trade costs in high-income countries were on average equivalent to a 170 percent ad valorem tariff. Although influential in raising policy makers' awareness of trade costs, the Anderson and van Wincoop result is misleading in that they calculate the cost of moving a good from the factory gate to the point of sale in another country, which includes many elements that would also apply to domestic sales. A better approach is to define *trade costs* as the difference between the cost of doing domestic and international trade, whether in money, time, or uncertainty.[23] Trade facilitation refers to measures aimed at reducing trade costs.

Trade costs are hard to measure. Nuno Limão and Anthony Venables (2001) found a nice natural experiment to show that trade costs vary by country of destination. The World Bank ships many containers of miscellaneous goods from Baltimore to almost every country in the world; the cost of these shipments varies greatly by destination and the cost does not depend only on distance. Limão and Venables ascribed the variation to differences in port costs in the destination country, but it seems clear that trade costs are much broader than just costs at the port.

A useful way to look at trade costs is to examine the difference between the free-on-board (fob) value of goods at the port of export and the cost-insurance-freight (cif) value when the good is landed in the importing country, but not including tariffs. This is simplistic in ignoring behind-the-border trade costs such as trade finance or regulation compliance. Moreover, suitable data only exist for a few countries (Hummels 2007). Measuring trade costs as (cif value—fob value)/fob value, Australian import data show that average ad valorem trade costs on Australian imports fell from 8.0 percent in 1990 to 4.9 percent in 2007, which can be compared to Australia's average applied tariff of 3.8 percent in 2006 (Pomfret and Sourdin 2010). Mode of transport matters (average ad valorem trade costs are lower for air than sea) and the large cross-country variation in trade costs is not strongly related to distance or bulk. The Australian data do suggest that institutions matter, and delay-causing corruption is a bigger obstacle to trade in GVC goods such as electronics than to trade in goods commonly conceived as time sensitive (e.g., food and fashion items).[24]

The reduction in tariffs is a force for greater intra-trade in a customs union, as happened in Europe in the 1960s and 1970s, but in the twenty-first century, reducing trade costs may be even more important. Reducing trade costs through measures such as simplification of customs procedures will generally be nondiscriminatory, benefiting all trade partners, although it may help some trade partners more than others. Thus, the trade effects from most trade facilitation measures will be overwhelmingly trade creation, with minimal trade diversion. Moreover, trade costs affect the composition as well as the level of trade, and low trade costs are especially important for participation in GVCs.

The GVC phenomenon is often dated from the late 1980s, coinciding with the reduction of tariffs in high-income countries to below 5 percent on average and restriction of NTBs after the Kennedy and Tokyo Rounds.[25] Trade costs in money, time, and uncertainty are anathema to GVCs, which rely on minimizing inventories at each point in the chain. Most GVCs rely on just-in-time delivery, and any uncertainty would require GVC participants to hold larger inventories, reducing the benefits of fragmenting production. Although referred to as "global," a common feature identified by empirical studies is that much of the phenomenon occurred within three sets of regional value chains based in Europe, Asia, and North America.[26]

In Europe, an early indication of the relationship between economic integration and GVC participation was the establishment and success of the Ford Fiesta factory in Spain in the 1970s and 1980s. The EEC recognized the importance of reducing trade costs in order to further economic integration and undertook trade facilitation in the form of the EC92 Single Market program, the removal of physical borders in Schengenland, and the reduction of financial costs of international trade by adopting the euro as a common currency.[27] GVC participation has been an important source of economic benefits for the Eastern European countries that joined the EU in the 2000s, especially in the car industry, and it is a major component of the 2015 Trade for All strategy.

The GVC phenomenon raises many issues that are still not fully understood. The fragmentation of production with ever finer levels of specialization by tasks is in key respects an extension of the basic ideas of Adam Smith and David Ricardo about the benefits from the division of labor and the gains from trade resulting from specialization by comparative advantage. In the key GVC sectors (cars, electronics, and apparel), it is clear that integrated national industries are no match for goods produced along GVCs, and consumer demand for global brands of cars, smartphones, and clothes appears insatiable. At the same time, globalization increases volatility on the production side as component manufacturers will be hurt by disruption at any point on the GVC or reduced demand for the final product. In 2008–2009, the fall in world trade was substantially greater than the fall in global output, and the phenomenon can be ascribed in part to disruption of GVCs (Bown 2018).

Quantifying GVC Impacts: The Head-Mayer Approach

GVCs are hard to analyze because they come in many forms and the phenomenon is dynamic. Improvements in information technology permit coordination of more complex GVCs, and infrastructure developments can enable regional GVCs to link up—for example, regular rail services between China and Europe since 2011 have facilitated creation of Eurasian value chains (Pomfret 2019a). Building on several strands of trade theory, Keith Head and Thierry Mayer have extended the monopolistic competition model described in the Appendix to Chapter 3 to include the supply-side decisions of a GVC lead firm that is producing several varieties of a product.

The monopolistic competition model focuses on consumers' responses to differentiated products. In a multivariety GVC setting, the lead firm must make four decisions about the location of production which involve supply as well as demand considerations: from which factory to source each variety, where to distribute the product, which varieties to offer in each market, and how much to supply to each market. In the global car industry in 2016, the twenty-one main brands assembled cars in fifty-two countries and sold them in seventy-six national markets; in 98 percent of cases, each model supplied to a market came from a single source country, and geography and trade agreements influenced these source-to-market decisions. Based on the model-level data, Head and Mayer (2019) find evidence of significant internal and external economies of scale in production and that the fixed costs of entering a market are larger than trade costs as normally estimated.

Policy or other shocks affect firms' choice of which markets to serve and what subset of varieties to offer in each market. Standard trade theory focuses on frictions between production and consumption locations in the form of tariffs, NTBs, or trade costs. Within GVCs, there are two added frictions: distance from the lead firm adds to monitoring and other costs and explains the prevalence of regional rather than GVCs, and there are costs to entering and maintaining a presence in a market. Deep trade agreements recognize these frictions insofar as they include topics such as harmonization of standards, protection of investments, facilitation of movement of professionals and skilled workers, and intellectual property rights, all of which mainly affect the relations between lead firms and production or distributions partners.

Unlike simpler monopolistic competition theories or computable general equilibrium models, Head and Mayer do not invoke the Armington assumption of elasticities varying only by location but allow for differing elasticities across varieties—for example, the elasticity of substitution between a Polish-assembled Fiat 500 and a UK-assembled Range Rover will be much lower than the elasticity of substitution between the Fiat 500 and a BMW Mini assembled in the UK. Head and Mayer also reject the spaceless analysis of monopolistic competition and place the lead firm's decisions on production location in a gravity model.

Because of the geographical elements, regional disintegration is a significant determinant of outcomes, although magnitudes vary depending on the elasticities. Production locations will change and prices increase due to less efficient spatial allocation of production.[28] If the United States had abrogated the North American Free Trade Agreement in 2017, Head and Mayer estimates that car output would have fallen by 40 percent in Mexico and by 67 percent in Canada, and consumer surplus would have declined significantly in all three countries. By contrast, they estimate that Brexit will have a smaller impact on production in the UK but a larger negative impact on consumer surplus in the UK due to the rise in car prices. Conversely, regional integration can increase production efficiency and give a larger boost to national output due to reduced market entry costs—for example, estimated gains to Canada from the Comprehensive Economic and Trade Agreement with the EU include a 7 percent increase in car output and increased Canadian consumer surplus by 1.8 percent, while the impact on the EU is less significant due to the small market share of Canadian car production in EU markets.

The Head-Mayer model is an important extension of the monopolistic competition model described in the Appendix to Chapter 3, and it highlights the greater potential for economic benefits from deep integration in the presence of GVCs. Neither model is applicable to all trade, but GVCs are a growing phenomenon and the car industry is a leading player.[29] Moreover, the car industry is a high-profile industry in the EU.

CHAPTER FIVE

Post-Lisbon Challenges and Responses

THE DECADE AFTER the signing of the Lisbon treaty in 2007 might have been a time for drawing breath after the widening and deepening of the previous decade and a half, but the European Union (EU) was hit by three major challenges. Each challenge had origins in the integration process and the specific path toward European economic integration. However, the Greek debt crisis, the refugee crisis, and the British referendum on leaving the EU all came as more or less unanticipated shocks

Behind the unanticipated shocks, the EU faced a range of deeper integration issues. How should public goods, such as external border control, be funded? If this requires expansion of the EU budget, to what extent is the balance of fiscal policy decisions shifted from national capitals to Brussels? Even without an increase in the size of the EU budget, who coordinates EU fiscal policy? In the absence of coordination, is it just a by-chance aggregate of national policies? The criticism of uncoordinated fiscal policy in the eurozone was voiced by the International Monetary Fund (IMF) in the 2010s when monetary policy was largely inactive at the zero lower-bound interest rate, effectively leaving the eurozone short of macroeconomic policy instruments. To what extent should banking regulations and state aid for the financial sector, which had both remained primarily national competences, be subject to EU rules?

As a federation of nation states that had differing priorities and experienced divergent national developments (low investment in Germany, high government spending in France, and low productivity growth in Italy), the eurozone faced adjustment problems. With independent exchange rates, purchasing power parity and the Balassa-Samuelson effect would lead to equilibrating exchange rate changes; but what is the equilibrating mechanism in a currency union with incomplete deep integration?[1] Moreover, if national governments pursue different labor market, social security, and other policies, will the playing field be uneven, punishing countries where workers, pensioners, or others are treated more generously and encouraging races to the bottom? The answer to the last question may be to coordinate structural reforms on which governments agree in principle but have differing time horizons.

The EU also responded to changes in the world economy. Policies were increasingly designed to be smart and sustainable, a reference to increased concern about environmental issues and climate change in particular. Shifts in global economic power led to the EU having to pay attention to the rise of China, and the 2016 US presidential election brought to power a president who showed disregard for the World Trade Organization (WTO)–based multilateral trading system. The EU had to reconsider its role in the world economy as well as vexed questions of further enlargement and the eastern border of "Europe."

In sum, in the 2010s, the EU faced both immediate crises and systemic challenges that were to a greater or lesser extent consequences of the integration process of the previous half century. The EU response can only be understood in the context of the deeper and wider economic integration envisaged in the Maastricht and Lisbon treaties, as well as the incomplete Single Market in areas such as the banking sector and capital markets and need for common external migration policies for an integrated internal labor market. The responses to challenges highlighted the mixed attitudes of Europeans to closer economic and political union.

5.1 Financial Integration and Financial Crises

In the early twenty-first century, the EU faced several related but distinct financial issues. All EU members had banking laws and central banks that had managed to maintain financial and macroeconomic stability in the late twentieth century. Removal of restrictions on capital mobility in the early 1990s and adoption of the euro in the late 1990s changed things for EU members, although the full impact would not be felt for several years. The European Central Bank (ECB) took over monetary policy, but banking regulation and functions such as lender of last resort remained the responsibility of national governments.

5.1.1 The Need for Banking Regulation

The need for banking regulation arises from potential market failures due to asymmetric information, adverse selection, and moral hazard. Banks act as intermediaries between many small depositors and borrowers who have lumpy projects requiring capital that cannot be repaid on demand. The small depositors do not know banks' balance sheets or the extent of their nonperforming loans, so governments try to counter the asymmetric information either by prudential measures, such as forcing banks to hold reserves of safe assets like cash or government bonds, or by providing deposit insurance for banks' customers.

Preferred regulatory instruments have changed over time. Reserve requirements and interest rate ceilings have declined in popularity because they restrict the efficient flow of capital. Encouraging prudential behavior by imposing reserve requirements leads to financial repression— that is, too few loans to private sector businesses with good investment projects. Imposing interest rate ceilings leads to adverse selection; if the interest rate is too low and there is excess demand for capital, banks will ration capital by financing the safest loans, excluding borrowers with good but risky ideas. Since the 1990s, many banks have conducted stress tests to determine their ability to withstand adverse economic developments, and since 2007, such tests have been conducted by public authorities. Uncoordinated prudential oversight may lead to home bias if banks worry about the greater riskiness of loans in a foreign country; within the EU, coordination and strengthening of prudential oversight would discourage home bias.[2] The European Banking Authority was established in 2011, originally in London but relocated to Paris in 2017, to assess risks and vulnerabilities in the EU banking sector through regular risk assessment reports and pan-European stress tests.[3]

All EU member countries provide explicit or implicit deposit insurance, although this creates moral hazard and encourages too risky behavior by banks.[4] Potential losers from over-risky behavior are either insured (i.e., the depositors) or do not see the cost until too late (i.e., the taxpayers who pay the insurance bills and costs of bailing out banks that are rescued). Unconstrained by the potential losers, banks seek out borrowers willing to pay the highest interest rates on loans, which are probably for risky projects. If the bank's owners or managers have little of their own capital at stake and receive incentives based on profits, they will make greater returns on such loans and suffer limited losses if the borrower defaults. Even a cautious bank will have to follow such a strategy if other banks' high interest rates on deposits attract funds from insured depositors who are unconcerned about the soundness of banks' balance sheets.

Apart from financial sector regulation, governments also accept a role for their central bank as the lender of last resort in order to avoid bankruptcy of a solvent financial institution. Banks have a maturity imbalance between their liabilities (deposits that can be withdrawn on demand or with limited notice) and assets (loans). If there is a run on a bank with customers seeking to withdraw their funds, the bank may face a liquidity crisis because its loans cannot be recalled before maturity. In such a situation, the national central bank will automatically provide loans if the bank is fundamentally solvent. Stress tests try to forestall the necessity for such action by checking for potential cash-flow problems and identifying potential nonperforming loans that could turn a bank's liquidity crisis into a solvency crisis. An added problem for regulators is that many nonbank financial intermediaries offer similar services to banks, and if bank regulations become too intrusive or burdensome, banks may be displaced by less-regulated near-banks such as credit unions.

5.1.2 The Crises of 2007–2010

Between 2007 and 2010, the global economy experienced three major crises that were interconnected but essentially different. Although the period is often referred to as that of a global financial crisis, there was a North Atlantic financial crisis in 2007–2008 that was followed by a global economic crisis when world trade plummeted in 2008–2009 and by a public finance crisis that dominated EU financial management after 2010.

The 2007–2008 financial crisis was largely driven by poor loans for real estate and their packaging in complex financial instruments or granted too freely to borrowers with poor capacity to service debts. As real estate prices fell in the United States, many subprime borrowers found that their outstanding home loans exceeded the value of their property; loan defaults, foreclosures, and desperation sales added to the downward pressure on house prices.[5] When real estate prices collapsed in the UK, Spain, and some smaller European economies (e.g., Ireland, Iceland, and Latvia), governments intervened to insure depositors in the financial institutions and in some cases to nationalize the insolvent banks or nonbank financial institutions. Pressure on public finances led to austerity programs in which governments cut back spending.

The immediate financial crisis was over by 2009, although it had longer-lasting consequences for many people who lost out by becoming overindebted or being dispossessed of their houses and for a few who became rich. By the end of 2008, policy attention in the United States had shifted to groups such as car producers that were suffering from reduced demand as consumers delayed renewal of major durable goods. A striking feature (despite the "global financial crisis" label) was the lack of financial contagion, unlike the 1997–1998 Asian financial crisis that led to Russian default and the collapse of Long-term Capital Management in the United States. In 2007–2009, events in the United States, UK, and Spain triggered no financial crisis in South America, Asia, Africa, Australia, or Canada. In the EU countries that were not directly involved, fears of contagion were not borne out.

The origins of the 2007–2008 financial crises were financial reforms in the 1980s and 1990s. Deregulation and financial innovation combined with deposit insurance created moral hazard. Easy credit led to greater and more sophisticated leveraging by the most innovative financial institutions. Within the EU, this process was notable in the UK, Spain, and some of the smaller economies but notably absent in France, Germany, or Italy.[6] The divergent national financial histories can in part be attrib-

Table 5.1   Faster and Slower Financial Reformers, Nominal GDP in US Dollars, 1992 and 2007

	1992	2007	% change		1992	2007	% change
USA	6,286.8	13,811.2	119.7	Germany	2,062.1	3,297.2	59.9
UK	1,074.0	2,727.8	154.0	France	1,372.8	2,562.3	86.6
Spain	612.6	1,429.2	133.3	Italy	1,265.8	2,107.5	66.5
Ireland	54.3	255.0	369.6	Greece	128.4	360.0	180.4
OECD	19,764.1	38,219.0	93.4	World	24,533.6	54,347.0	121.5

Source: Pomfret (2010, 26) based on data from World Bank *World Development Indicators.*

uted to the failure to establish common rules and a single market for banking. Even with hindsight, it is unclear whether a more or less liberal policy regime was better. In the decade and a half before 2007, the less regulated, more dynamic financial sectors were associated with faster economic growth. Table 5.1 compares economic growth in four of the financial-sector-reforming, and crisis-hit, countries with four roughly similar-sized slower-financial-sector-reforming countries.

Although there was little financial contagion, financial crises in two of the world's five largest economies did trigger a global economic crisis by reducing global demand for goods. Reduced household wealth led to lower consumption demand, including demand for imports, and collapse of world trade between the third quarter of 2008 and the third quarter of 2009. The impact on world trade was made worse, and less predictable, because of global value chains (GVCs). The impact was uneven not only across sectors (e.g., heavier on cars whose purchase could be delayed) but also across producers (e.g., VW was better placed than other carmakers because of its good recent model range) and across countries (e.g., Eastern European countries that were more dependent on continental EU markets suffered less than countries more dependent on US or UK markets). Overall, the global economic crisis was relatively brief; world trade had recovered by 2010.

A number of countries experienced difficulties funding their public sector deficits and ran into debt problems. Some of these sovereign debt

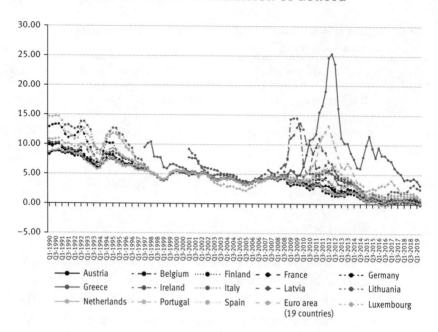

Figure 5.1 Interest Rates in Eurozone Countries, 1990–2019
Source: OECD.

crises were related to the 2007–2008 financial crisis because governments became involved in expensive bailouts—for example, Ireland's government guaranteed not only depositors but all creditors of Irish banks. Other debt crises, notably in Greece, were essentially independent of the 2007–2009 financial and economic crises.

Adoption of the euro contributed to the sovereign debt problem because lenders assumed that with no exchange rate risk, all eurozone government bonds were equally risky. This led to interest rate convergence as the eurozone was established in 1999 (Figure 5.1) and to excessive borrowing by some countries. With lower interest rates, debt servicing was less of a burden, and countries with debt problems could refinance rather than deal with the source of their high debts—until Greece revealed the severity of its debt problem in late 2009. Finally recognizing that not all euro-denominated sovereign debt was equally risky, creditors identified Portugal, Italy, Ireland, Greece, and Spain (the

PIIGS) as potential problem cases, and interest rates diverged sharply in 2010–2012.

The divergence was triggered by Greece's debt-servicing problems and also contributed to the sovereign debt crisis by making refinancing more expensive for all indebted countries. In May 2010, Greece was the first eurozone country to request official financial assistance, and with default imminent, emergency loans and packages were offered to Greece. Rescue packages were also offered to Ireland (November 2010 and February 2012), Portugal (May 2011), Spanish banks (July 2012), and Cyprus (May 2013). The major creditors were banks in EU countries without real estate bubbles (France, Germany, and Cyprus), "prudent" banks that had avoided real estate lending and focused on "safe" government loans or government-guaranteed loans.[7]

5.1.3 The Greek Financial Crisis

The Greek sovereign debt crisis was the most severe and resolution the most difficult. Although membership of the eurozone facilitated the debt explosion after 2001, the underlying cause of Greece's debt burden lay in public spending exceeding revenues over more than three decades. When Greece entered the eurozone in 2001, shortly before the issue of notes and coins on 1 January 2002, the government officially claimed to meet the criteria of a budget deficit equal to less than 3 percent of gross domestic product (GDP) and a debt/GDP ratio of less than 60 percent. The claim was supported by creative accounting—for example, by moving pensions and other payments outside the government budget. Greek governments continued to report manageable deficits and debt/GDP ratios, even though for twenty years up to 2000, government borrowing added up to more than double the sum of reported fiscal deficits, and this was continuing. According to ex post IMF estimates, the general government debt increased from €150 billion in 2001 to over €350 billion in 2011 (Figure 5.2).

In October 2009, a new Greek government under George Papandreou entered office and found that the treasury was empty. The government decided to come clean about true levels of revenues and expenditures, although it took time to establish the facts. Some features were clear: the

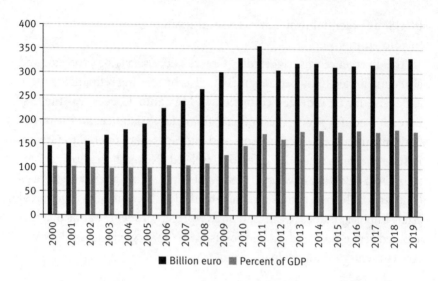

Figure 5.2 Greece, General Government Debt, in Billion Euros and as a Percentage of GDP,
2000–2019
Note: Consolidated general government gross debt at face value, outstanding at the end
of the year in the following categories of government liabilities: currency and deposits,
debt securities and loans. The general government sector comprises central, state, and
local government and social security funds.

Source: Eurostat.

public sector wage bill had doubled between 2000 and 2010 in real terms
and many areas were hugely overstaffed (railways, schools, etc.), prestige projects (e.g., the 2004 Olympics) had gone far over budget with little
legacy, the retirement age had been reduced in many jobs to fifty-five for
men and fifty for women, and many individuals and firms did not pay
taxes. The new government thought that the 2009 budget deficit was
3.7 percent of GDP but two weeks later declared that it was 12.5 percent.
It turned out to be over 15 percent. After Papandreou's acknowledgment
that previous Greek governments had misrepresented the fiscal deficit,
the interest rate spread between Greek and other eurozone countries'
debt began to widen (Figure 5.1). In 2010, holders of Greek government
debt heard more serious warning bells as the country faced default.

Between April and June 2010, all the major credit-rating agencies
downgraded Greek government bonds to junk status. In April 2010, over
half of the bank holdings of Greek sovereign debt was held by French

(33%), German (15%), and Dutch (5%) banks (Roos 2019, 236). For the EU countries whose banks were major creditors, the initial priority was to avoid Greek default and forestall failure of their banks. In May 2010, the EU, IMF, and ECB pledged €110 billion to help avert financial collapse in Greece. The 2010 bailout was important for providing a breathing space during which Greece could continue to service its debts while foreign banks could reduce their exposure to Greek debt.[8]

The May 2010 bailout was conditional on Greece cutting its budget deficit to 8.1 percent of GDP by the end of 2010 and to 3 percent of GDP by 2014. These steps were not taken. For Greek residents, cuts to spending from the pre-2010 debt-fueled levels were labeled "austerity," but for outsiders, there was no evidence that the Greek government was serious about reducing, let alone removing, the large public sector deficit. In 2010, Greece's general government deficit was 11 percent of GDP, and the deficit / GDP ratio increased to 13 percent in 2013. Meanwhile, other eurozone countries such as Latvia, Portugal, and Ireland took a big ax to their fiscal deficits; between 2010 and 2013 the deficit / GDP ratio was cut from 9 percent to 1 percent in Latvia, from 11 percent to 5 percent in Portugal, and from 32 percent to 6 percent in Ireland.[9]

In May 2010, the Securities Market Programme (SMP) allowed the ECB to purchase distressed bonds. Between May 2010 and September 2012, the ECB purchased €210 billion of vulnerable eurozone members' bonds in the secondary market. Because the ECB could not fund budget deficits, it was not allowed to buy bonds directly from member governments, but the SMP mechanism was a form of debt relief because it pushed down the price of a government's debt. In September 2012, the SMP was replaced by the Outright Monetary Transactions scheme, which had a similar goal of providing bondholders with an exit strategy. However, under both schemes, ECB activity was conditional on the primary issuer observing negotiated conditionality. This was a powerful weapon because, when the ECB did identify noncompliance and withheld purchases (e.g., with respect to Greek and Italian bonds in November 2011), the interest rate spread increased for the primary issuer pushing up the price of primary debt for both Greece and Italy, whose governments quickly backed down from the strategies that were ignoring previously negotiated conditions.

After the first Greek bailout, it was clear that the solution would involve burden sharing between creditors and the debtor. In the second EU-IMF bailout for Greece, approved by EU finance ministers in February 2012, the €130 billion in official assistance was accompanied by a 53.5 percent debt write-down—or "haircut"—for private Greek bondholders. However, by then, the large foreign banks had much reduced their holdings of Greek debt and the burden was largely felt by domestic Greek creditors. As a condition of the second bailout, Greece was required to reduce its debt-to-GDP ratio from 160 percent to 120.5 percent by 2020. Greece and its private creditors completed the debt restructuring on March 9. The deal encountered popular resistance in Greece, but a June 2012 election returned a government committed to the program. In September 2012, ECB president Mario Draghi committed to buying eurozone members' debt in the secondary market and doing "whatever it takes" to forestall default or collapse of the eurozone.

The 2010–2012 Greek crisis and EU response raise two questions: why not default on the debt and why not leave the eurozone? Neither Greece nor its creditors (nor other EU countries) wanted these outcomes. Default would exclude Greece from almost all capital markets, including trade finance to cover the time lag between exporters shipping goods and importers receiving and paying for goods. Compromise was less assured after 2012 because the rest of the EU—not just rich northern members who foot the bill but also poorer countries that had implemented genuine public spending cuts—were more willing to consider Greece exiting the eurozone (Grexit). Some partners may not have cared either way; the Greek economy is tiny in the EU context, about half of the gross metropolitan product of greater Paris (and roughly the size of the economy of greater Miami or Sydney).

The EU / IMF / ECB bailout aid was to be distributed in tranches to keep the pressure on Greece to honor its commitments. To secure release of the installment of almost $9 billion in rescue loans due in July 2013, the government introduced austerity measures. Plans to put twenty-five thousand civil servants, including teachers, municipal police officers, and school janitors, into a "mobility plan" by the end of the year, docking their wages ahead of forced transfers or dismissals, generated the most public anger, prompting labor unions to hold a general strike. The government survived and was able to reenter the bond market in 2014, relieving some financial pressure. But austerity measures remained unpopular.

A new anti-austerity government stood for renegotiation of bailout terms, debt cancellation, and increased public spending. On 30 June 2014, Greece missed a €1.6 billion payment to the IMF—the first developed country to default on an IMF payment. EU opinions were divided: ECB executive board member Benoît Coeuré insisted, "Greece has to pay, those are the rules of the European game," but French finance minister Michel Sapin warned that "if this new government was elected, it's also because Greece has lost 25 percent of its national wealth in the space of five years. That's extremely heavy, extremely hard for people to bear." A July 2015 referendum in Greece voted for rejection of bailouts, but the government negotiated acceptance.[10]

In 2017, tensions over Greece's third bailout grew as the IMF warned that the country's debt was unsustainable and that budget cuts EU creditors were demanding would hamper Greece's ability to grow. EU representatives agreed to more lenient budget targets but declined to consider any debt relief. Greek Prime Minister Tsipras agreed to implement deeper tax and pension reforms even as he faced domestic pressure over a weakening economy and rising poverty. A June 2018 plan allowed Greece to extend and defer repayments on part of its debt for another ten years and gave €15 billion in new credit. Greek finance minister Euclid Tsakalotos said it marked "the end of the Greek crisis" and the prime minister, Alexis Tsipras, claimed that "Greece is once again becoming a normal country, regaining its political and financial independence." Capital markets responded positively in July 2019, when Greece issued its first seven-year bond since 2010; the target of €2.5 billion was modest but offers exceeded €13 billion, pushing down the yield down to 1.9 percent.[11] With Greece subject to enhanced surveillance for the next decade, reaction on the ground was muted. Greece is expected to stick to austerity measures and reforms, including budget surpluses, for over forty years, and adherence will be monitored quarterly.

The overall picture is that Greece survived primarily on loans from the eurozone after 2010, when it lost market access to funds because of a ballooning budget deficit, huge public debt, and an underperforming economy, matched with an expansive welfare system. The country was plunged into an unprecedented recession from which it started to recover only in 2018, posting economic growth of 2 percent after its economy had shrunk by more than 26 percent since 2010. Wages had fallen by nearly 20 percent since 2010, with pensions and other welfare payments cut by 70 percent in the same period. The size of the public sector had been reduced by 26 percent. Unemployment had dropped slightly but remained at 20 percent, with youth unemployment at 43 percent, sending thousands of young Greeks abroad. The €320 billion debt mountain (almost 180% of GDP) was still the highest debt ratio in the EU, but Greece's borrowing costs stood at about 4 percent, compared with 24 percent at the peak of the crisis.

Although the Greek crisis cannot be separated from eurozone membership, it is unclear just how much the euro contributed to the crisis and its unfolding. The crisis would have hit sooner if Greece had not had the opportunity to borrow at German interest rates during the first decade of the twenty-first century. However, the euro did not cause the crisis in any meaningful sense; that has to be laid at the door of successive Greek governments and the banks who lent to Greece without recognizing the danger of loans turning bad. The unfolding of the crisis through the three bailouts between 2010 and 2015 has many similarities to the Latin American bailouts of the 1980s. Creditor banks, with the support of their governments, prioritized recovering as much of their loans as possible. The 2010 bailout provided a breathing space when debts continued to be serviced while the foreign banks divested their Greek bonds. After 2012, the priority was to wind down Greek debt with as little fuss as possible, a process that involved transferring risk to domestic Greek banks and EU taxpayers. The ECB remained involved and used its monopoly over euro emissions and power to purchase Greek debt in the secondary market to ensure that Greek governments remained on track with the conditionality.

Although the ECB was reported as threatening that Greece would have to leave the eurozone if it went off-track, that option—and indeed anything to do with the common currency—appeared not to be a driving force behind the unfolding of the Greek debt crisis. The Greek crisis did, however, impact the eurozone by invigorating discussion of banking and capital reforms that might be desirable in themselves as well as pillars supporting the eurozone.

5.1.4 Banking Union and Capital Market Reform

The European Central Bank as it operated in the 2000s was responsible for monetary policy but lacked many other powers normally held by central banks. For example, because mutualization of EU members' debts was not permitted, the ECB could not act as lender of last resort to banks in difficulty. Financial regulation and supervision as well as monitoring the Stability and Growth Pact (SGP) were responsibilities of the EU Commission, not the ECB. The SGP had been established at the same time as the single currency in order to ensure sound public finances, but it did not prevent the emergence of serious fiscal imbalances in EU members. Many critics of the eurozone's institutional structure questioned the prospects of currency union without a banking union or fiscal policy coordination, and the Greek and other financial crises were a catalyst for rethinking the ECB's responsibilities and the institutional framework of the eurozone.

Fiscal rules, as in the five convergence criteria for euro adoption (Section 4.1), are nontransparent, procyclical, and divisive. Some progress on definitions and transparency had been made in the Maastricht Treaty and by Eurostat, but Greece evaded them in the 2000s. Fiscal rules can be procyclical because during recessions, budget deficits increase as tax revenues fall and social security payments increase; if the deficit passes the 3 percent threshold, the government may be obligated by the fiscal rules to cut spending or raise taxes at a time when they want to use expansionary fiscal policy to stimulate economic activity. The rules are divisive because national governments differ on priorities such as how they weight unemployment versus inflation. Helping countries with a liquidity crisis by giving loans conditional on fiscal retrenchment often leads to a populist backlash, and having rigid bailout rules exacerbates crises (as in Greece in 2010–2012 and 2015).[12]

The EU's efforts during the 2010s to improve its macroeconomic governance centered on legislative packages to reinforce the SGP. Measures to strengthen the monitoring of members' macroeconomic policies started with the European Semester, introduced in 2010 and revised in

2015, which ensures that eurozone members discuss their economic and budgetary plans with their EU partners at specific times of the year. The "Six Pack," which became law in December 2011, introduced a new macroeconomic surveillance tool, the Macroeconomic Imbalance Procedure, and the "Two Pack," which entered into force in May 2013, requested that eurozone members present draft budgetary plans for the following year in mid-October. The procedural reforms were reinforced by the Intergovernmental Treaty on Stability, Coordination and Governance in the Economic and Monetary Union (TSCG) that entered into force on 1 January 2013.[13]

The TSCG is a stronger version of the SGP and has been ratified by all EU27 countries. The TSCG includes the Fiscal Compact, which has been adopted by the nineteen eurozone countries plus Bulgaria, Denmark, and Romania.[14] The Fiscal Compact requires countries to have a balanced budget rule in domestic legislation, to establish an automatic mechanism to correct potential deviations from budget balance, and to have a national independent monitoring institution to provide fiscal surveillance. For the countries bound by the Fiscal Compact, the national budget has to be in balance under the treaty's definition, which is a more nuanced version of the SGP's 3 percent of GDP criterion.[15] The TSCG also contains the "debt brake" criteria outlined in the SGP, which defines the rate at which debt levels above the limit of 60 percent of GDP shall decrease.

Although commentators have criticized the TSCG for being "long on good intentions but rather short on substance" (Gros 2012, 1), the cumulative impact of the procedural innovations and the Fiscal Compact represent a significant step toward increased fiscal cooperation. The regular cycle of meetings and reporting that tracks members' budget drafts through the year gives the TSCG more enforcement substance than the original SGP. However, the arrangement is still intergovernmental rather than a fiscal union, and its ability to preempt future crises will only be apparent when the next precrisis situation occurs.

In 2010, the EU created two temporary funding programs, the European Financial Stability Facility and the European Financial Stabilisation Mechanism, that provided financial assistance conditional on the implementation of reforms to Ireland and Portugal between 2011 and

2014, and short-term bridge loans to Greece in July 2015. In September 2012, these temporary programs were replaced by the European Stability Mechanism, an intergovernmental arrangement providing instant access to assistance for eurozone members in financial difficulty, with a maximum lending capacity of €700 billion in the form of loans or as new capital to banks in difficulty. In 2015, the ECB introduced the Public Sector Purchase Programme (PSPP) under which it could buy bonds issued by eurozone central governments, agencies, and European institutions; the institutions that sold the securities can use the revenue to buy other assets and extend credit to the real economy, contributing to an easing of financial conditions.

In June 2012, the EU committed to establishing a banking union consisting of a single supervisory mechanism, a single resolution mechanism, and a European Deposit Insurance Scheme. Large parts of the bank regulatory and supervisory framework were transferred from the national domain to the euro area in November 2014 when the ECB was assigned a supervisory function and the Single Resolution Board (SRB) was created as an area-wide resolution authority; the former is intended to forestall bank failure, whereas the SRB deals with the situation after a bank failure. The ECB reviewed banks five times after 2014 and before the COVID-19 pandemic, making significant progress in improving asset quality and bank solvency.[16] The SRB is building up its resources by levies on financial institutions, intended to amount to €55 billion by the end of 2023, which will permit full mutualization of the costs of resolution. The SRB is also designing procedures to ensure as much bail-in as possible—that is, resolution of insolvent banks will be a cost on owners in the first instance with use of public funds as a last resort.

A June 2018 summit on euro area reform reaffirmed commitment to a European Deposit Insurance Scheme, to be introduced after sufficient reduction in banks' legacy risks.[17] Deposit insurance is desirable to address the asymmetric information between banks and their depositors but introduces moral hazard because bank owners or managers can seek higher returns by making riskier loans knowing that if the loans turn bad, the taxpayer will bail out the bank's depositors. In the eurozone, different national deposit insurance schemes distort competition in banking because depositors will, other things equal, be attracted to the jurisdictions that provide the most generous guarantees. However, national governments are cautious about mutualizing deposit insurance because they may consider some members' banks less safe than their own banks. Those governments will insist on cleaning up all eurozone banking systems (e.g., by credible stress tests combined with effective measures), while advocates of a European Deposit Insurance Scheme argue that the scheme is a necessary component of banking union and should not be delayed indefinitely. The sequencing problem has, so far, stymied introduction of the scheme.

Despite progress toward banking union, the central objectives of the banking union proved to be elusive. The banking sector remains largely unprofitable with little evidence of improved efficiency or competitiveness. Perceived benefits of risk diversification by integrating eurozone banking markets did not occur, and the large euro area banks struggled to hold their position in the competitive global marketplace. Apart from services for expatriates, cross-border retail banking remains rare in the EU; ING has offered online banking services and Santander penetrated some non-Spanish markets and HSBC some non-British markets, but these are minor exceptions.[18]

Incomplete banking union leaves banks vulnerable to national government pressure and also to subnational government actions. The lobbying power of the financial sector, which varies across countries, can make agreement difficult even when eurozone members express a shared commitment to a goal. A recognized ultimate goal of banking sector reform is to promote bail-in—that is, the cost of sustaining a troubled financial institution should be borne by the owners rather than the taxpayers. The greater the role of bail-in, the smaller the moral hazard and excessively risky lending; consequently, the need for stress tests to monitor a bank's creditworthiness or for drawing on deposit insurance is reduced. Although governments agree on the goal of maximizing bail-in, bank owners and managers prefer to have limited liability.[19] Small banks may be captured by local governments seeking funding for prestige projects or other activities that do not yield adequate returns.[20]

Financial sector reform remains incomplete in part due to failure to address the links between sovereign borrowers and national financial systems. Lender of last resort to banks remains a national responsibility;

even if lending to distressed banks is under an ECB program, the ECB is not an unconditional lender of last resort and liability for repayment is national. Farhi and Tirole (2018) have demonstrated that such links between banks and sovereign borrowing create a doom loop that transforms a bank crisis into a public debt crisis. In the early 2010s, apart from Greece, the doom loop of contagion between banks' balance sheets and sovereign debt was evident in Ireland, Italy, and Spain.

In 2018, the Commission proposed creation of Sovereign Bond-Backed Securities (SBBS), a new financial instrument that would take the form of liquid assets backed by a predefined pool of eurozone central government bonds. SBBS are a market-led solution to promote financial integration, reduce home bias in investors' portfolios, and facilitate the diversification of sovereign exposures. SBBS should contribute to financial sector stability by further weakening the link between banks and their governments by allowing banks to invest in a type of low-risk liquid asset that is less dependent on the solvency of one particular nation-state while still benefiting from a more favorable regulatory treatment than traditional securitization products.[21]

In sum, a consequence of the sovereign debt crises that broke out after late 2009 has been serious rethinking of the appropriate institutions to accompany a single currency in a more deeply integrated EU. The process has been messy and slow, and some of the measures described above may work and others may not. Together, they represent a tentative step toward more integrated approaches to fiscal policy, a banking union, and sovereign debt relief. Their effectiveness depends on implementation as well as on declarations of intent, and the strength of implementation may only be revealed when the next crisis occurs.

Crisis management in the 2010s and responses to the need to address banking and financial sector reform have dominated thinking about the euro. The answer to the deeper question of whether the euro has been a success depends on the extent to which the microeconomic benefits of reduced transactions costs outweigh the macroeconomic costs of lost policy independence.[22] Clearly, if there are irreconcilable differences in desired monetary policy (as in Czechoslovakia in 1990 or Yugoslavia in 1992) or gross macro mismanagement (as in the ruble zone in 1992–1993), then a common currency is unsustainable. In Europe, monetary policy consensus plus the transactions costs benefits of a single currency for an integrated market have been decisive. Among eurozone members, there has been general agreement since the early 1980s on the priority of maintaining price stability, and ECB management of monetary policy has been competent; in that setting, the macroeconomic costs of lost policy independence are small. The microeconomic benefits in terms of reduced private and public sector transactions costs are hard to quantify but likely to be large, especially since establishment of the Single Market and progress toward deeper integration. In its first two decades, despite financial crises, the euro faced no existential challenge; eurozone membership increased from eleven to nineteen countries with no exits.

5.2 Labor Market Integration and Refugee Crises

The Treaty of Rome included freedom of movement of labor as an objective, but in the twentieth century, cross-country labor mobility within the EU was notoriously low compared to within federal economies such as the United States, Canada, or Australia. Following the enlargements to include Eastern European countries in 2004 and 2007, there is evidence of increased labor migration especially between new and old EU members, but migration within the EU remains much smaller as a percentage of population than in federal countries.[23] The net economic consequences of migration should be positive as labor moves from a lower productivity to a higher productivity workplace, although as with removing restrictions to trade in goods, there will be distributional effects; other things equal, labor in the low-wage country and owners of other factors in the receiving country benefit from labor migration, and labor in the receiving country and other factors in the sending country lose. Indirect consequences of easier movement of people include increased demand for foreign goods, spread of information about potential trade partners in the migrants' home country, reduced costs and risks of cross-border trade, and increased direct foreign investment and cross-border financial flows.

After 2004, workers from the ten new members were able to enter the labor market in Ireland, Sweden, and the UK, whereas the other twelve

EU members restricted migration during a seven-year transition period. This could have provided a natural experiment of the impact of internal migration. However, the evidence of labor market impacts is weak and inconclusive. Blanchflower and Shadforth (2009) found evidence of significantly weaker wage growth for groups of workers competing directly with new arrivals and document that the increasing numbers of foreign workers led to "fear of unemployment" that helped to control wage pressure. However, Dustmann et al. (2013) find a positive effect on native wages if the impact is analyzed along the wage distribution; downward pressure is restricted to the bottom percentiles but increases in the upper parts of the distribution mean that the overall effect on native wages is positive. Wadsworth (2018) observes that in all the literature on the effect of Eastern European migrants on the UK labor market, results tend to range from weak to insignificant. At the upper end of the wage distribution, the UK, as first mover in accessing the pool of talented Eastern European workers, was able to attract the best and brightest migrants, and this may have discouraged British workers from training for some high-skilled positions. However, Mountford and Wadsworth (2019) conclude that this was not a major driver of labor market developments.[24]

In the twenty-first century, labor mobility has been facilitated by the Schengen Agreement that is (apart from the opt-outs by the UK and Ireland) part of the EU's *acquis communautaire,* and hence required of new members. By the 2010s, the Schengen Area included twenty-two of the twenty-eight EU members (Cyprus, Romania, Bulgaria, and Croatia had yet to implement) and four nonmembers (Norway, Iceland, Liechtenstein, and Switzerland). Counterparts to free internal movement of people have included introduction of a uniform Schengen visa policy, cooperation on criminal and judicial matters, and definition of national responsibilities for asylum seekers.

Removal of barriers at national borders has reduced trade costs and facilitated movement of travelers. Beneficiaries from Schengen include cross-border commuters who clearly gain in time saved as Schengen connects national labor markets in border regions. A 2009 EU study reported that over 200,000 people commuted across the Swiss border to work—that is, 6 percent of all employees in Switzerland—and 127,000 people commuted across the Luxembourg border to work—that is 43 percent of all employees in Luxembourg (Ademmer et al. 2015). Dismantling border controls in Schengenland may have caused redundancies among border officials, although increased cross-border cooperation mitigated this effect by providing new tasks for the officials, and it led to greater cooperation on criminal and judicial matters as it became easier for criminals to slip across borders to evade pursuit. By facilitating cross-border travel, Schengen may also shape positive attitudes toward the EU, although greater mobility among higher-skilled, better-educated individuals may contribute to polarization of attitudes toward integration.

Labor migration is related to monetary union. A common currency eases comparison of wages and the costs of migration, although this is likely to be a minor consideration. Labor mobility is expected to improve the prospects of currency union—that is, bring the new currency area closer to an optimum currency area, because exchange rate changes to deal with asymmetric shocks are less necessary if adjustment can be achieved by labor movements (Mundell 1961). The evidence on whether labor mobility does play such an adjustment role is mixed. Arpaia et al. (2018) and Huart and Tchakpalla (2019) both find evidence of labor mobility in response to changes in relative unemployment rates in the EU, but the magnitude of the response remains small.[25]

In sum, the total number of internal migrants in the EU has not been large. Although cross-border migration may reduce wage inequality and act as a macroeconomic stabilizer, the magnitude of these effects is limited. There is some evidence of migration by complementary rather than competing workers—that is, migrants fill empty niches rather than displace host-country workers. In the lower wage countries, the benefits from emigration are widely spread (among workers), and those remaining in the country face no culture shock of seeing immigrants. In the higher wage countries, although there is political resistance to migrants, anti-immigrant sentiment is often targeted against extracommunitarians from countries with more obvious cultural differences to the receiving countries' population.

Freer internal movement has led to tighter external border controls that have made it harder for nonmember citizens to cross-border commute. In 2005, Frontex was created to coordinate border operations on Schengenland's frontiers.[26] Workers from Eastern European countries such as Moldova or Ukraine or from southern Mediterranean countries formerly commuted, often semilegally, for seasonal work (e.g., in agriculture); this is less feasible with tighter borders. Granting Schengen visa access became a foreign policy tool for the EU—for example, in relations with European Partner countries to the east or with Mediterranean countries. Visa access is granted to countries in return for political reform or adoption of EU practice, which may include improving document security and border management to facilitate the EU's border controls. Once granted, a Schengen visa allows travel throughout the zone, perhaps stimulating more positive feelings toward EU countries.

A major unforeseen consequence of Schengen was the need to determine common policies toward refugees. European countries signed the United Nations Convention Relating to the Status of Refugees in 1951, with sympathy for displaced persons amid memories of World War II but with little expectation that numbers might be large. Under the convention, refugees can request political asylum if they are unable or unwilling to return to their country of origin owing to a well-founded fear of persecution, and when applicants cannot document persecution but conditions prevent safe return to their country of origin, they may receive "complementary protection" as long as the adverse conditions persist.

To apply for political asylum, refugees need to present themselves to authorities in the signatory state. However, Schengen country embassies do not grant visas for this purpose, and airlines do not accept passengers without visas, so refugees arrive by foot across a land border (e.g., Turkey / Greece) or by sea.[27] To prevent shopping for the country providing best conditions for refugees, asylum seekers must apply at their point of entry into the Schengen zone. The Dublin Convention enshrines the principle that the first member state where an asylum claim is lodged is responsible for a person's asylum claim.[28] In July 2017, the European Court of Justice declared that despite the high influx of refugees in 2015, the Dublin Convention still applied, giving EU member states the right to deport migrants to the first country of entry into the EU.

Following the 2011 Arab Spring and subsequent repression or state breakdown, irregular migration across the Mediterranean increased. In late 2014, with the war in Syria approaching its fourth year and Islamic State making gains in the north of the country, the exodus of Syrians intensified. At the same time, others were fleeing violence and poverty in countries such as Iraq, Afghanistan, Eritrea, Somalia, Niger, and Kosovo. Many came through southeast Europe to Austria and Hungary. German chancellor Angela Merkel saw it as Germany's duty to welcome refugees, and in 2015, Germany accepted a million refugees—a controversial outcome for many Germans—whereas leaders of other EU member countries such as Hungary or Poland saw it as their duty not to accept any refugees because their presence would challenge the country's culture.

Refugee acceptance could be seen as a public good. The EU as a whole has an obligation to accept refugees, but the burden of implementation falls on host countries. Dustmann et al. (2017) note that "the different exposures to refugee inflows and the lack of any effective European-level mechanism to 'spread the burden' of hosting refugee populations, led many countries to implement procedures aimed at reducing inflows into their territories."[29] However, even with goodwill, spreading the costs of providing a public good can be difficult. Among other issues are different views of what the host should provide, different wishes of the migrants about preferred destinations, different absorptive capacities of hosts (including the "cultural" objections of some Eastern European governments), and so forth. When the EU adopted by qualified majority voting a burden-sharing agreement to allocate refugees among partner countries, the Czech Republic, Hungary, and Poland voted against the decision and failed to implement it; the Czech Republic took 12 refugees (out of a quota of 2,000), and Hungary and Poland refused to accept any of their 140,000 allocation. These actions would have ramifications in 2020 that are described in Chapter 6.

The total number of refugees entering the Schengen Area in 2015 was 1.8 million (Frontex data, quoted by Petroni 2020, 231). Differences in acceptance policies led some Schengen countries to "temporarily" reimpose controls at national borders, first Germany in September 2015, followed by Austria, Sweden, France, and Denmark; the controls were prolonged several times. Other EU member countries (e.g., Bulgaria, Hungary, and Slovenia) erected physical fences to keep out migrants. However, the flow of illegal migrants appeared to moderate after an EU-Turkey agreement in March 2016 in which Turkey, in return for financial assistance of €6 billion over five years, committed to restrict departure of refugees hoping to move on to Europe. Debates about revision of the Dublin Convention remained bogged down in disagreement, but President Donald Tusk captured the prevailing mood in a September 2018 speech: "The migration debate showed that we may not agree on everything, but we agree on the main goal, which is stemming illegal migration to Europe" (quoted in Petroni 2020, 235). Although the flow moderated in 2017–2019, the issue could be ignored; it would reemerge when Turkey terminated its commitment in February 2020.[30]

The EU budget provides some funding for patrolling the Mediterranean Sea, but the costs of processing asylum seekers are still an excessive burden on the frontline countries (Hatton 2017). Frontex, as established between 2006 and 2010, was a lean organization with an annual budget around €100 million and 300 staff; it remained the task of each member state to control its own borders, while Frontex was vested to ensure that they all did so with the same high standard of efficiency. In 2016, the Border and Coast Guard was created within Frontex to strengthen enforcement.[31] However, with a budget that rose to €330 million and 750 staff in 2019, Frontex's reach remained limited.[32]

If implementing and funding asylum system were EU competences, it would be a sizable budget item, although less than spending on the common agricultural policy (CAP) or structural / regional policies. On the principle of subsidiarity, national authorities would still be involved in, for example, provision of housing and social services for refugees. The dilemma is that although the status quo is unacceptable, the alternative vision is politically impossible because distribution of the costs of providing the public good is thwarted by governments who refuse to accept any responsibility.

People movements have become a threat to EU solidarity because they are driving populism and hence threatening the liberal democracy foundations of the EU. Populist parties remain a minority in most members, with typically no more than 10 percent to 25 percent of votes, but they have leverage due to deep disagreements over policy toward informal immigrants. To what extent should such immigrants be treated as refugees or as illegal economic migrants? Should refugees be distributed among EU member countries according to negotiated quotas, which raises issues of quota sizes and of implementation within the Schengen Area, or should they be returned to the country of first arrival?

The impacts of migration are difficult to measure. There is little agreement among economists of whether there are huge potential gains from moving people from low-productivity to high-productivity locations (e.g., Hamilton and Whalley 1984) or whether such movements depress average productivity in the currently high-productivity locations (Borjas 2015). The time horizon is important—for example, following the 2004 EU enlargement, immigration from Eastern Europe contributed to an economic boom in the UK between 2004 and 2007, but the micro impacts and cultural reactions to migration contributed to the outcome of the 2016 referendum on whether the UK should leave the EU.[33]

5.3 Brexit

When the UK joined the European Communities in 1973, the *acquis communautaire* that it accepted did not extend far beyond the customs union and CAP.

From the late 1970s to the early 1990s, the UK stood apart from the majority as it negotiated opt-outs on monetary integration and on Schengen, as well as obtaining a special budget arrangement. Following the Maastricht Treaty (1993), which committed signatories to deeper integration and monetary union on the path to closer union, a strong Eurosceptic movement emerged in the UK, including the UK Independence Party (UKIP).[34] In the 2014 elections for the European Parliament, UKIP won more votes than any other party in the UK. The British government held a referendum in June 2016 on UK membership in the EU, offering the simple choice—*leave* or *remain*? By a 52–48 majority, voters chose *leave*. Prime Minister David Cameron, who had supported *remain*, resigned the following day.

Support for *leave* in the referendum came primarily from older, more rural, less educated, and less economically successful voters, who felt left behind by economic integration and globalization (Sampson 2017, 175–178). Evidence is unclear on whether they specifically voted to shift control from the EU to the UK or were scapegoating the EU for wider concerns associated with globalization. Nevertheless, the historical record suggests British reservations about federalism and a more transactions-based view of European integration going back at least to the 1980s negotiations about "fair" budget contributions to balance what the UK paid in and what it got out of membership. In 2016, the UK debate focused on economic costs and benefits of EU membership, with some attention to migration but virtually no focus on bonds of Europeanness.

There was no relevant precedent for withdrawal from the EU. Previous exits were special cases inapplicable to Brexit. In 1962, when Algeria gained independence from France, it also ceased to be part of the European Communities. In 1985, Greenland, following Denmark's granting of home rule, exited the EU. In 2012, Saint Barthélemy, following secession from the French overseas region of Guadeloupe, withdrew from the EU and became an Overseas Country and Territory (OCT).[35]

The new prime minister, Theresa May, set out her strategy for negotiating Britain's EU exit (Brexit) in a February 2017 white paper.[36] The paper stated that the UK would not seek to remain in the EU's Single Market and would pursue a new strategic partnership with the EU, including a customs arrangement that would allow the UK to sign new trade agreements with other countries. In March 2017, the UK triggered exit negotiations by invoking Article 50 of the Lisbon treaty which provided for a two-year deadline before Brexit in March 2019. May then made the disastrous decision to call a general election in May 2017 in hopes of strengthening her position. In the election, the Conservative Party lost its majority in Parliament and would henceforth govern with the support of the Democratic Unionist Party which was committed to maintaining the status of Northern Ireland within the UK.

After the referendum, the EU27 moved quickly to coordinate their response. Negotiation was an EU competence, and the twenty-seven agreed on general principles that would be pursued by the EU27 negotiator Michel Barnier. These principles included upholding the EU's core values of promoting peace and the well-being of its peoples, negotiating an orderly withdrawal according to the road map in Article 50 of the Lisbon treaty, and treating the UK as a third country (Laffan 2019). In contrast, the UK did not have a clear negotiating position beyond May's red line of leaving the Single Market.[37]

The withdrawal negotiations were expected to cover three central issues: the UK's outstanding financial liabilities to the EU based on commitments made while a member, the future status of EU citizens in the UK and of UK citizens in the EU27, and the framework for future UK-EU relations. In practice, the decision on future EU-UK trade relations was postponed, with the EU in particular emphasizing the importance of concluding the Withdrawal Agreement prior to serious discussion of future relations. On 14 November 2018, EU and British negotiators agreed on a legally binding 585-page text, setting out the details of the UK's divorce from the EU. The agreement contained numerous legal resolutions, especially affecting commerce. It defined how Britain's financial debt should be calculated and the terms under which it would be paid; the main components were the UK's outstanding obligations as a net contributor to the 2014–2020 EU budget and more distant commitments such as unfunded pension rights accrued by EU employees during the UK's membership.[38] The agreement preserved the existing residency and working rights of UK citizens living elsewhere in the EU and of EU citizens living in the UK up until the end of the Brexit implementation period set for 31 December 2020.

Although the EU27 were united and the British government had signed the agreement, it quickly became clear that the agreement would not be ratified by the UK parliament. The government postponed the vote in hopes of avoiding defeat, but when the vote was finally taken on 15 January 2019, the agreement was rejected by 230 votes—the largest ever parliamentary defeat of a British government. Despite repeated attempts by the government to push it through, the agreement failed to obtain parliamentary approval, leading Theresa May to announce on 24 May that she would resign as prime minister. Although opponents of the agreement had diverse objections, a key sticking point turned out to be the proposed method of avoiding the return of a physical border between the UK's Northern Ireland and the Republic of Ireland.

Dismantling the border between Ireland and Northern Ireland was an important, and popular, part of the 1998 Good Friday Agreement that ended "the Troubles" in which over 3,500 people had died since 1969. If the UK exited the customs union, then the current arrangement was untenable. Logically, there were three, and only three, mutually exclusive options, each of which was unacceptable to an important UK stakeholder:

1. UK stays in the customs union, which was unacceptable to Brexiteers and breached the cornerstone of Prime Minister May's strategy (i.e., quitting the Single Market).

2. UK exits the customs union and re-erects border controls in Ireland, which was unacceptable to Ireland and to many members of the UK parliament.

3. Northern Ireland remains in the customs union, requiring controls on trade between Northern Ireland and the rest of the UK, which was unacceptable to the Democratic Unionist Party on whose support the UK minority government after the 2017 general election relied.

The deal reached by UK and EU negotiators in November 2018 included agreement on a backstop that would see Northern Ireland staying aligned to rules of the EU Single Market, which meant that goods coming into Northern Ireland from elsewhere in the UK would need to be checked for conformity to EU standards. The backstop sparked a backlash, including resignation of several UK cabinet ministers, concerned that it breached the red line of leaving the Single Market. The Democratic Unionist Party opposed the backstop for separating Northern Ireland from the rest of the UK. The backstop arrangements would apply unless and until both the EU and the UK agreed they were no longer necessary, which exacerbated concerns of opponents that it would leave the UK permanently tied to the EU.

In the first half of 2019, the situation was deadlocked as the British government could not command a parliamentary majority and had to request an extension of the 29 March deadline. However, the UK parliament seemed to be paralyzed while waiting for the Conservative Party to find a new prime minister, until Boris Johnson was appointed on 24 July, two months after Theresa May announced her resignation. Johnson announced his determination to lead the UK out of the EU on 31 October with or without a new agreement. However, the majority of Members of Parliament voted to block the no-deal option of letting time run out until the UK quit the EU on the new deadline of 31 October 2019 without a binding agreement on the UK's outstanding financial liabilities to the EU, on the future status of EU citizens in the UK and of UK citizens in EU countries, and on Ireland. Such a no-deal would surely poison UK-EU relations and negotiations over future trading relations.

Meanwhile, Johnson attempted to revise the agreement with the EU27. To break the deadlock over Ireland, he proposed a customs regime that would more effectively separate Northern Ireland from Great Britain. In an extraordinary Saturday session of Parliament, Johnson's strategy was defeated, to which he responded by calling a general election. After his party gained an increased majority in the 12 December election, Johnson was able to obtain parliamentary support for the Withdrawal Agreement and ensure Brexit on 31 January 2020. In retrospect, 2019 was largely a wasted year for Brexit negotiations, as the adamant parliamentary objections to the agreement were overturned by the voters. The only significant change to the agreement during 2019 was a hardening of the future customs border between Great Britain and Northern Ireland, prevention of which was the issue on which the Democratic Unionist Party had supported May's minority government.

How to assess the economic consequences of Brexit? When the UK joined the EU in 1973, it was at a short-term cost (trade diversion was greater than trade creation due to the CAP), but forty-five years later, the CAP was much less distortionary. Using a gravity model to study the effect of EU membership on UK's trade, Mulabdic et al. (2017) estimated that deep integration increased UK goods and services trade by about 42 percent between 1995 and 2012 and value-added by about 14 percent. Because of EU membership, UK's services trade more than doubled and UK exports of services to new EU members had been especially buoyant. They also found that the increase in domestic value-added in gross exports from the UK was driven by stronger GVC links: the UK's "forward linkages" (supply of inputs to EU customers) increased by about 30 percent due to deepening integration, whereas its "backward linkages" (demand for inputs from EU suppliers) increased by almost 40 percent thanks to EU membership.[39]

As in classic customs union theory, Brexit is second best and could in principle be welfare reducing or welfare increasing.[40] We might expect a mixture of (negative) trade destruction due to new trade barriers on EU-UK trade and trade diversion, which may be positive if the new UK tariff is lower than the EU tariff. However, with an average EU tariff of 4 percent and expected low UK tariffs, the price wedges will be small and welfare effects limited. There will also be the relatively small financial benefits of retaining tariff revenue on UK imports and of no longer making net contributions to the EU budget.

Any option involving departure from the Single Market is likely to disrupt value chains crossing the EU-UK border and most likely lead to reduction in the UK's participation in GVCs. Using a gravity model that includes domestic and GVC linkages between goods and services sectors and bilateral tariffs that have direct and indirect effects on production, Vandenbussche et al. (2017) predict the impact of Brexit in terms of value-added, production, and employment for the whole set of EU countries and estimate Brexit would reduce economic activity in the UK approximately three times more than in the rest of the EU.

The UK will also face some sector-specific costs of not being in the Single Market—for example, concerning the financial sector and airlines.[41] The EU passporting system for banks and financial services companies enables firms that are authorized in any member of the European Economic Area (EEA) to trade in any other EEA state with minimal additional authorization. Non-EU firms do not have passporting rights on financial services; Djankov (2017) estimated that UK financial sector revenue would fall by between 12 percent and 18 percent without passporting rights. The impact of loss of passporting will vary; Schoenmaker (2017) argues that retail banking and insurance are unlikely to suffer much, but wholesale banking is vulnerable. In particular, London could lose its attractiveness as the EU base for non-EU financial institutions which in 2014 had £2,040 billion in assets in London, compared to EEA banks' assets of £530 billion in London.[42]

The empirical literature forecasting the economic consequences of Brexit followed two main approaches. Dhingra et al. (2017) simulated Brexit using general equilibrium models of the UK and EU economies with various assumptions about the specifics of the post-Brexit agreement. They examined the impact of changes in tariffs, nontariff barriers to trade, and intra-EU trade costs, although the last two are hard to quantify. Dhingra et al. found that the UK would suffer from higher import prices and reduced ability to specialize according to comparative advantage. They concluded that even in the optimistic case of no tariffs on EU-UK trade, the UK will suffer a permanent 1.3 percent fall in per capita consumption, and in the pessimistic case of trade at most-favored nation (MFN) tariffs the loss is 2.7 percent. This is consistent with other computable general equilibrium (CGE) modelers' results (e.g., Hantzsche et al. [2019] estimated that for comparable scenarios, GDP per capita will be reduced by 2 percent and 3 percent). They may, however, be underestimates because CGE models are poor at including special but important cases, such as the financial sector or airlines to answer questions such as, will London remain a financial center? Will EasyJet remain competitive?

The second approach was to use a gravity model to quantify the determinants of bilateral trade and then use estimated import and export functions to measure the effect of changes in trade flows. This approach, sometimes referred to as reduced-form estimates because there is no real theoretical underpinning, is summarized in Dhingra et al, (2017, section 6.2) and in Sampson (2017, 172–173). It avoids the black-box nature of CGE modeling and is driven by empirical relationships. In general, these reduced-form studies produced larger estimates of loss to the UK. The difference may be because trade is correlated with other benefits of integration that are not picked up in CGE models—for example, the impact on productivity.[43]

A third approach used by Born et al. (2019) is to create a synthetic country whose performance tracked that of the UK before the Brexit referendum to trace the counterfactual outcome of Britain without Brexit.[44] They conclude that the Brexit vote caused an output loss of between 1.7 percent and 2.5 percent by the end of 2018, which they ascribe primarily to uncertainty and predict that the loss will rise to 4 percent by 2020.

In a world of heterogeneous firms and production fragmented along value chains, predicting changes in trade flows needs a microeconomic component missing from the approaches just described. Brexit may reduce the attractiveness of the UK as a destination for foreign investment or as a GVC participant, and some studies predict large loss of car assembly operations as companies like BMW shift tasks from UK to EU locations.[45] Such phenomena are hard to predict because investment decisions are multicausal; Serwicka and Tamberi (2018) estimate that foreign direct investment in Britain fell by almost one-fifth between the year before and the year after the Brexit referendum.[46] Other studies point to costs of limiting labor migration, whereas pro-Brexit studies focus on benefits of deregulation (e.g., Minford 2019, based on an unsubstantiated assumption that the cost of EU regulations amounts to 6 percent of GDP). The deregulation benefits are easy to overestimate insofar as UK ministers agreed to EU regulations, many of which will remain unchanged after Brexit; for example, among the most economically costly regulations are limits on working hours, but these and other social protection or product safety measures are unlikely to be abolished.[47]

There is a strong consensus among economists that the economic costs of Brexit will significantly exceed its benefits. Beyond doubt in the short term, uncertainty was a major issue, already having a negative economic impact after announcement of the referendum in 2015 (Graziano et al. 2018). In the long term, Brexit is expected to have negative consequences in terms of growth and productivity making the UK "permanently poorer" (Baldwin 2016), although magnitudes will depend on post-Brexit trade arrangements. Economic effects of leaving the customs union on goods producers could be small because external tariffs are low and there are few exceptions. In the twenty-first century, trade costs are more important than tariffs and a key issue is the impact on GVC participation. Leaving the Single Market will increase trade costs, and the extent to which this damages GVC participation is likely to be product specific. Uncertainty led firms to change their investment plans or choice of GVC partners already after the 2016 referendum in anticipation of the impact of Brexit. Services trade is important to the UK and half of this is financial services, which will certainly be damaged by the loss of passporting rights. British airline companies could also be hit by compliance difficulties to fly in EU airspace and removal of access to routes between destinations in the EU27. Long-term effects, such as the impact of trade and GVC participation on productivity or the impact of exiting the Single Market on flows of capital and labor, could be more important but are hard to capture empirically.

Does disintegration matter? The answer depends on circumstances. In a customs union with high external trade barriers, disintegration may be good—for example, in unions such as the East African Community and the Central American Common Market which unraveled in the 1970s when trade diversion exceeded trade creation. In a more fragmented world, disintegration may cause economic disruption. Collapse of the Austro-Hungarian and Ottoman Empires in 1919 was followed by hyperinflation and other symptoms of economic distress in east and southeast Europe, contributing to outbreak of war in 1939. Dissolution of the Soviet Union in 1991 led to major disruption of supply chains and deep recession for most of the 1990s. In these cases, economies integrated by transport, financial, and commercial policies were not easily untangled into separate units, especially when successor states adopted inward-looking economic policies. In a globalized world with low trade barriers and low trade costs, regional integration or disintegration matter less for economic health but may still have nontrivial effects.[48] Such economic costs and benefits may not matter if there is a commitment to federal Europe rather than a transactional view of the EU, or in the cases of Norway and Switzerland which do not want to be part of the EU but are rich enough to pay to be in the EEA. Moreover, and relevant to the UK case, economic disintegration can set in train indirect consequences that are hard to predict.[49]

5.4 Cohesion Spending and Smart, Sustainable, and Inclusive Growth

After the adoption of the Social Charter in the Maastricht Treaty, a striking phenomenon in the twenty-first century has been the limited realization of a European social policy (Graziano and Hartlapp 2019). This is despite a series of high-level social policy packages during the 2010s (in 2010, Europe 2020; in 2012, the Employment and Youth Employment Package; in 2013, the Social Investment Package; and in 2017, the Pillar of Social Right). In the Youth Guarantee in 2013, EU members made a commitment to ensure that all people under the age of twenty-five years receive a good-quality offer of employment, continued education, apprenticeship, or traineeship within a period of four months of becoming unemployed or leaving formal education. However, the steps taken to implement such goals at the EU level have been negligible. In practice, the social policy competences of the EU are constrained by the member countries' determination to retain national control in this area.

Nevertheless, within the Single Market, the national monopolies in welfare state provision are being undermined. Greater labor mobility has stimulated many legal cases where denial of access to national welfare states has been challenged and decisions by the EU Court take precedence. Market forces can undermine monopolies, especially in areas where market forces and private provision are increasingly prevalent, such as health. Removing obstacles to cross-country competition in insurance or finance can also indirectly challenge welfare state monopolies by offering alternative means to achieving social goals—for example, saving for retirement or insuring against high medical bills. Such processes are in their infancy but are likely to become more important as the Single Market develops.

The main EU tool for addressing income inequality has been cohesion spending. However, the effectiveness of European structural and investment funds is debated. Between Maastricht and Lisbon, there was a struggle between national governments (especially the richer net contributors to the EU budget) and the Commission (supported by poorer countries) over the implementation of cohesion spending. A key issue was additionality—that is, the principle that EU funds for a project must be in addition to, rather than a substitute for, national spending. To enforce the principle, the Commission needed a level of involvement that national governments, acting as "gatekeepers" who governed public spending within their country, could thwart. A second issue was "partnership" in the sense of the Commission working directly with subnational authorities. Both issues were effectively over whether national governments would permit the Commission to bypass them in order to work with lower levels of government in the poor regions that qualified for cohesion funds.

Reforms in 2006 aimed to make the process more coherent, with the goal of increasing EU competitiveness as well as effectively addressing inequalities. In 2004, the Sapir Report advocated that cohesion funds should go to only the new members joining the EU in or after 2004, and some countries proposed that no cohesion funds should go to regions in the richest states (Bache 2015, 249–251). Although the Commission pushed these ideas, they were resisted by the Council, and the principle that cohesion spending is based on regions rather than nations was retained into the 2014–2020 EU budget cycle when both Spain and Italy received large amounts, intended for the poorer regions of those relatively affluent countries, exceeded only by Poland (Figure 5.3). The largest recipient of cohesion spending was Poland, but seven other Eastern European countries and Portugal received larger support per capita.

Transport policy has contributed to convergence of incomes between the older western and newer eastern EU members. The EU coordinates and cofinances cross-border transport infrastructure investments in the Trans-European Transport Network (TEN-T). Construction of new road corridor segments has been concentrated in Eastern Europe since 2004 and has promoted growth. Goldmann and Wessel (2020) provide evidence that a new corridor segment increases economic growth not only in the narrowly defined region in which it is located but also has positive spillover effects to neighboring regions. They argue that the positive effects are unrelated to road density in the region (i.e., the benefits arise from improved interregional connectivity) and are greatest when the new segments reduce bottlenecks.[50]

The EU has adopted a 2020 Strategy for Smart, Sustainable and Inclusive Growth with eleven objectives. The strategy is based on labor mo-

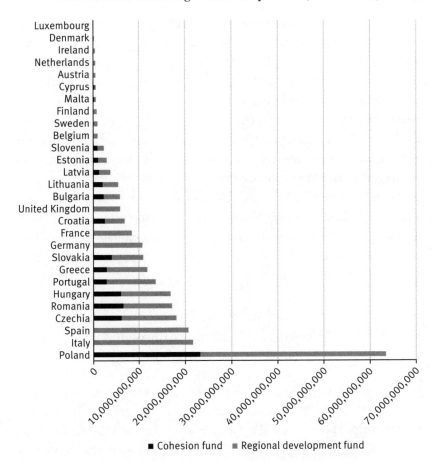

Figure 5.3 EU Allocation of Cohesion Spending by Nation, 2014–2020
Note: Excludes interregional RDF allocation of 9,410,036,960 euros.

Source: Eurostat.

bility leading to people moving to higher wage locations where they will be more productive and on cohesion policy encouraging development where poor people live. Whether there is a contradiction in this dual basis largely depends on the determinants of the geography of production. If agglomeration effects are important, then the stress should be on rural-urban migration. On the other hand, if falling trade costs and the death of distance are important, then rural areas can become attractive GVC participants.

The EU has maintained a high-profile leading role on climate change. In 2010, the commissioner for climate action was created as a new post on the EU Commission, and the EU targeted a unilateral 20 percent cut of its greenhouse gas emissions by 2020. The target of keeping the increase in global warming below 2^0C (Section 3.4) was revised to "well below 2^0C" at the 2015 Paris climate summit. At the Katowice climate conference in December 2018, the aim was to finalize detailed rules and guidelines. The EU has taken an active lead in these developments through the High Ambition Coalition.[51] The Commission that entered office on 1 December 2019 under Ursula von der Leyen announced that addressing global climate change would be its top priority, and President von der Leyen pledged to increase the EU's climate target from a 40 percent reduction in carbon emissions by 2030 to a 50 percent to 55 percent cut by the same date.

5.5 Unfinished Business: Enlargement and Eastern Partners

The eventual eastern border of the EU remains imprecise, but it is clear that the Western Balkan countries qualify geographically for EU membership. The Thessaloniki Declaration from the EU–Western Balkans summit in June 2003 asserted that "the future of the Balkans is within the European Union." However, apart from Croatia's accession to the EU in 2013, not much actually happened over the next fifteen years (Figure 5.4).

Progress has been uneven. Although Macedonia became a candidate in 2005, negotiations were held back by a name dispute with Greece that was not resolved until 2018; the country was officially renamed the Republic of North Macedonia in February 2019. Montenegro has been a candidate since 2010, Serbia since 2012, and Albania since 2014. Bosnia submitted an application in 2016. Kosovo's Stabilisation and Association Agreement with the EU came into force in 2016.[52] Membership talks have started for Serbia and Montenegro. In May 2019, the European Commission recommended that talks should start with Albania and North Macedonia, but in October, Denmark, France, and the Nether-

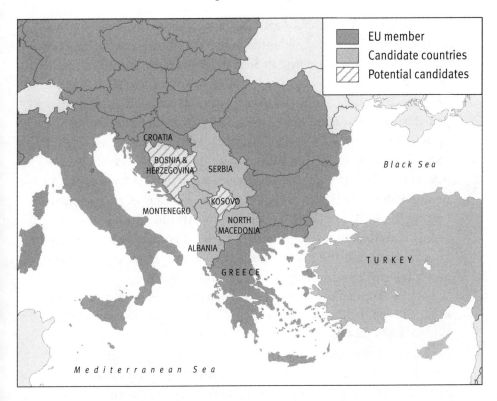

Figure 5.4 The Western Balkans and the EU

lands refused agreement to open membership negotiations with Albania, and France vetoed proceeding with North Macedonia.

The process has been slow in part due to digestion of previous enlargements and in part due to doubts about the candidates' readiness.[53] In a process known as Copenhagen++, the EU tightened the accession criteria in November 2006 and also started requiring solution of long-term disputes as a condition for accession. The latter was an innovation; such a condition would have prevented UK and Irish accession in 1973 during Ireland's Troubles or the accession of Cyprus in 2004 when a large part of the island was under Turkish Cypriot control.

An April 2018 Commission progress report identified various idiosyncratic obstacles on the Western Balkans economies' road to EU accession and several common themes: lack of competitiveness, big external deficits, high public debt, rigid labor markets, weak governance, a large informal economy, and infrastructure deficiencies. A second EU–Western Balkans summit held in Sofia in May 2018 reaffirmed the place of the Western Balkans in Europe but made little concrete progress.[54] The president of the European Commission, Jean-Claude Juncker, suggested before the summit that Serbia and Montenegro could join the EU by 2025, but German chancellor Angela Merkel quickly clarified that each Western Balkan country would join only when it was ready. The May 2020 EU–Western Balkans (virtual) Zagreb summit focused on addressing the COVID-19 epidemic without mention of enlargement, beyond the six Western Balkans partners (Albania, Bosnia and Herzegovina, Serbia, Montenegro, the Republic of North Macedonia, and Kosovo) recommitting to carry out and effectively implement the necessary reforms toward European values and principles.

For countries farther east, the situation is even more confused. Although Europe has no obvious geographical boundaries to the east, there is little doubt that current members doubt the suitability of any of the twelve non-Baltic former Soviet republics or of Turkey as members of the EU. In the twenty-first century, a new pyramid of preferences has been created among former Soviet republics: Estonia, Latvia, and Lithuania are EU members; Georgia, Moldova, and Ukraine have deep integration short of membership; Azerbaijan and perhaps Armenia and Belarus are in limbo; the five Central Asian republics are largely ignored; and since 2014, Russia has been subject to sanctions.

An alternative way to see these countries is through the prism of bloc rivalry, especially since the 2008 war between Russia and Georgia[55] and initiation of the Russian-led Eurasian Economic Union (EAEU) in 2010.[56] In May 2009, the EU launched the Eastern Partnership (EaP) with six partner countries: Armenia, Azerbaijan, Belarus, Georgia, Moldova, and Ukraine. The EaP neither promises nor precludes the prospect of EU membership. It offers deeper integration with EU structures by encouraging and supporting partners in political, institutional, and economic reforms based on EU standards, as well as facilitating trade and increasing mobility between the EU and the partner states. A key long-term objective is lifting the EU visa requirement for the citizens of partner states; in the shorter term, the EaP envisages visa facilitation and readmission agreements (already signed with Ukraine, Moldova, and Georgia) followed by "visa dialogue," the aim of which is to determine the conditions each country needs to fulfill to have the Schengen visa requirement lifted.

The scope of participation in the EaP and the level of integration with EU structures varies from country to country, depending on internal situations and aspirations. The first step is a bilateral Association Agreement which forms a framework for cooperation on a wide range of issues and is also aimed at bringing the partner closer to EU standards of governance. The Association Agreements contain three parts: (1) political dialogue and foreign and security policy; (2) justice, freedom, and security; and (3) economic and sectoral cooperation. The next stage is negotiation of a Deep and Comprehensive Free Trade Agreement (DCFTA) with not only liberalization of trade in all areas by lifting customs barriers and trade quotas but also harmonization of partner countries' trade-related legislation with EU standards and the *acquis communautaire*. Because membership of the WTO is a precondition for entering into DCFTA negotiations, Azerbaijan and Belarus, which are not WTO members, cannot start negotiations. The other four DCFTAs were scheduled to be ratified at the EU's November 2013 Vilnius summit, but the timetable was upset in September 2013 when Armenia declared that it would be joining the EAEU and no longer wished to have a DCFTA with the EU. Georgia, Moldova, and Ukraine signed DCFTAs in 2014, which were provisionally implemented after 2014; by 2017, citizens of Georgia (except for Abkhazia and South Ossetia), Moldova, and Ukraine could travel visa-free to the Schengen countries, while citizens of other Commonwealth of Independent States (CIS) countries still required visas.

The tensions in Armenia and, especially, Ukraine appeared to highlight the need to choose between alignment with the EU or with the EAEU. Ukraine's vacillation between the DCFTA and the EAEU culminated in pro-EU protests in Kiev and the overthrow of President Yanukovych in February 2014. Russia's response included annexation of Crimea and support for separatist forces in eastern Ukraine, which led to sanctions against Russia by the EU, United States, and others, and countersanctions by Russia.

At the November 2017 EaP summit in Brussels, the EU and Armenia signed a new agreement which focuses on customs issues and trade facilitation; the agreement does not include tariffs, because Armenia's EAEU common external tariff schedule is nonnegotiable and Armenia already benefits from the EU's GSP+ scheme. The final text of the November 2017 EaP summit mirrored that of previous summits, stating that "the summit participants acknowledge the European aspirations and European choice of the partners concerned, as stated in the association agreements" but stopping short of promises of future membership. In his summit statement, European Commission President Juncker was explicit: "This is not an enlargement or accession summit."

The bleak political relations between the EU and Russia contrast with an important transport development. Overland connections between Europe and China were practically nonexistent since Vasco da Gama discovered the sea route round the Cape of Good Hope around 1500. The Trans-Siberian railway was built between 1891 and 1905 primarily for military reasons and carried little freight outside the Russian Empire and later Soviet Union. Although physical rail track existed for EU–East Asia trade, such trade was dominated by sea transport during the economic rise of East Asia in the second half of the twentieth century. In contrast, since 2011, EU rail connections to China through Belarus, Russia, and Kazakhstan have carried exponentially increasing amounts of freight (Pomfret 2019a, 2019b).

The number of city pairs providing freight services between the EU and China has increased rapidly, especially since 2015. As more cities offer services, some successfully and others not, it is hard to keep track of numbers, but in both Europe and China, over fifty cities are Landbridge termini. The most reliable volume data are those from the Eurasian Rail Alliance (Table 5.2), which reports growth from 46,000 containers in 2015 to 280,500 in 2018, and extrapolating the rough doubling each year, they predict a million containers will be transported in 2020.[57]

In Europe, indicators of the increased salience of the rail Landbridge include the holding of an annual Silk Road Summit attended by hundreds of logistics service providers (the third in November 2019 was in Venlo, the Netherlands, and the fourth was held online in November 2020) and the EU Commission engaging in how to relate the EU-China ser-

Table 5.2   Volume of Traffic on China-EU-China Container Trains, 2015–2018

Year	Number of twenty-foot equivalent containers (TEUs)
2015	46,000
2016	104,500
2017	175,800
2018	280,500

Source: Eurasian Rail Alliance at www.utlc.com.
Note: The Eurasian Rail Alliance (UTLC) was founded by Belarus, Kazakhstan, and Russia in 2014 to provide services for container block trains running between China and Europe.

vice to the Trans-European Transport Network (TEN-T) as a top priority in 2020 (Walton 2019).[58] The TEN-T, including guidelines for the development of a Trans-European Rail Network, dates from July 1996, but extension to Eastern Europe was slow and, despite statements of intent to look east in 2011, only in 2017 were Eastern Partnership states included. Connectivity via Russia to China has always had a strategic dimension, and EU Commission policy is within the framework of the EU's 2016 Global Strategy.[59] The Eurasian Landbridge matters because the situation in Eurasia is changing rapidly since 2011.

5.6 Relations with China

During the second half of the twentieth century, by far the most important nonmember country for EU members was the United States. Japan and East Asian newly industrializing economies posed economic problems in the 1980s but never carried the same political, strategic, and economic weight as the United States. The Soviet Union posed the major military threat to Western Europe during the Cold War, but economic interactions were minor. Russia's economic importance after dissolution of the Soviet Union almost entirely concerned energy, mainly natural gas, supplies, which created divisions among EU member countries but diminished in significance after the collapse of oil prices in 2014. Relations with China were peripheral. After the opening of China's economy in 1978–1979, EU policies mirrored earlier relations with high-performing East Asian economies as the EU took antidumping actions and other measures against imports from China, but relations remained low profile at least until after China's WTO accession in 2001.[60]

Economic relations strengthened in the twenty-first century, although China focused more on bilateral relations with individual European countries rather than with the EU. In its 2006 Strategy, the EU placed new emphasis on China, and at the ninth EU-China summit in 2006, it was agreed to start negotiations on a new comprehensive framework agreement. Steps were taken to upgrade the relationship after 2007, with agreements on geographical indicators, maritime and aviation agreements, and many economic and trade dialogues. However, there were setbacks, as in 2008 when the annual summit was canceled by China in response to several EU heads of government meeting the Dalai Lama. In 2013, a comprehensive program for closer relations was agreed as the EU-China 2020 Strategic Agenda for Cooperation was launched, but relations soured in 2016 over political disagreements—for example, on South China Sea issues. An indication of the relative importance to China of economic relations with the EU since 2013 has been the presence of Prime Minister Li Keqiang, rather than President Xi Jinping, as head of the Chinese delegation at the EU-China summits.

Investment flows in both directions appear to have been driven primarily by financial considerations. The most controversial Chinese investments in Europe were in the Greek port of Piraeus.

In October 2009, Greece leased two of the port's three terminals from the Piraeus Port Authority (PPA) to the China Ocean Shipping Company (COSCO) for a thirty-five-year period at an annual rent of €100 million. Under COSCO's management, Piraeus went from being the world's ninety-third biggest container port in 2010 to the forty-fourth biggest in 2015, by which time Piraeus was the eighth busiest container port in Europe and third in the Mediterranean. In 2016, COSCO bought a 51-percent stake in PPA for €280.5 million under its plan to make Greece a transshipment hub for rapidly growing trade between Asia and Eastern Europe. In January 2018, COSCO announced a €500 million investment plan to upgrade the port for container shipping, cruise ships, and ship repairs, largely for luxury yachts, with the aim of developing Piraeus as a major entry port to the EU.

Critics of Chinese investment saw Piraeus as an example of China using debt dependence to gain access to strategic maritime facilities, as in Sri Lanka and potentially in Djibouti (Hurley et al. 2018). However, Piraeus does not have obvious control over shipping lanes and COSCO appears to have made a financially astute investment, buying an under-realized asset when Greece needed funds. The inflow of Chinese funds in the 2010s helped to relieve Greece's debt burden.[61]

Western European countries saw a different strategic threat, relating Chinese operations in Piraeus to China's policies toward the countries of Central and Eastern Europe. The 2011 China-CEE National Economic and Trade Forum started the 16 + 1 cooperation between China and the Central and Eastern European countries. The sixteen consist of eleven EU members plus Albania, Bosnia and Herzegovina, North Macedonia, Montenegro, and Serbia (Figure 5.5). Annual summits have been held since 2012.[62] Trade and investment—especially Chinese exports to Eastern Europe and investment by China in the Eastern European countries—have grown rapidly since 2011, although it is from a very low base, and how much of this would have happened in the absence of the 16 + 1 framework is unclear.[63] At the 2019 summit in Dubrovnik, Greece joined the group to make it 17 + 1.

The overall economic significance of the 16 + 1 arrangement has been small, especially in comparison to progress made since 2011 on the China-EU rail Landbridge. The headline project is a high-speed rail link between Belgrade and Budapest, which could be seen as a first step in upgrading rail connectivity between Piraeus and the Baltic countries and is often listed by China as part of the Belt and Road Initiative. Modernization of the 350-kilometer Belgrade-Budapest line to allow speeds of up to 200 kilometers per hour was begun in Serbia in 2017, with expected completion in 2023, but progress has been slow, reportedly associated with Hungarian reservations about taking on debt through concessional financing from China. Other Chinese-funded projects include the China-Serbia Friendship Bridge across the Danube in Belgrade and highway projects in North Macedonia and Montenegro.

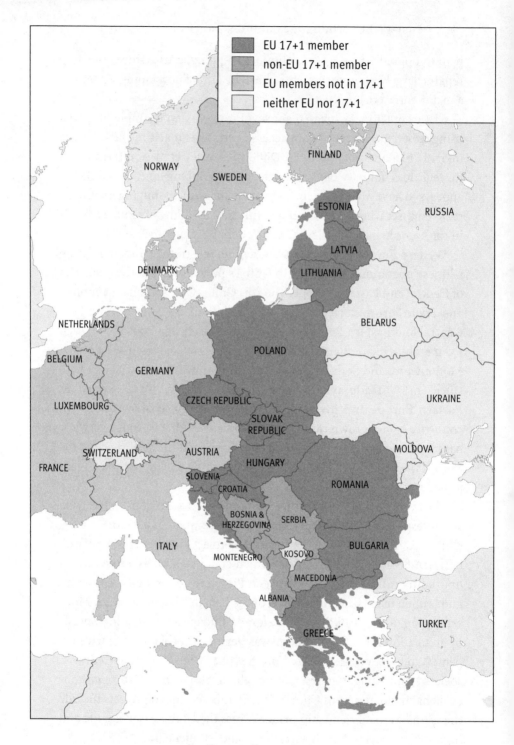

Figure 5.5 The 17 + 1 Group

Meanwhile, the 16 + 1 grouping was opposed by other EU countries (especially Germany) for undermining EU cohesion and seen as unwelcome interference in internal EU structures (Oehler-Sincai 2018).[64] Issues surrounding tenders for infrastructure projects were a bone of contention, but China began to address these in 2017 and 2018—for example, by changes in the regulations for Budapest-Belgrade railway construction projects. Two days before the G20 Hamburg summit in July 2017, President Xi Jinping met German chancellor Angela Merkel in Berlin; the big photo opportunity was outside the panda enclosure at Berlin's Tierpark zoo where Meng Meng and Jiao Qing had just arrived on a fifteen-year loan, sealing friendship with panda diplomacy.[65]

In the joint statement at the end of the July 2018 16 + 1 summit in Bulgaria attended by China's premier, Li Keqiang, all parties agreed that the 16 + 1 cooperation is not a geopolitical tool but a pragmatic cooperation platform where cooperation is carried out in accordance with EU rules and is conducive to strengthening rather than weakening the EU. After the July 2018 summit, Li went to Berlin where Angela Merkel, in contrast to Donald Trump's antagonistic rhetoric toward Beijing, praised China for opening itself to foreign investments and confirmed that Germany and China want to maintain the status quo regarding Iran's nuclear agreements.[66]

The chain of events in 2017 and 2018 illustrated that whatever China's objectives had been in establishing the 16 + 1 framework in 2011, in the global environment after the 2016 US election, China was keen to strengthen cordial political relations with the EU. In October 2018, the first EU-China joint military exercises were held in Djibouti. Relations with Eastern Europe have shifted toward inclusion in the more cooperative relationship between China and Europe that has emerged from the Eurasian rail Landbridge.[67] Several Eastern European cities have become Landbridge destinations and Łódź in central Poland is the main Eastern European hub. However, President Xi appeared to be keeping options open as he announced that he would chair the 17 + 1 summit in Beijing in April 2020 and he would attend the September 2020 EU-China summit in Leipzig. These plans would be disrupted by the COVID-19 epidemic (Section 6.4).

5.7 The EU in the Global Economy

The EU has always been a large trading bloc but has not played a commensurate leadership role in the global economy. For most of its history, the focus has been on the internal market and domestic economic concerns. Although the EU was one of the Quad, together with the United States, Japan, and Canada, that shepherded the Uruguay Round to conclusion with establishment of the WTO in 1995, the EU's role was reactive rather than leading as it responded to criticisms of the CAP and the pyramid of trade preferences. This has changed in the twenty-first century as the mentality behind the protectionist agricultural policy and the new protectionism against imports from East Asia in the 1980s has been replaced by a more confident outward-oriented approach to international trade. Important landmarks on this transformation path were the 2006 Global Europe strategy paper and the 2015 Trade for All strategy. In 2017, with the inauguration of a US president who challenged the international economic order, the EU had to assume a role among countries committed to the WTO-based multilateral trading system, both as a leader and seeker of allies.

The European Commission launched the Global Europe strategy in October 2006. It was endorsed by the Council and followed by the introduction of a renewed "Market Access Strategy" in April 2007. The purpose of the Global Europe strategy was to reinforce the EU's competitiveness by opening up markets and creating opportunities for European business. The strategy focused mainly on "behind the border" measures such as investment and government procurement liberalization, competition policy, and intellectual property rights enforcement. The Global Europe strategy was linked to the Single Market in aiming to increase EU firms' competitiveness both in Europe and on the world market. The EU was prepared to open up its markets even at the cost of shrinking labor-intensive low-technology sectors such as clothing (about which it could do little after termination of the Multifibre Arrangement at the end of 2004) or shoes. Recognizing that two-thirds of EU imports were inputs into manufacturing processes, the EU acknowledged that openness to imports would enhance the competitiveness of its exports.

The EU wants to integrate investment rules into its broader trade agreements. Prior to the entry into force of the 2007 Lisbon treaty, trade was an EU competence and investment was a national competence. Individual EU countries signed bilateral investment treaties (BITs) whose terms varied. Recognizing the interdependence of trade and investment decisions in a world of GVCs, the EU is attempting to coordinate trade and investment policies (e.g., in the 2007 Lisbon treaty). However, even in 2018, when negotiations on an Australia-EU free trade agreement began, investment was excluded because some members resisted the shift to EU competence and the EU Court had not yet ruled.[68] For opponents of such mission creep, the problem is that in a world of GVCs, *any* policy may affect competitiveness and trade and hence be deemed an EU competence. Even when investment has been included in EU trade agreements, a challenge has been to ensure dispute settlement procedures are fair and independent (as in trade agreements with Canada and Vietnam)—concepts that are often open to disagreement.

The Global Europe strategy signaled a new emphasis on competitiveness nurtured by exposure to the global economy, but it did not set out a trade policy vision. Despite increased diversity following the 2004 and 2007 enlargement, the EU members agreed on a trade policy based on shared values beyond trade liberalization that was set out in the 2015 Trade for All strategy (Box 5.1). The new strategy responds to the growth of GVCs, the increased importance of services trade, and the growth of e-commerce. It addresses concerns of the general public about transparency and perceived challenges to certain societal values—for example, no agreement will require an EU member to reduce the level of any public services such as water, education, health, and social services. The Commission will encourage the Council to disclose negotiating mandates, publish draft chapters submitted to its negotiating partner, and reveal finalized texts earlier. The EU will step up its efforts to promote a fact-based debate within member states and enhance its dialogue with civil society and to do more to show the impact of a trade agreement after it has been applied (Cernat 2019).

New-generation trade agreements cover goods, services, intellectual property, investment, government procurement, access to energy, trade facilitation, competition, and regulatory cooperation. The approach was to start with smaller partners and then move on to negotiations with larger partners. An agreement with the Republic of Korea was signed in 2010 and entered into force in 2015.[69]

BOX 5.1 Objectives of the 2015 "Trade for All" Strategy

The EU will focus attention on, inter alia, achieving the following:

(i) A more effective policy that tackles new economic conditions and lives up to its promises by:

- Updating trade policy to take account of the new economic realities such as global value chains, the digital economy, and the importance of services.
- Supporting mobility of technicians, experts, and service providers.
- Setting up an enhanced partnership with the member states, the European Parliament, and stakeholders to better implement trade and investment agreements.
- Including effective SME provisions in future trade agreements.

(ii) A more transparent trade and investment policy by extending the TTIP transparency initiative to all the EU's trade negotiations.

(iii) A trade and investment policy based on values by:

- Responding to the public's expectations on regulations and investment: a clear pledge on safeguarding EU regulatory protection and a strategy to lead the reform of investment policy globally.
- Expanding measures to support sustainable development, fair and ethical trade, and human rights, including by ensuring effective implementation of related FTA provisions and the Generalized System of Preferences.
- Including anticorruption rules in future trade agreements.

(iv) Progress in negotiations to shape globalization by:

- Reenergizing multilateral negotiations and designing an open approach to bilateral and regional agreements.
- Strengthening EU presence in Asia and setting ambitious objectives with China.
- Requesting a mandate for FTA negotiations with Australia and New Zealand.
- Exploring launching new investment negotiations with Hong Kong, China; the Separate Customs Territory of Taiwan, Penghu, Kinmen, and Matsu (Chinese Taipei); and the Republic of Korea.
- Starting new ASEAN FTA negotiations with the Philippines and Indonesia, as and when appropriate.

Source: From "Trade for All: Towards a More Responsible Trade and Investment Policy"—adopted by the Commission on 14 October 2015.

In Latin America, the EU started negotiations with Mercosur (Argentina, Brazil, Paraguay, and Uruguay) that were paused in 2012, restarted in 2016, and concluded in June 2019.[70] The EU envisioned an agreement with the Andean Community countries (Bolivia, Colombia, Ecuador, and Peru), but initial negotiations were only completed with Peru (provisionally applied from March 2013) and Colombia (provisionally applied from August 2013); Ecuador joined the trade agreement in January 2017. A similar agreement was negotiated with Central American countries in June 2012 and was provisionally applied by Costa Rica, El Salvador, Honduras, Nicaragua, and Panama in August 2013, and by Guatemala in December 2013. Negotiations with Mexico reached an agreement in principle in April 2018.[71]

More recently, the EU has engaged in negotiations with the other G7 countries. Negotiations for a Transatlantic Trade and Investment Partnership (TTIP) between the EU and the United States began in 2013 but were discontinued by the United States in November 2016. The Comprehensive Economic and Trade Agreement (CETA) between the EU and Canada entered into force provisionally in September 2017, awaiting ratification by all EU member states before entering fully into force. The EU-Japan Economic Partnership Agreement was signed in July 2018 and entered into force in February 2019. Subsequently, the EU moved on to launch negotiations with like-minded middle economic powers, with Australia and with New Zealand in June 2018, and to conclude the Mercosur negotiations in June 2019.

New-generation agreements cover goods, services, intellectual property, investment, government procurement, access to energy and raw materials, customs and trade facilitation, competition (including subsidies and state-owned enterprises), and regulatory cooperation. They contain commitments on customs duty reduction, access to services markets (to be able to fully take advantage of the tariff engagements), and tools to reduce or eliminate nontariff barriers to trade such as technical regulations or unjustified sanitary barriers. In addition, the EU emphasizes areas that are important in terms of values such as sustainable development and the protection of human rights.

However, not all of the areas are acceptable to all partners—including EU members in some cases.[72] A Trade and Sustainable Development chapter was included in the agreements with Korea, Japan, Canada, and Mercosur based on the premise that increased trade should not come at the expense of the environment. However, there are questions of whether such agreements are also protection devises. Restrictions on tropical forestry in the Mercosur agreement, with the laudable intent of restricting depletion of the Amazonian rain forest, benefit competing EU forestry and in the long term forestall competition from cheaper Brazilian beef raised on the cleared land. More generally, the agreements may impose EU regulatory norms on countries with looser or different rules—for example, New Zealand's weaker measures against environmental degradation by agriculture before 2019.[73]

Underlying the evolution in external trade policy was a fundamental shift in response to the increasing importance of international value chains (see Appendix to Chapter 4). In the twentieth century, EU trade policy makers responded to pressure from vested interests seeking protection from competing imports, most clearly with the CAP but also with trade restrictions on many manufactured goods—for example, cars and clothing. In the twenty-first century, with the increasing importance of GVCs, the removal of import-restricting policies and the reduction of regulatory burdens became drivers of trade policy. This was explicit in the 2015 Trade for All strategy.

At the same time, a conflicting force is challenging GVC-driven trade policies. In contrast to the requirements of GVCs, a globalization backlash drives calls for more protectionism and less support for trade agreements (Dür et al. 2020). Growing popular opposition to trade liberalization may be partly related to the perception that GVCs contribute to a greater concentration of wealth in the hands of the few in the twenty-first century, reflected in higher shares of the top 1 percent of wealth holders. Globalization is also associated with a hollowing out of labor markets in high-income countries as manufacturing tasks requiring semiskilled or unskilled workers have moved to emerging economies. Technology rather than policy explains a large part of these changes, but the two are often conflated. Populist politicians can attract voters who feel threatened by globalization. Nevertheless, at least in the first two decades of the twenty-first century, EU trade policy moved in the direction of greater openness to trade.

Measuring the Effects of Changes in Preferential Treatment

CGE and Gravity Models and Big Data

Predicting economic effects by comparing the situation with and without a tariff in a partial equilibrium model worked reasonably well when integration was about preferential tariffs in settings such as formation of the customs union in the 1960s or the first enlargement in 1973 (Appendix to Chapter 2). More ambitious assessments used computable general equilibrium (CGE) models to capture indirect effects ignored in Figure 2A1, but they did not change fundamental conclusions. In the twenty-first century, measuring the impact of membership in the Single Market or of preferential treatment under the EU's trade policy toward nonmembers is much more difficult because these agreements go beyond simple tariff arrangements. To address the added complexity, empirical studies have increasingly relied on CGE models or variations of the gravity model. These models have in turn become more complex since the 1990s, as powerful computers have become more accessible and large data sets more available and manageable.

CGE Models

A CGE model mimics the structure of the economy in a set of simultaneous equations. If we expect indirect effects on labor markets or exchange rates to be substantial, then this is a significant improvement over the partial equilibrium model of Figure 2A1. A suitably detailed CGE model can also pick up sectoral and other variations in treatment such as would be associated with the deeper integration of the Single Market or in deep trade agreements such as CETA. For these reasons, a reputable CGE model has become the approach of choice when policy makers seek quantification of the effects of major economic policy changes.

The principal drawback of relying on CGE models is that it is difficult for any but CGE modelers to debate the results. A typical model involves a large number of equations, most of which include parameters whose estimated value may be open to debate, and the equation structure and parameter choice will determine the results. The most trusted models have been subject to extensive scrutiny and testing, but there is always a concern that the results emerge from an opaque black box.

An example of how to respond to the criticisms about the difficulty of verifying the results from CGE models is the Global Trade Analysis Project (GTAP) network of researchers and policy makers conducting quantitative analysis of international policy issues. The standard GTAP model is a multiregion, multisector CGE model, with perfect competition and constant returns to scale, originally developed by Thomas Hertel of Purdue University together with Alan Powell and Peter Dixon of the IMPACT project in Melbourne, Australia, during the 1990s. The group was soon expanded to become a consortium including the World Bank and the Australian Productivity Commission. The focus of the GTAP model has been on international trade, with explicit treatment of transport margins and handling substitution between goods from different countries by the Armington assumption.[74] The network also maintains a consistent database on international trade. Using the GTAP database and core CGE model, many authors were able to work on estimating the effects of the Uruguay Round after its conclusion in 1994, and the narrow range of estimates contributed to their credibility. By 2019, the GTAP network had spread to more than seven thousand participants in over 150 countries. Such interaction among modelers contributes to consistent standards. At the same time, it is desirable to have competing CGE models to challenge reliance on particular assumptions and structure.

A weakness of applying many CGE models to analyze discriminatory trade policies is the common interpretation of the Armington assumption to imply that the elasticity of substitution between imports from any pair of countries is the same. The simplifying assumption may be inappropriate, especially at disaggregated levels of trade. For example, bringing Mediterranean products such as olive oil or tomatoes into the CAP after Spain's accession would impact more on countries specializing in such goods—for example, Tunisia or Morocco—than on other nonmembers and any preferential treatment for one of these partners that was not granted to the other could have an uncertain impact.[75] A recent example is EU measures against palm oil imports from Malaysia or Indonesia; although based on environmental concerns, the restrictions clearly hurt palm oil exporters, but the two major suppliers are further concerned about how they are treated relative to their competitor and indirectly relative to other countries.[76]

Gravity Models

The most successful model for analyzing bilateral trade patterns is the gravity model, which explains trade between two countries by the size of their economies and the distance between them. This is a plausible model; after all, larger economies have more to sell than smaller economies and larger economies generate more demand than smaller economies and it is obvious that, other things equal, transport costs are negatively associated with distance. In its simplest form, the gravity model is

$$T_{i,j} = f(Y_i, Y_j, D_{i,j}),$$

where the subscripts i and j refer to a pair of countries, $T_{i,j}$ is the bilateral trade between i and j, Y_i and Y_j represent the national incomes of the two countries, and $D_{i,j}$ is the distance between them. The model was originally developed by Dutch planners Jan Tinbergen and Hans Linnemann in the 1950s and 1960s and proved successful in explaining bilateral trade patterns, but it occupied a small place in the trade literature because the results seemed obvious and unexciting.

The gravity model has enjoyed a renaissance since the mid-1990s as people have focused on understanding deviations from the basic model. An influential study by John McCallum (1995) examined US-Canada trade. The two countries had a free trade agreement, simple border-crossing procedures, a common language, and other features that might be expected to make the border virtually meaningless for trade. Yet, when McCallum examined bilateral trade flows among the forty-eight contiguous US states and ten Canadian provinces, he found that the simple gravity model worked well for within-country trade, but the results were substantially different when a trade flow was between a state and a province—a difference captured by a dummy variable that was large and significantly different from zero. In another influential study, Rose (2000) ran a gravity model of bilateral trade that included a dummy variable when the two countries had a common currency; he found that countries with a common currency traded about three times as much with each other as similar pairs of countries that used different currencies.[77]

The gravity model has become a workhorse that has proven useful for studying many aspects of international trade. However, the simple model is atheoretical and has obvious problems. Trade between two countries may depend on other trade flows—for example, if country j forms a customs union with another country, that could affect its trade with country i due to trade diversion. There may also be features of some countries that affect their trade with all countries—for example, due to its economic regime, North Korea has less bilateral trade with all countries than would be predicted on the basis of distance and economic size. Anderson and van Wincoop (2003) developed a theoretical underpinning for the gravity model and established the desirability of including country fixed effects in regression equations to take into account the multilateral resistance terms; exports from country i to country j depend on trade costs across all possible export markets, and imports into country i from country j depend on trade costs across all possible suppliers.

The use of gravity models has become more frequent because large bilateral trade data sets have become readily accessible and computing power has mushroomed so that it is easy to run regressions. With many thousands of observations, standard errors are low and statistical significance tests often satisfied, even when the economic significance of the variable in question may be dubious. The common use of dummy variables in a gravity model to track the importance of particular features must be done with care (Baldwin and Taglioni 2006). Reasons why trade between a pair of countries may deviate from the general pattern described by the simple gravity model include cultural affinity (a common language or shared history has a positive impact), geography (coastal nations trade more and landlocked countries trade less), and borders, but these are highly correlated with one another.[78] Dummy variables are a simple construct and may be picking up more than their creator bargains for.

Recent theoretical developments have validated structural gravity models which include variables that take into account structural relationships, such as a common colonial past, as well as country fixed effects. Estimation methods have improved over ordinary least squares, which is poorly suited to data sets with many zero values, heteroskedasticity, and other problems. Current practice is to use the Poisson pseudo-maximum-likelihood estimator with fixed effects. Even though the search for the theoretically most appropriate specification and estimation method is clearly desirable, the varied approaches actually used is a further reason for caution in accepting results. Nevertheless, the gravity model has proven to be a powerful tool for identifying drivers of bilateral trade flows, which is a central issue in analysis of economic integration.

Complex Preferential Schemes and Large Databases

Techniques like CGE modeling, gravity models, or cross-country growth econometrics have flourished since the 1990s because of the exponential growth of computing power and convenience of desktop and laptop computers. The same phenomenon has driven the availability of large data sets for almost all economic variables.

Trade data are typically organized according to the Harmonized Commodity Description and Coding System (HS) which has been developed and maintained by the World Customs Organization since 1988.

The HS breaks commodities into ninety-nine chapters. In the six-digit HS code, the first two digits designate the chapter, the next two the heading (of which there are 1,244), and the last two the subheading (of which there are 5,244). Thus, world trade between the world's two-hundred-plus economies using six-digit data is captured in over two hundred million (>200 × 199 × 5,244) observations.[79] Analysis over time increases the database into billions of annual observations.

An example of the use of large data sets is the recent literature addressing the EU's preferential trade policies. Because the system of tariff preferences has evolved over time into a complex range of product-specific and partner-specific tariff rates, it is desirable to conduct analysis at the product level. Cipollina et al. (2017) used data on EU imports in 2004 at the eight-digit level (10,174 products) from 234 exporters, which allowed them to identify product-specific relative preference levels—that is, to take into account that the value of preferential tariff access depends not only on the difference between the preferential and MFN tariff rates but also on how one's competitors are treated. They included these measures in a gravity model to estimate the impact on trade volumes and found no convincing empirical evidence of preferential tariffs' impact on trade flows.

The cautious conclusion is appropriate. Although they conclude that one-quarter of the trade flows would not have occurred without tariff preferences, preferential tariffs have little impact overall and in some sectors are offset by other measures—for example, SPS and other nontariff measures as well as high trade costs mean that "agricultural preferences do not appear to be very effective" (Cipollina et al. 2017, 219). For around half of imports from beneficiaries of EU tariff preferences, the MFN tariff is zero. There are also potentially serious but hard to evaluate econometric issues such as the large number of zero values, potential endogeneity in the gravity model (preference recipients often have high bilateral trade with the EU for historical reasons which may explain why they receive preferential treatment—that is, causality runs from trade to tariff treatment rather than the other way around), and the Armington assumption about elasticities of substitution between goods from different countries.[80]

CHAPTER SIX

The European Union in the 2020s

As the European Union (EU) has become wider and deeper, the nature of European integration has clearly changed. The initial steps in the European Coal and Steel Community (ECSC) and the Treaty of Rome led to a customs union in the 1960s with some supranational policies (on trade and agriculture) but with a weak executive (the Commission) and national vetoes. Following the EC92 Single Market program and the Maastricht Treaty, the EU became a much more integrated economic space with a common currency, a wider range of common policies, and stronger supranational institutions in the twenty-first century, a situation consolidated in the 2007 Treaty of Lisbon.

Since the Lisbon treaty, the EU has been challenged by a series of shocks that have tested the strength of the economic and monetary union. The financial crises of 2007–2008 and more specifically the Greek crisis since 2010 were seen by some observers as a fatal blow to the euro—an opinion proven to be false as no country abandoned the common currency and the number of adopting countries increased. The financial crises did, however, highlight the lack of progress on creating a single market in financial services with appropriate common regulations. The unanticipated surge of migrants claiming refugee status that began after the 2011 Arab Spring highlighted a darker side to the border-free zone created by the Schengen Agreement; the Schengen countries had a common visa regime but no common policy toward irregular migrants and deep-seated resistance in some member countries to accepting refugees. Finally, the vote for Brexit in the 2016 UK referendum represented the most dramatic expression of Euroscepticism, as the anti-integration mood evident to varying degrees in several member countries was taken to the ultimate step by one of the largest members. By 2020, the challenges had been met, but the unfinished business of financial sector reforms, agreement on external border management and refugees, and reducing the attraction of Euroscepticism is still to be addressed in the 2020s.

Through the crises of the 2010s, the EU showed remarkable resilience and ability to continue with business as usual in continuing to strengthen the internal market and develop a common external position. In analyzing the impact of economic integration in Europe, it is important to remember that this has been a long-term project characterized by slow progress toward long-term goals. Path dependence has meant that decisions taken at one point affected later outcomes, and in many instances, reform of policies no longer considered appropriate has been difficult, taking decades in the case of the agricultural policy or commercial policy after 1990. In completing the Single Market, markets for services have been much more difficult to integrate than goods markets.

The 2014–2019 Juncker Commission was more active as an executive branch than previous Commissions and Jean-Claude Juncker himself more visible as head of the EU government, representing the Commission at G7 and G20 summits and at bilateral summits involving the EU.[1] The issue of who leads the EU is, however, complicated by the position of the European Council president created in the Lisbon treaty (Herman van Rompuy 2009–2014, Donald Tusk 2014–2019, succeeded by Charles Michel) and the power of the largest members' leaders. The division intended since the Lisbon treaty is that the president of the Commission speaks as the EU's government whereas the president of the European Council is a strategist. Creation of the position of High Representative for Foreign Affairs and Security Policy (Catherine Ashton 2009–2014, Federica Mogherini 2014–2019, followed by Josep Borrell) has been less successful in moving the EU toward a common foreign and security policy.[2] The high representative position matters because external relations, especially with the United States and China, appear likely to dominate EU policy making in the 2020s.[3]

In sum, in the 2010s, the EU had a crisis-ridden decade with the sovereign debt, migration, and Brexit crises. At the same time, the institutional structure was strengthened with the six-year Commission and budget cycles and forceful leadership from Commission President Juncker, Council President Tusk, foreign affairs supremo Mogherini, and European Central Bank (ECB) head Draghi. By the end of 2019, with the Greek debt crisis winding down, migration and refugees out of the headlines, and Brexit done, skies looked clearer for the new Commission under Ursula von der Leyen and the new head of the ECB, Christine Lagarde.

This chapter starts with an assessment of internal and external issues facing the new Commission. The Commission's stated intention of focusing on a green deal prioritizing the environment was quickly sidelined when, early in 2020, it was forced to focus on the COVID-19 pandemic. Designing and financing EU measures to counter the negative economic consequences of the epidemic reawakened debates over the extent to which sovereign debt obligations should be mutualized across the EU and over whether assistance to members should be in the form of grants or loans. Section 6.1 analyzes the revival of the three crisis issues of the 2010s (sovereign debt, refugees, and Brexit), which reemerged in 2020. Sections 6.2 and 6.3 discuss the issues facing the EU over the longer term with respect to the EU's internal functioning and the EU's relations with the rest of the world. Section 6.4 offers an overall assessment of European economic integration seventy years after creation of the ECSC.

6.1 The von der Leyen Commission and COVID-19

The new Commission under Ursula von der Leyen that took over on 1 December 2019 signaled that the environment would be a major theme of their six-year term. The ambitious program aimed to reduce emissions by 50 percent to 55 percent before 2030, with the long-term goal of a climate-neutral EU by 2050. Intended policies included an improved emissions trading scheme and a carbon border tax as well as institutional reform, moving away from unanimous decision making on climate and energy to qualified majority voting (QMV). This will be placed in a context of international leadership on climate change.

The European Green Deal announced by the Commission on 11 December 2019 provided a road map with actions "to boost the efficient use of resources by moving to a clean, circular economy and to restore biodiversity and cut pollution." It outlined investments needed and financing tools available to ensure a just and inclusive transition to a climate-neutral EU in 2050 and noted that reaching this target will require action by all sectors of the EU economy, including investing in environmentally friendly technologies; supporting industry to innovate; rolling out cleaner, cheaper, and healthier forms of private and public transport; decarbonizing the energy sector; ensuring buildings are more energy efficient; and working with international partners to improve global environmental standards. Through a Just Transition Mechanism, the EU would provide financial support (at least €100 billion over the period 2021–2027) and technical assistance to help people, businesses, and regions most affected by the move toward the green economy.

In practice, the Commission's activities were blown off course by an epidemic that in January 2020 seemed to be an Asian problem of little concern to Europe. However, by the end of February 2020, Europe was facing a health crisis in which the EU appeared almost absent. As the epicenter of the COVID-19 epidemic shifted to Europe, responses in the first half of March were national, and decisions to close national borders challenged the Schengen zone of border-free Europe.

A major problem was the speed and variation of COVID-19's spread. The first mover in late February, Italy, was cautious with limited, weakly enforced quarantine areas; as the number and spread of cases increased rapidly, Italy turned to full lockdown on March 12. France, Spain, Germany, and the smaller EU countries followed at varying speeds and with diverse measures, including closure of national borders. Although President Macron in particular emphasized the need for European and international cooperation in his TV messages to the nation, it was not until the EU leaders met in videoconference on 10 March that EU collaboration was visible.

Commission President von der Leyen followed up on 11 March with a video address to the Italian people, whose opening paragraph in Italian ended with a call for solidarity with the worst-hit EU member state: *in Europa siamo tutti italiani.* Continuing in English with Italian subtitles, von der Leyen offered all necessary support to Italy in its fight against COVID-19. On 18 March, Christine Lagarde, the head of the ECB, launched an emergency €750 billion package to ease the impact of the pandemic, tweeting "there are no limits" to the ECB's commitment to the euro, in an echo of previous ECB president Draghi's 2012 promise to do everything necessary to help Greece. Nevertheless, and especially in Italy, there was widespread belief that the EU had done nothing to help European citizens in the crisis.[4]

A fundamental problem for policy makers addressing COVID-19 was that it was new, and nobody knew which responses would work best. The initial policy of the United Kingdom (UK) (still technically in transition from the EU until the end of 2020) was based on the theory of herd immunity; as infection spreads and people who recover have immunity, the pool of susceptible people shrinks to the point where the epidemic is halted. However, when Prime Minister Johnson was confronted with estimates that the number of deaths would be at least 250,000 and more likely half a million, he suddenly reversed policy on 16 March. For most EU governments, who were following to varying degrees the World Health Organization–recommended approach of testing, tracking, isolating, and thus reducing the burden on hospitals while better treatment responses were developed, the UK go-it-alone approach seemed highly irresponsible.[5]

Several EU governments resorted to national policies in areas of obvious EU competence. On 3–4 March, France, Germany, and the Czech Republic banned export of key medical equipment. On 15 March, they were convinced to drop restrictions on sales within the EU as the EU imposed exports restrictions on $12 billion worth of key products to non-EU members. The direct negative impact on trade partners (primarily Italy in the first half of March, and Switzerland, Norway, and the United States after 15 March) is clear and retaliatory measures were likely to further reduce mutual gains from trade; any exemptions from bans would increase the paperwork and costs of trade. An example of national export restrictions disrupting supply chains occurred when Romania banned exports of a critical input used by Hamilton Medical, the

Switzerland-based global market leader in the manufacture of ventilators.[6] In the Hamilton case, an EU export restriction put at risk EU imports needed to fight COVID-19.

The pandemic challenged the notion of subsidiarity that is enshrined in the EU's Maastricht Treaty. Italy's original response was to delegate policy to the provinces in which the outbreak began; when this proved inadequate, responsibility was shifted to regional governments and ultimately the national level. The need for coordination was clear, but implementation starts locally. At the EU level, there is a similar problem of determining what needs to be standardized in EU-wide policies toward COVID-19 (e.g., respect for Schengen) and what can be national or local decisions—for example, closing schools or the level of lockdown (if essential businesses are to remain open, do food shops include cake shops or chocolate shops or wine merchants?). What is clear is that the scientific response to COVID-19 should be global.[7]

The epidemic posed a challenge to EU solidarity as the leaders sought agreement on common financial measures. The main rift was between the most COVID-affected countries, Spain and Italy, who complained that the EU was not doing enough, and the frugal four countries (Austria, Denmark, the Netherlands, and Sweden), who resisted extra EU spending, especially in the form of unconditional grants. A Eurogroup ministerial summit on 8 April ended in disagreement as ministers failed to accept a proposal from France and Italy to share out the cost of the crisis by issuing corona bonds. However, the next day, the ministers agreed on a €500 billion package that included €240 billion from the European Stability Mechanism to guarantee spending by indebted countries under pressure, €200 billion in guarantees from the European Investment Bank, and a European Commission project for national short-time working schemes.

Although negotiations dragged on, a compromise was reached at the July 2020 council meeting where the twenty-seven heads of government eventually agreed on a fund to help countries recover from the COVID-19 recession. The €750 billion COVID package was innovative in allowing the Commission to incur debt on an unprecedented scale to fund the recovery and in agreeing to distribute €390 billion as grants (i.e., substantial intra-EU fiscal transfers). The frugal four did, however, insist on an emergency brake by which a government can object to a recipient government's spending plans, delaying and complicating the grant. The frugal four were also bought off by increased rebates on their contributions to the EU budget (special deals that are anathema to federalists). In May 2020, Chancellor Merkel and President Macron proposed a package of bonds and grants that was supported by the commission. At a July 2020 council meeting, the heads of government agreed on the Next-Generation EU package consisting of €750 billion in loans (€360 billion) and subsidies from a Recovery and Resilience Fund (€390 billion) to be added to the €1,075 billion Multinational Financial Framework (the EU budget) for 2021–2027.

At the July 2020 summit, negotiations over the size of the package, conditions for receiving funds from the package (use of funds must target carbon neutrality, green jobs, and the digital economy), and the role of the Commission and of the European Parliament in assessing planned use of funds dragged on over five days before the twenty-seven heads of government agreed on the Next-Generation EU package to help countries recover from the COVID-19 recession. The €750 billion package was innovative in allowing the commission to incur debt on an unprecedented scale to fund the recovery and in agreeing on substantial intra-EU fiscal transfers. Although allocation of funds across member countries was agreed in July 2020, member governments must prepare recovery and resilience plans which will be assessed by the European Parliament and will be the basis for the Commission releasing funds.[8] Media coverage focused on conflicts between northern and Mediterranean countries over the balance between grants and subsidies or concerns of the frugal four (later joined by Finland) about the size of the budget, the Visegrád-Four's concerns over the share going to Eastern Europe or southern Europe, and Hungary and Poland's desire to avoid any political conditionality related to democracy or rule of law. These were serious debates. However, the key innovations for economic integration related to the Commission's ability to issue bonds and to the Commission's own resources.

The Recovery and Resilience Fund (RRF) grants represented a substantial increase in the EU budget that was frontloaded; the RRF funds were intended to be disbursed in 2021–2024. Debate over how the larger

Commission budget will be funded will inevitably arise in the 2020s, reviving an issue that dates back to France's empty chair in the 1960s and the UK budget renegotiation in the 1980s. Since 2004, contributions based on national income have provided over three-fifths of EU revenue, as the share from customs duties and value-added tax–based revenues has fallen. The RRF grants and bond servicing costs will increase EU expenditures at the same time as EU revenues will be reduced due to lower budget contributions promised to the frugal four in the July 2020 package and loss of the UK as a net contributor.[9] The EU's "own resources" will have to increase either as taxes to be collected by the EU or as increases in national contributions. At the July 2020 summit, EU taxes on plastic waste, carbon, and digital services were discussed, although only the first, estimated to raise about €7 billion a year, was approved.[10] Common debt and common taxes are first steps toward fiscal union and toward greater European Parliament responsibility for budgetary oversight.

6.2 The 2010s Crises Reborn

The COVID-19 epidemic dominated headlines in 2020 but should not obscure the significance of other events. After the refugee crisis of 2015 when Germany accepted a million migrants and the EU imposed "burden sharing" that was opposed by some members, the EU backed down on common action in 2017 as the magnitude of the crisis ebbed. Nevertheless, the ramifications were felt on 2 April 2020, when the European Court of Justice condemned and fined the Czech Republic, Hungary, and Poland for failing to accept their allocation of refugees in 2015 as decided by QMV of the Council. The Czech Republic took twelve refugees (out of a quota of 2,000), and Hungary and Poland refused to accept any of their 140,000 allocation. Although the three countries had voted against the Council's decision, the Court found that it was appropriately a decision by QMV.[11] The Court's decision was little noticed by a Europe in the midst of the COVID-19 epidemic.

The February 2020 decision by Turkey, the host of the most Syrian refugees by far, to allow refugees to move on to Europe caused more immediate concern, especially in frontline countries Greece and Bulgaria.[12] The EU response in 2020 was much less welcoming to refugees than in 2015 and may even have condoned harsh treatment of would-be immigrants in order to discourage further refugee waves (Clapp 2020). Media coverage of events on the borders of the Schengen zone was drowned out by coverage of COVID-19.

In Hungary's case, the Court's ruling on refugees was overshadowed by Prime Minister Orban's decision to have parliament grant him powers to rule by decree, ostensibly to fight the epidemic, but without time limit. The move, which was from the start applied to areas unrelated to COVID-19, seemed clearly intended to give the central government power over the local governments including that of Budapest controlled by opponents of Orban's party since the elections of October 2019 (Bonvicini 2020). This and other actions by the Hungarian and, to a lesser extent, the Polish government raised the question of how to enforce the first of the Copenhagen criteria (stable democratic institutions that promoted respect for the rule of law) when respect for the rule of law was flouted by a democratically elected government.

The COVID-19 epidemic raised a deeper challenge to the legitimacy of EU institutions. Christine Lagarde's commitment that "there are no limits" to the ECB's commitment to the euro had encountered some pushback in northern EU members from politicians who feared a bottomless pit of loans for feckless southern members. The EU Council did negotiate a package of EU-backed relief on 9 April in addition to the ECB commitment. However, in Germany, a case was brought before the constitutional court in Karlsruhe challenging the right of the ECB to acquire debt from EU members even though a challenge to the ECB's actions had already been dismissed by the European Court of Justice. The German court's ruling was mixed, but it opened the door to future challenges to ECB decisions and even to decisions of the European Court of Justice. The precedence of EU law over national law is fundamental to the EU. The Karlsruhe ruling about the legality of ECB instruments under German law and perhaps even more its explicit criticism of the European Court of Justice ruling on the matter, which should be final, are serious challenges to the EU. The immediate case will be fudged, but the lingering issue is fundamental.

Thus, both the refugee and sovereign debt issues, which by 2019 had appeared to be resolved or at least dormant, continued to raise fundamental questions about the EU's foundations. The third 2010s crisis, Brexit, was formally resolved after the UK's December 2019 election. The UK officially left the EU on 31 January 2020. However, 2020 was a transition year before Brexit would be complete. Most importantly, future relations between the EU27 and the UK had to be negotiated.

For the framework for future EU-UK trade, the official negotiating positions were that the EU hoped to maintain close economic relations with the UK but would not compromise on the indivisibility of the four freedoms of the Single Market (movement of goods, services, labor, and capital), whereas the UK wanted to leave the Single Market and sought a trade agreement that would allow the freest possible trade in goods and services between the EU and UK as well as leaving the UK free to negotiate its own future trade relations with non-EU countries. The EU insistence on a comprehensive deal reflected deep concern about possible "unfair competition"; if the UK deregulates in the future by terminating EU regulations in areas such as labor, state aid, and the environment, then that will give UK businesses an advantage over competitors in the EU Single Market. The EU sought commitments that the UK will keep in line with its competition rules, whereas the UK says as a sovereign country it cannot do that (and indeed the ability to set its own regulations was a major motive behind Brexit). The UK prefers to negotiate on topics separately. For example, the UK wants access to the central intelligence database of the EU's law enforcement agency, Europol. EU leaders are not keen on such sharing; once you've left the club, forget the perks. In the phrase most often used, "You can't have your cake and eat it," to which the UK responds by threatening to exclude EU fishing boats from UK waters; if we are no longer in the club, then forget the perks. You can't have your fish and eat it.

Both sides aspire to a free trade agreement. UK leaders refer to the Canada-EU trade agreement as a simple minimalist free trade option. However, the Comprehensive Economic and Trade Agreement (CETA) is not a no-tariffs / no-quotas agreement; British farmers would not like the array of protectionist measures applied by the EU27 to agricultural imports in CETA. Moreover, EU negotiators see many terms agreed with a country on the other side of the Atlantic Ocean as inapplicable to a trade partner linked by rail or a short sea crossing. The option of joining Norway, Iceland, and Liechtenstein in the European Economic Area (EEA) was unacceptable to the UK government because it involved most of the costs of being in the EU without a seat at the decision-making table and remaining subject to EU court decisions.[13] This left the two alternatives of signing a UK-EU trade agreement or trading under most-favored nation terms as independent World Trade Organization (WTO) members

And then there is Ireland. The stumbling block in passing Theresa May's deal with the EU was the return to a harder border in Ireland. Boris Johnson's magic wand removed that obstacle by negotiating the Irish protocol to leave EU regulations in place in Northern Ireland and introduce a mechanism for checking compatibility as goods crossed the Irish Sea between Great Britain and Northern Ireland. Implementation was always a potential issue as Johnson argued that there would be no threat to Northern Ireland's place in the UK.[14]

Much depends on the negotiators' desire for the agreement that both sides say they want. British Brexiteers accuse the EU of trying to undo Brexit by imposing their regulatory regime, whereas EU officials see the British attempt to negotiate issue by issue and kicking hard issues down the road as an attempt to force the EU into last-minute concessions. If red lines become too immutable and goodwill in short supply, then neither side will make sufficient concessions and the potential for no deal is increased. That would be a lose-lose outcome. It would be most harmful to the English voters who supported Brexit and will uncork the bottles of Irish unification and Scottish independence.

The WTO option was seen by many Brexit supporters as a clean break, an acceptable default option in the absence of reaching a UK-EU trade agreement.[15] The process could be to take EU commitments at WTO and replace "EU" by "UK" and then gradually amend any commitments that the UK did not want to retain. However, the break would not be so clean because the UK is party to EU agreements with third countries, which may no longer apply. For example, EU trade agreements include tariff-rate quotas on over one hundred products—for example, on beef, that would have to be reallocated, including allowance for EU-UK trade. All renegotiations would be two-sided as trading partners may not wish to extend the same WTO+ privileges to the UK as they had to the EU.[16] Most costly of all, physical entry of goods into the UK and from the UK to the EU27 will be subject to customs inspection after 2020.[17]

6.3 Internal Issues: Completing the Single Market, Cohesion and Convergence

The Single Market in goods was created in a two-stage process of first eliminating tariffs on trade among member countries and only later, once the benefits from the customs union had been established, were nontariff barriers (including trade-distorting regulations) tackled after the 1986 Single European Act. Creating a Single Market in services is more difficult because there are rarely at-the-border taxes on services. Generalization is difficult due to the heterogeneity of the services sector; in most cases, regulations are the overriding barrier to trade and market integration requires reinforcement of the Commission's regulation-setting role in the face of strong domestic resistance to change—for example, by professional services associations (Section 3.5).[18]

A fundamental challenge arises when there are good reasons for regulation, such as consumer protection in the face of asymmetric information, but genuine differences exist among EU members over how to regulate. There may also be transparency issues. The nature of the regulations may be indirect—for example, restrictions on direct foreign investment in areas where the service provider needs to have a physical presence in a market or local spatial planning rules may restrict entry of retail establishments.[19]

Slow progress accompanied by specific breakthroughs has often been the outcome, as in the example of telecommunications.[20] Since 2002, the EU has attempted to establish a common regulatory framework for telecommunications which will foster end-to-end competition and restrict the need for regulation to cases of significant market power, which will be gradually eliminated; an update in 2008 found eight cases of significant market power and a 2014 update found four cases of significant market power. However, although the EU has a common framework, national telecommunications regulators operate differently and there are no EU-wide licenses to operate; few EU citizens look beyond their national market for a service provider. Nevertheless, one of the most dramatic changes for EU consumers occurred on 15 June 2017 when, after ten years of negotiation, roaming charges ended in the EU; after that date, Europeans traveling within the EU paid domestic prices for phone calls, short message service (SMS), and data.

In passenger transport, liberalization has proceeded in different ways. After deregulation in 1992 allowed EU carriers to fly between any EU countries, Ryanair started to expand, but rapid growth followed the launch of the company's website in 2000 and increased efficiency of check-in and other operations; by 2019, Ryanair's fleet consisted of 419 Boeing 737s, compared to two small aircraft in the late 1980s. Intercity bus transport emerged after national deregulation in Germany. Flixbus established its first Bavarian routes in 2013, followed by entry into the liberalized French market in 2015 and other Western European markets in 2015 and Eastern Europe in 2016, by which time Flixbus was serving 1,700 destinations in twenty-eight countries.[21] Like Ryanair, Flixbus was criticized for poor customer relations and basic level of service, but enough travelers loved the low prices for both companies to flourish and strengthen economic integration. Railway deregulation has had less dramatic impact, with major changes such as the Eurostar route under the Channel or high-speed networks being primarily national rather than EU initiatives.

The transport changes reflect the interaction between policy change, at the EU level and the national level, and technological change. The internet revolution dates from the mid-1990s—that is, after the EC92 program to create the Single Market—and it has been transformational in many service activities. Europe has clearly lagged behind the United States and China in responding to the challenge and the EU has belatedly acknowledged the need to create a Digital Single Market (DSM). The DSM has been pursued since 2015 with three pillars: access to online products and services, conditions for digital networks and services to grow and thrive, and growth of the European digital economy. Implementation of the strategy centered on the Directive on Copyright in the Digital Single Market released by the European Commission in

September 2016, which ran into extensive public opposition, especially on issues related to fees for citing news stories (the "link tax") and responsibilities of website services to ensure that no uploads breach copyright restrictions; both were seen as threats to freedom of expression on the internet. More popular among internet users, if not content providers, was the data protection package adopted in May 2016 that included the General Data Protection Regulation (GDPR) giving all EU citizens the right to protection of their personal data.

There is overwhelming empirical evidence that service activities are an important and increasing component of value-added in all parts of the economy and that efficient servicification is a necessary condition for competitiveness in manufacturing.[22] Hence, the continuing barriers to services trade within the EU will remain a source of concern. In the 2020s, the Commission will worry more about Europe's competitiveness and about whether poorer member countries may be left behind.

A critical challenge for the integrated EU is to reduce the size of income differences across countries and regions. Although cohesion has always been a goal, it has been a stronger feature since the 2004 enlargement brought a group of substantially poorer countries into the EU. The new members did well in the short run, including before formal accession when the prospect of entering the EU was associated with faster economic growth and convergence toward the income levels of the older EU member countries. However, the new members were especially vulnerable to collateral damage from the crises that began in 2007–2008 and convergence slowed to a crawl in the early and mid-2010s. A crucial question is whether the convergence of the poorer countries' income levels toward those of the more affluent EU members can be revived in the 2020s.

The growth patterns are well known, although specific numbers vary from study to study depending on the choice of countries, dates, and output or productivity measure. Åslund (2018) compares gross domestic product (GDP) growth of the eleven Central and Eastern European economies that joined the EU in 2004, 2007, and 2013 with that of the twelve pre-2004 eurozone members.[23] Growth in the eleven averaged 5.7 percent per year between 2000 and 2007, compared to a eurozone average of 2.2 percent. Between 2010 and 2016, the eleven countries' growth rate averaged 2.1 percent; average growth in the older EU members was even slower, but the point is that with such slow growth, any convergence will be over a very long time. Growth rates picked up in Eastern Europe in 2017 and 2018, reigniting debates over convergence.

Several authors—for example, Åslund (2018) and three International Monetary Fund economists (Papi et al. 2018)—are optimistic that conditions for convergence are strong in Eastern Europe, with policies, institutions, and human capital endowments all favorable for catch-up growth. Shortage of risk capital and lagging research and development are the main causes for concern. Emigration may be taking more productive workers away from the new members, although this is hard to document, and with falling populations, estimated growth in per capita income is higher. Papi et al. (2018) also emphasize that the structure of the population matters, and an aging population in Eastern Europe may lead to divergence.

An ongoing debate questions whether free markets and social protection are compatible in the EU. While some leaders—for example, the UK's prime minister David Cameron before the Brexit vote—have emphasized the need to focus on the core business of free trade within the Single Market, others have been concerned about the erosion of national welfare states as members engage in a race to the bottom in removing constraints to competitiveness—for example, the "no" campaign in France's 2005 referendum that sank the proposed Constitutional Treaty. The Maastricht Treaty sought to balance the two objectives of growth and inclusion by emphasizing both economic and social aims, and this was continued in the Lisbon Treaty under the formula of a "social market economy." However, the "social market economy" formula gives hardly any guidance about appropriate policies: "what are the limits of market integration, what kind of (social) policies should the EU strive for and, ultimately, what should a well-functioning social market economy look like" (Claasen et al. 2019, 4). Member states have jealously guarded their national control over elements of the welfare state such as unemployment and health insurance, pensions, and access to education.

In September 2015, the European Commission launched a new political initiative—the European Pillar of Social Rights (EPSR)—with the stated aim of strengthening the social *acquis* of the EU and promoting upward social convergence across eurozone countries. In particular, the Commission presented the EPSR as a reference framework intended to address the gaps in existing EU employment and social policy legislation. To this end, the Commission identified twenty common principles and rights divided into three main categories: (1) equal opportunities and access to the labor market, (2) fair working conditions, and (3) social protection and inclusion. In January 2017, the European Parliament voted in a resolution supporting the EPSR.

These principles were put at the center of the interinstitutional proclamation adopted at the Gothenburg social summit in November 2017. Nevertheless, the actual content and scope of the EPSR remain blurred. As a policy initiative, the EPSR mainly serves to restate some principles and rights already enshrined in the EU treaties and secondary legislation, to update the so-called social *acquis,* and finally to reinforce the monitoring of social and employment issues (Versan and Corti 2019). The lack of EU progress in creating common social policies and the weakness of cohesion policies to stimulate convergence highlight the gap between European integration and economic integration within federal nation-states.

6.4 External Issues: Looking beyond the Neighborhoods

For the EU, China has become the major foreign policy challenge as the burgeoning economic relationship with strong win-win outcomes from trade and investment have to be balanced against political concerns over China's authoritarian regime that does not share EU values. In 2018, the EU was China's largest trading partner and China was the EU's second largest trading partner after the United States. The dilemma was exacerbated by the US swing toward conflict with China in 2017 with an open trade war. The EU shares US concerns about the WTO compatibility of Chinese support for state-owned enterprises and use of nontransparent subsidies and about forced technology transfer from foreign investors in China, but the EU has reservations about the confrontational approach of the United States and takes a more nuanced approach. The

EU's March 2019 strategy paper described China as being simultaneously a cooperation partner, a negotiating partner, an economic competitor, and "a systemic rival promoting alternative models of governance."[24] The EU-China summit on 9 April 2019 concluded with agreement to finalize a China-EU Comprehensive Investment Agreement in 2020, to cooperate on WTO reform, and to work together to resolve the WTO appellate body crisis—all in contrast to the more confrontational US approach to China (González and Véron 2019, 17). There are potential divisions within the EU as some members prioritize improving economic relations with China over a more circumspect common EU foreign policy; most stridently, Italy in 2019 advocated warmer relations with China and broke EU ranks by signing a memorandum of understanding about participating in the Belt and Road Initiative.[25]

Differences between the EU and the United States have also arisen over relations with Iran. After the signing of the Joint Comprehensive Plan of Action to monitor Iran's nuclear program and subsequent lifting of United Nations sanctions in January 2016, President Xi visited Tehran, and rail services between China and Iran began that month. An EU delegation headed by High Representative Federica Mogherini visited Tehran in April 2016, and EU-Iran trade and investment picked up despite difficulties of doing business in Iran and US retention of primary sanctions against Iran (Adebahr 2018). The situation deteriorated after the 2016 US election, although it was not until May 2018 that President Trump announced US withdrawal from the Joint Comprehensive Plan of Action and imposition of secondary sanctions against any businesses dealing with Iran.

A third source of tension between the EU and the United States is the future of the WTO-centered multilateral trading system. The Trump administration clearly did not consider the United States to be constrained by the international trade law of the WTO and undermined the effectiveness of the WTO by refusing to approve new appointments to the appellate body. In summer 2018, President Trump introduced restrictions on imports of steel from the EU. The EU responded by imposing tariff rate quotas on several categories of steel imports in February 2019; the complex array of restrictions applied not only to imports from the United States. In May 2020, with the steel industry hurt by falling demand due to the COVID-19 pandemic, the EU announced a revised set of steel safeguards which impacted negatively on a number of steel exporters, several of which filed a complaint at the WTO.[26]

In July 2019, at a meeting in Nice, the EU agreed with Canada on two ways to work around US obstructionism.[27] First, they propose rewriting the EU-Canada CETA rules to serve as an initial model of a multilateral Investment Court System that will provide a more transparent and accountable alternative to most investor-state dispute settlement arrangements. Second, as an alternative to the WTO dispute settlement process that is nonfunctional due to US opposition to any new appointments of appellate judges, a shadow appellate body will rule on future disputes between the EU and Canada using retired appellate judges. Brussels and Ottawa have effectively issued an open invitation to other governments to participate.[28]

The EU is under pressure to rethink its partnership agreements. In Africa, the slow progress in implementing the Economic Partnership Agreements foreseen by the 2000 Cotonou Agreement (Section 4.2) suggests that the model was unattractive to the EU's partners. The signing of the African Continental Free Trade Area by forty-four of the African Union's fifty-five members in March 2018 offered an opportunity for a new start for collaboration with the EU as it signaled greater willingness of the African countries to open their markets to foreign competition. Relations with neighbors to the south and east will continue to be problematic despite ongoing EU financial assistance.[29]

6.5 Assessment

Has European integration been a good thing? Opinion surveys in the original six signatories of the Treaty of Rome still place peace as the EU's biggest achievement, and the contrast between three increasingly destructive Franco-German wars in the seventy-five years to 1945 and the absence of war in Western Europe in the seventy-five years after 1945 is sharp. It is harder to evaluate the economic consequences of European economic integration because it is difficult to specify the counterfactual; what would the European economy have looked like if the UK had led

Western Europe to a limited free trade area agreement after World War II, or if there had been no economic integration? Campos et al. (2018) use synthetic controls—that is, the experience of hypothetical countries that are similar to EU members—to evaluate the impact of EU accession on incomes and labor productivity. They find a positive impact on per capita GDP in all new members except Greece, although there is large variation in the size of the impact.

European economic integration has been a continuous process of widening and deepening since 1950. The political background is clear and different political decisions could have been taken, especially in the early stages, but in fact the process of ever closer union in Europe has been led by economic integration. The structure of this book emphasizes the discontinuous nature of economic integration as big steps were followed by the challenges of implementation and consolidation. It has been a decades-long process that still continues. The outcome so far is a unique level of integration, not as deep as in established federal states but far deeper than any other association of independent nations.

Such deeper integration is not welcomed by all, as shown by Brexit or the Danish referendum to maintain the national currency or Sweden's reluctance to adopt the euro. More federally minded countries welcome extension of common social and political standards, whereas other governments—notably Hungary and Poland—resist pressures to follow norms of liberal democracy or to accept QMV in areas such as accepting refugees. Differing appetites for closer union lead to calls for, or fears of, a two-tier Europe. However, the groupings can be fluid. For example, in May 2020, debates over financial support for poor countries hit hardest by the COVID-19 pandemic (i.e., Italy and Spain), the principal opponents to cash transfers were the frugal four (Austria, Denmark, the Netherlands, and Sweden); those four countries are split 2–2 on the euro and all are closer to Copenhagen criteria social and political standards than the governments of Hungary or Poland. At the July 2020 Council meeting, as so often in EU history, the twenty-seven heads of government did eventually achieve agreement on the regular budget and on the fund to help countries recover from the COVID-19 recession. However, one casualty was reduced future-oriented funding including for environmental policies.

If a multitier Europe does emerge, the touchstone for being in the first tier is likely to be adoption of the common currency. Members reluctant to adopt the euro will find themselves effectively excluded from decision making as the eurozone members' meetings set the agenda for and pre-agree decisions at EU Council meetings. Those outside the core may end up in a room with the non-EU EEA members, or they can follow the UK through the exit door. Within the EU, Brexit has made second-tier status less desirable because the noneuro group has lost its largest member. Ironically, Brexit may have unified and strengthened the EU, while weakening the union of England, Wales, Scotland, and Northern Ireland.

The uncertainty of predicting the future course of European integration can best be appreciated by looking at the past. At every step forward, the integration project has encountered pessimism about its future: the European Defence Community debacle in 1954, President de Gaulle's empty chair in 1967, Margaret Thatcher's Bruges speech, several lost referenda, skepticism about the euro—the list goes on. So does the EU.

Measuring the Effects of Economic Integration

Identifying the Counterfactual

Overall assessment of the economic costs and benefits of European integration has been challenging. It is difficult to isolate integration effects from other determinants of long-term performance (Eichengreen 2007; Crafts 2016). Economic growth has many drivers, and the no-integration counterfactual is hard to specify.

Early arguments linked increases in savings and investment rates in response to market expansion to higher economic growth. This is, however, likely to be a transient effect as the economy shifts to a higher level of output and income per head but without impacting the long-run growth rate (Solow 1956). Following the development of endogenous growth theory, several writers related economic integration to higher long-run growth through its impact on production of knowledge capital (Baldwin 1989; Rivera-Batiz and Romer 1991; Grossman and Helpman 1991). However, empirical evidence of the long-run growth impact of EU integration is unconvincing. In the growth econometrics literature that flourished in the 1990s, inclusion of an EU variable sometimes had a statistically significant positive coefficient (e.g., Henrekson et al. 1997) and sometimes did not (e.g., Vanhoudt 1999), suggesting a tenuous relationship between EU membership and economic growth, other things equal—a conclusion restated in Badinger's 2005 review of the literature on growth effects of EU integration.[30] Moreover, simply including an integration dummy in a growth econometrics exercise is methodologically problematic (Baier and Bergstrand 2007).

The economic consequences of a major institutional change such as the Single Market occur over many years and at different speeds—for example, trade effects impact sooner than changes in investment or in attitudes. Measurement is further complicated by two other features. First, the impact is likely to be gradual; perhaps beginning before a policy change such as joining the EU, because people anticipate the change, and then taking time to work through the economic system as attitudes change, as capital comes up for renewal, as new skills are acquired, and so forth. Second, because time horizons cover many years, it is difficult to sort out the impact from other contemporaneous changes; although it is tempting to make before-and-after comparisons, the comparison should be with and without, which requires knowledge of the counterfactual world without the change that is being assessed.

Long time lags reinforce the difficulty of identifying a plausible counterfactual; what would the European economies have looked like in the twenty-first century without the Single Market program? A recently popular approach is to construct a synthetic control. For example, to assess the impact of joining the EU, the postaccession performance of the new member is compared to that of an artificial country that performed identically to the EU member before accession. Typically, a synthetic control can be created from a small number of "donor" countries—for example, in Campos et al. (2019) synthetic Spain is composed of 37.3 percent Brazil, 35.8 percent New Zealand, and 26.8 percent Canada, which means that a unit consisting of those weights most closely mimics Spain's economic performance before joining the EU in 1986. Between 1986 and 1996, Spain's GDP per capita was on average 13.7 percent higher than the GDP per capita of synthetic Spain, indicating a positive impact of EU accession.

Campos et al. (2019) find that all countries joining the EU between 1973 and 2004, except Greece, benefited from accession by having higher per capita GDP ten years after accession than their synthetic control (Table 6A1). The net benefits were smallest for the countries joining in 1995, presumably because Austria, Finland, and Sweden already enjoyed substantial access to the integrated EU market through the European Communities–European Free Trade Association free trade in manufac-

Table 6A1   Percentage Increase in GDP per Capita and GDP per Worker Ten Years
after EU Accession due to EU Integration, Using Synthetic Controls

	GDP per capita	GDP per worker			GDP per capita	GDP per worker
Denmark	14.3%	−0.6%		Czech Rep	5.6%	3.7%
Ireland	9.4%	8.6%		Estonia	24.2%	20.5%
UK	8.6%	8.5%		Hungary	12.3%	17.7%
Greece	−17.3%	−14.1%		Latvia	31.7%	19.4%
Portugal	16.5%	12.3%		Lithuania	28.1%	24.1%
Spain	13.7%	3.7%		Poland	5.9%	9.4%
Austria	6.4%	12.9%		Slovakia	0.3%	−1.8%
Finland	4.0%	4.5%		Slovenia	10.4%	12.8%
Sweden	2.4%	2.6%				

Source: Campos et al. (2019, Table 1).
Note: Effect for 2004 cohort is dated from 1998 when accession appeared certain.

tures agreement. Net benefits were highest for the three Baltic countries that had the lowest preaccession per capita GDP and hence greatest
scope for convergence. Although most of the results in Table 6A1 are
plausible, the Slovakia estimate is surprising.

Campos et al. (2019) also found that the per capita GDP differences
continued to increase after ten years. All of the countries in the left-hand
side of Table 6A1 had larger effects if the difference was taken up to their
final data point, 2008. For the 1973 cohort, the integration effect by 2008
was 24 percent for Denmark and the UK and 49 percent for Ireland—
that is, after thirty-five years, Irish GDP per capita was almost half as
large again as it would have been outside the EU.[31]

The synthetic control method has been used by Lehtimäki and Sondermann (2020) to evaluate the impact of the Single Market. They created a synthetic EU12 (47 percent United States, 37 percent Israel,
15 percent Japan, and 1 percent Australia) that best predicted EU macroeconomic performance between 1964 and 1992 and compared the performance of the synthetic EU to that of the actual EU12 between 1993
and 2014. As reported in Section 3.1, the EU countries outperformed the
synthetic EU slowly in the mid-1990s and then substantially in the decade

to 2008. The authors' initial comparison ran to 2014, but they caution that in the years after 2008, the component countries in synthetic EU and the actual EU12 countries faced specific shocks so that the synthetic EU became a less useful proxy for the counterfactual; most clearly, the United States experienced a severe financial crisis in 2007–2009, and several EU12 countries ran into sovereign debt crises in 2010.

How serious is the problem of idiosyncratic shocks? They will always be present—for example, in Lehtimäki and Sondermann (2020), the divergence in the decade 1998–2008 may have reflected differential impact of the resource boom that dominated the world economy over that decade on the synthetic control countries and on the EU12. The problem is likely to be more severe in less stable global conditions and if the treatment variables are less important. Thus, we may have more confidence in applying the synthetic control method to EU membership than to the Single Market or to euro adoption (Fernández and Perea 2015; Puzzello and Gomis-Porqueras 2018).

Abbreviations

ACP	African, Caribbean, and Pacific countries
Benelux	Belgium, the Netherlands, and Luxembourg
BIT	bilateral investment treaty
BRI	Belt and Road Initiative (China—announced 2013, launched 2017)
CACM	Central American Common Market
CAP	common agricultural policy
CETA	Comprehensive Economic and Trade Agreement— unofficially, Canada-Europe Trade Agreement
CGE	computable general equilibrium
cif	cost insurance freight (value of a good at the point of import)
CIS	Commonwealth of Independent States (former Soviet republics)
CJEU	Court of Justice of the European Union
CM	common market (see Box 1)
COVID-19	Coronavirus disease 2019
CU	customs union (see Box 1)
DCFTA	Deep and Comprehensive Free Trade Agreement
DSM	Digital Single Market
EAC	East African Community
EAEC	European Atomic Energy Community (Euratom)
EAEU	Eurasian Economic Union (established 2015)
EaP	Eastern Partnership (with Armenia, Azerbaijan, Belarus, Georgia, Moldova, and Ukraine)
EBA	Everything But Arms (arrangement for least-developed countries)

EC	European Communities (see Box 0)
ECB	European Central Bank
ECSC	European Coal and Steel Community
EDC	European Defence Community
EEA	European Economic Area
EEC	European Economic Community (see Box 0)
EFTA	European Free Trade Association
EMS	European Monetary System
EMU	economic and monetary union
ENP	European Neighbourhood Policy
EPA	Economic Partnership Agreement
EPC	European Political Community
EPSR	European Pillar of Social Rights
ERM	exchange rate mechanism of the EMS
ESCB	European System of Central Banks
ESM	European Stability Mechanism
ESMA	European Securities and Market Authority
ETS	Emissions Trading Scheme (of the EU)
EU	European Union (see Box 0)
EVFTA	EU-Vietnam Free Trade Agreement
FDI	foreign direct investment
fob	free on board (value of a good at the point of export)
FTA	free trade area (see Box 1)
G7	Group of Seven (United States, Japan, Germany, United Kingdom, France, Italy, and Canada)
G20	Group of Twenty
GATS	General Agreement on Trade in Services (1995)
GATT	General Agreement on Tariffs and Trade (1947)
GDP	gross domestic product
GDPR	General Data Protection Regulation
GSP	Generalized System of Preferences (1971)
GSP+	EU Special Incentive Arrangement for Sustainable Development and Good Governance
GUAM	Georgia, Ukraine, Azerbaijan, Moldova

GVC	global value chain
HS	Harmonized Commodity Description and Coding System
ICT	information and communication technologies
IIT	intra-industry trade
IMF	International Monetary Fund
IPA	investment protection agreement
IT	information technology
MCA	monetary compensation amount
MFA	Multifibre Arrangement (terminated 2004)
MFN	most-favored nation
NAFTA	North American Free Trade Agreement
NATO	North Atlantic Treaty Organization
NDCs	Nationally Determined Contributions (on climate change)
NTB	nontariff barrier to trade
OCA	optimum currency area
OCT	Overseas Country and Territory (of the EU)
OECD	Organisation for Economic Co-operation and Development
OEEC	Organisation for European Economic Co-operation
PHARE	Poland and Hungary: Assistance for Restructuring their Economies program
PIIGS	Portugal, Italy, Ireland, Greece, and Spain
PSPP	Public Sector Purchase Programme (of the ECB)
QMV	qualified majority voting
R&D	research and development
RRF	Recovery and Resilience Fund (2020)
SEA	Single European Act (1987)
SBBS	Sovereign Bond-Backed Securities
SGP	Stability and Growth Pact (adopted in 1997)
SHEIC	safety, health, environmental, investor / saver, and consumer
SMP	Securities Market Programme (2010)

SMS	short message service
SPS	sanitary and phytosanitary measures
SRB	Single Resolution Board
TACIS	Technical Assistance to the Commonwealth of Independent States
TBT	technical barriers to trade
TC	trade creation
TD	trade diversion
TEN-T	Trans-European Transport Network
TFEU	Treaty on the Functioning of the European Union (Lisbon Treaty)
TRQ	tariff rate quota
TSCG	Intergovernmental Treaty on Stability, Coordination and Governance
UEFA	Union of European Football Associations
UK	United Kingdom (of Great Britain and Northern Ireland)
UKIP	United Kingdom Independence Party
VER	voluntary export restraint agreement
Visegrád-Four	Czech Republic, Hungary, Poland, and Slovakia
WHO	World Health Organization
WTO	World Trade Organization (established 1995)

$ refers to the US dollar

£ refers to the British pound sterling

€ refers to the euro

List of Boxes, Tables, and Figures

Notes

1 A BRIEF HISTORY OF EUROPEAN UNION

1. This was the outcome, but the negotiations at Versailles in 1919 were more complex and the negotiators more aware of the difficulties than this simple statement implies (Macmillan 2001).

2. Churchill made the call in a September 1946 speech in Zürich. By 1946, Churchill was out of office. His successor as prime minister, Clement Atlee, would dismiss the countries forming the ECSC in 1950 as "six nations, four of whom we had to rescue from the other two." However, Foreign Minister Ernest Bevin had an internationalist dream of going to London's Victoria station to "get a railway ticket, and go where the Hell I liked without a passport or anything else" (quoted in Charlton 1983, 43–44). Fifty years later, under the Schengen Agreement that dream would be possible almost anywhere in Western Europe except the British Isles.

3. Usherwood and Pinder (2018) provide a brief introduction to the EU from the federalist perspective; the EU is designed to transform the member nations into integral parts of a cooperative venture. Gilbert (2012) provides a more substantial political history emphasizing the role of the member states and their intergovernmental dealings.

4. As Cold War tensions mounted with the Berlin blockade and airlift, negotiations to strengthen the military alliance led to the North Atlantic Treaty, signed by US president Harry Truman in April 1949. The North Atlantic Treaty Organization (NATO) included the five Treaty of Brussels states plus the United States, Canada, Portugal, Italy, Norway, Denmark, and Iceland

5. This is the position ascribed to the head of the French Steel Association by François Duchêne (1994, 239). The quotations from Monnet's inaugural address are from Duchêne (1994, 235).

6. However, the ECSC was far from being a single market—for example, coal subsidies and price controls remained common as governments considered low household fuel costs to be essential for social stability and economic development (Eichengreen and Boltho 2010, 279).

7. Intergovernmental initiatives were not pursued. The European Payments Union became redundant as quantitative restrictions on currency transactions were eased and currencies became convertible in the second half of the 1950s. With

European reconstruction considered complete by 1960, the OEEC was converted into an intergovernmental think tank in 1961 and renamed the Organisation for Economic Co-operation and Development (OECD); with the inclusion of the United States and Canada, it was no longer a purely European institution.

8. Euratom was sidelined by France's new president, Charles de Gaulle, with the aim of keeping the French atomic energy sector fully under national control. The executive bodies of Euratom and the EEC were called commissions to emphasize their more limited power than the High Authority of the ECSC. All three communities would share the court and assembly (later renamed the European Parliament). An institutional innovation was establishment of the European Investment Bank, which opened in Brussels in 1958 and relocated to Luxembourg in 1968.

9. Additionally, the Six provided preferential access to goods from members' colonies and promised aid and investment to them.

10. Given that much of northwestern Europe's imports entered the customs union through Rotterdam, allowing the country of entry to keep the revenue would be unfair (in favor of the Netherlands), but trying to establish the final destination of imported goods would have been unnecessarily complex within a common market. In the period until the end of 1965, EEC funding was by national contributions, and the transition to an EEC budget was part of the 1965–1966 empty-chair conflict over how decisions should be reached. Formal agreement on the Community's own resources was finally approved in April 1970 with import levies going to the EEC together with transfer of up to one percent of value-added tax receipts.

11. Iceland joined EFTA in 1970, Finland in 1986, and Liechtenstein in 1991. Although retaining national trade policies, EFTA members did negotiate as a group to form a free trade area and reach other agreements with the EEC, and EFTA has trade agreements with other countries or groupings.

12. A 1962 application for membership by Spain was rejected in 1964 because fascist Spain was not a democracy.

13. When factory workers went on strike in sympathy with students demonstrating against capitalism, it briefly looked as though France's Fifth Republic might be overthrown. The government brokered agreement between the labor unions and the employers on a large wage increase, after which the workers returned to work and the revolt faded away. Nevertheless, the signal that de Gaulle's style of government had become out of tune with the times was clear, as was the fact that, after the wage increases fed through into higher prices, the French franc would have to be devalued.

14. Gibraltar and Greenland joined the EC as part of the British and Danish accession. Faroe Islands, although under Danish sovereignty, remained outside the EC. Faroe home rule was established on 1 April 1948 when the Faroe Islands became a self-governing community within the Kingdom of Denmark. When Den-

mark joined the EC on 1 January 1973, the Faroese government determined that the Faroe Islands would not be an EC member. The Faroe Islands have a free trade agreement with the EU, signed in 1991 and revised in 1996, and a 1980 agreement on fisheries that is renewed annually. Greenland automatically became a member of the EC with Denmark's accession in 1973. After the introduction of home rule in 1979, Greenland held a referendum on EC membership in 1982, following which Greenland chose to leave the EC with effect from 1 February 1985. Since its withdrawal from the Community, Greenland has special fisheries arrangements with the EU and is included as one of the so-called overseas countries and territories enjoying association arrangements (special relations) with the EU.

15. The Committee of Permanent Representatives (COREPER, from the French *comité des représentants permanents*), consisting of the heads or deputy heads of mission of the member states is the permanent body that prepares for European Council meetings and also liaises between the Commission and the Council of Ministers. The European Council discusses high-level issues and the outcomes are transparent. The Council of Ministers comprises ministers from each member state with responsibility for the policy area under discussion and takes decisions increasingly by qualified majority voting.

16. The act was ratified by nine countries in Luxembourg on 17 February 1987, and Denmark, Italy, and Greece signed it in The Hague ten days later. The changes were enshrined in the Maastricht Treaty.

17. The EEA agreement includes a common goal of reducing social and economic disparities in Europe. Since 1994, Iceland, Liechtenstein, and Norway have contributed to social and economic progress in the less wealthy countries, which until 2004 included Greece, Ireland, Northern Ireland, Portugal, and Spain and after 2004 included Bulgaria (from 2007), Cyprus, Czech Republic, Estonia, Greece, Hungary, Latvia, Lithuania, Malta, Poland, Portugal, Romania (from 2007), Slovakia, Slovenia, and Spain.

18. The Schengen Agreement was signed independently of the SEA due to lack of consensus over the pace of removal of border controls and over whether the EEC had the jurisdiction to abolish border controls.

19. This was not a formal agreement (Bozo 2005) but part of an ongoing accommodation between Kohl and Mitterrand from the December 1989 Strasbourg summit, where Chancellor Kohl committed to keeping Germany at the center of the European integration process during the drive for German reunification, to the Maastricht Treaty two years later. Among other issues, Kohl wanted to give greater power to the European Parliament, which Mitterrand resisted, and Mitterrand wanted a common European foreign policy to address concerns about post–Cold War security, but this was fairly toothless in the Maastricht Treaty.

20. The Snake and EMS and the 1985 Schengen Agreement had involved subgroups of EC members, but these had not been treaty obligations.

21. The treaty's 253 pages include many binding protocols and nonbinding declarations in response to national concerns. For example, the UK inserted a declaration requiring the EU "to pay full regard to the welfare requirements of animals," a protocol drafted by Denmark intended to ban Germans from buying holiday homes on the Danish coast, and Spain obtained a protocol that the EU budget process would be reformed to better reflect member countries' ability to pay and needs for assistance.

22. Spain and Portugal never left the ERM, but their currencies were frequently devalued between September 1992 and March 1995 (see Table 2.1).

23. Following the 2000 referendum on introducing the euro, which was defeated by 53 percent to 47 percent, Denmark remains in the ERM and the exchange rate of the krone against the euro cannot diverge by more than 2.25 percent. Denmark has no monetary policy independence and bears the costs and inconvenience of foreign currency and exchange transactions in return for the privilege of issuing its own banknotes.

24. Andorra, Monaco, San Marino, and the Vatican have formal agreements with the EU to use the euro as their official currency and issue their own coins. Kosovo and Montenegro have unilaterally adopted the euro and are not part of the eurozone.

25. At the October 1990 summit in Rome, Thatcher was effectively isolated in her opposition to all proposals for deeper integration. After a passionate defense of her position in the British parliament, she was criticized by leading members of her party and faced a leadership challenge in November. After failing to win on the first ballot, Thatcher stepped down and John Major became prime minister.

26. The idea was to make the Treaty on the Functioning of the European Union seem more like tidying up existing EU law and hence subject only to ratification by national parliaments. The only referendum was held in Ireland in July 2008, when the voters rejected the treaty; a second referendum in October 2009 gave the desired "yes" majority.

27. The principle is to keep decisions as close to the citizen as possible. The treaty allows action at the EU level only if the goals cannot be achieved by national actions of member states and provides a role for national parliaments to police subsidiarity in practice.

28. The lack of consensus was highlighted in 2008 when most EU members recognized Kosovo's independence, but Greece and Spain refused to do so.

29. Developing countries were divided between the benefits of bounteous food aid and the lower world prices received for agricultural exports. The complex sugar regime, for example, led to the EU becoming the largest exporter of white sugar with about two-fifths of the world market, including large exports to Nigeria and Algeria, which might otherwise have been markets for sugar exports from suppliers such as Mozambique (Baldwin and Wyplosz 2015, 230–231).

2 THE CUSTOMS UNION: SETTING EUROPEAN INTEGRATION IN MOTION (1957–1982)

1. The original intention was that external tariffs should be the simple average of preceding tariffs, which generally involved an increase in Benelux countries' tariffs, reduction in French and Italian tariffs, and West Germany somewhere in between, although there was much variation from product to product.

2. The 1963 Long Term Arrangement regarding International Trade in Cotton Textiles took textiles and clothing out of the GATT. It was extended to become the Multifibre Arrangement from 1974 through 1994 and the Agreement on Textiles and Clothing from 1995 until such protection expired on 1 January 2005. The customs union did not apply to military goods. State ownership and industrial or intellectual property rights remained in national jurisdictions, although they could weaken the integrated internal market and the common competition policy. Coal and steel were covered by the ECSC. Specific arrangements (e.g., Italy's agreement with Japan to limit car sales in the other country's market) were grandfathered.

3. If goods from the partners and a third country are close substitutes, then rules of origin cannot prevent trade deflection. Producers in the low-tariff FTA member will export to the partner country where prices are higher, and any short-fall in meeting domestic demand will be met by imports from nonmembers (Pomfret 2001, 185–188); under these conditions, a protective tariff will be ineffective, and the race to the bottom will resume.

4. In 1955, agriculture's share of employment was 9.3 percent in Belgium, 13.2 percent in the Netherlands, 18.5 percent in Germany, 19.4 percent in Luxembourg, 26.9 percent in France, and 40.0 percent in Italy.

5. Although export subsidies were illegal under GATT, agriculture was excluded from the 1964–1967 Kennedy Round, and the 1973–1979 Tokyo Round saw little effective external pressure for CAP reform.

6. Large farmers had higher productivity and more elastic supply so that the producer gain (area a in Figure 2A1) was greater for them. Also, the EU farmers' union COPA (Comité des organisations professionnelles agricoles, founded in 1958) had solely large farmers on its board and influenced CAP design in their favor.

7. As the customs union moved from importer to exporter, the size of the variable levy increased in order to prevent any imports, but revenues from variable levies ceased. Meanwhile, storage costs and export subsidies increased.

8. Michael Plummer, in a 1988 PhD dissertation at Michigan State University, undertook economic assessments of the impact of membership; parts were published as Plummer (1991a) on Greece and Plummer (1991b) on Spain and Portugal. Handley and Limão (2015) argue that reduced uncertainty about trade policy was an important reason why Portuguese accession helped economic performance.

9.   For quantitative estimates of these effects, see the Appendix to Chapter 6. In contrast to the short-run analysis in Section 2.4, Campos and Coricelli (2017b, 2–3) report econometric evidence of a long-term positive impact of UK accession, which they relate to the victory of business groups wanting to compete at the high-tech end of the European market over business groups content to sell in the less-demanding Commonwealth markets.

10. Baldwin (2016) focuses on how advances in information technology (IT) have reduced communications costs, so it is easier to troubleshoot any problems along the value chain. As tariffs have fallen, attention shifted to nontariff barriers and other costs of international trade (Sourdin and Pomfret 2012). Relevant trade costs include money, time, and uncertainty; GVCs are only feasible if inventories can be minimized by reliable just-in-time delivery. IT is part of the trade costs story—for example, tracking shipments—as well as allowing face-to-face contact over distance.

11. Algeria, as part of France, was in the EEC from 1957 until becoming independent in 1962. Greece, Portugal, and Spain graduated from the Global Mediterranean Policy when they became EEC members in the 1980s (Pomfret 1986).

12. The 1963 Yaoundé Convention and the 1975 Lomé Convention provided for generally free access to EEC markets for ACP exports of manufactures, subject to rules of origin (about 50 percent to 60 percent of value-added had to be domestic) and excluding textiles and clothing. CAP products were excluded, except for a special regime for sugar, and some stabilization schemes for minerals were included in various Lomé renewals.

13. However, when it came to devising its own GSP scheme, the EEC had little to offer. To keep Lomé beneficiaries distinct, the EEC's GSP tariffs were lower than MFN tariffs but above zero. A common criticism of both GSP and Lomé tariff preferences was that the EEC offered easy access for imports of aircraft or Jet Skis but not for textiles and clothing or for agricultural goods—the two things that low-income countries were most likely to export. This was a general problem with donor-determined assistance; developing countries would benefit more from low MFN tariffs in relevant goods, which started to happen only after 1995 with the phasing out of the Multifibre Arrangement, than from GSP schemes.

14. The first article prohibits all agreements that "may affect trade between Member States and may have as their object or effect the prevention, restriction or distortion of competition within the common market" and gives examples (such as price fixing, market sharing, output restriction, and discrimination between trading parties), although exemptions are possible where benefits exceed anti-competitive effects—for example, research and development agreements. The second article covers abuse of dominant position and lists prohibited practices, and allows no exemptions (Utton 2006, 112–113). The enforcement system was established in 1962 by Regulation 17 / 62 and updated and extended by Regulation 1 / 2003.

15. This is consistent with the limited results from the huge growth econometrics literature of the 1990s and 2000s. The only widely recognized result is that conditional convergence has occurred globally since the 1960s (Barro 2015), although there is little agreement about the conditioning variables, beyond generally favorable results for variables capturing human capital levels and openness. The Appendices to Chapters 3, 5, and 6 contain more discussion of these results.

16. Among other consequences, the exchange rate gap provided an incentive for smuggling, a phenomenon especially observed at the Irish border where cows moved across the border depending on MCAs in the Irish or the UK market. On the interaction between the CAP and the revival of monetary integration by Jenkins, Giscard, and Schmidt and on the longevity of the EMS, see Pomfret (1991) and Basevi and Grassi (1993).

17. Although the monetarist approach to macro policy is most associated with Margaret Thatcher in the UK and Ronald Reagan in the United States, the reassessment had already begun in the late 1970s by the Labour government in the UK and the Carter administration in the United States. The shift to a greater focus on price stability was almost universal in the 1980s whether by right-of-center or by left-of-center leaders, such as González in Spain or Mitterrand in France (Pomfret 2011, 148).

18. Artis and Taylor (1994) and Hu et al. (2004) provide evidence of the EMS's dampening effect on exchange rate volatility.

19. Despite creation of the euro, there were more independent currencies in Europe at the end of the 1990s than at the start of that decade (Pomfret 2016b). The reason for the breakup of the Yugoslav, Czechoslovak, and Soviet common currency areas was political disintegration followed by fundamental disagreements over monetary policy.

20. *Rewe-Zentral v Bundesmonopolverwaltung für Branntwein* (1979) Case 120 / 78.

21. Corden (1972) extended the partial equilibrium analysis to include economies of scale, which introduced some new considerations but reinforced rather than challenged the conclusions from Figure 2A1.

22. Trade diversion and unevenly shared benefits were the main reason, even though the trigger for collapse might have been more dramatic (Pomfret 2001, 299–300). Tanzania's invasion of Uganda to depose Idi Amin was the final blow to the EAC and the soccer war between Honduras and El Salvador terminated the operation of the CACM. In both cases, however, the economically stronger countries reaped benefits of industrial development, whereas the poorer, less industrialized countries (Tanzania and Uganda in the EAC and Honduras and Nicaragua in the CACM) countries found that they were importing more expensive goods that were often of inferior quality.

23. For example, Mundell (1964) and Petith (1977). Terms of trade effects are more controversial than most other effects because they are zero-sum—that is, improvement

in one country's terms of trade must be matched by deterioration in other countries' terms of trade.

24. Yannopoulos (1990) found some evidence of investment creation in EEC members due to the customs union. The preferential access offered to Mediterranean and ACP partners encouraged investment in export-oriented projects (Pomfret 1986, 63–75).

25. Aitken (1973) measured impacts at the economy-wide level, based primarily on changes in trade shares which could be picking up extraneous drivers. Sapir (2011) sees this as an early application of the gravity model, but use of the gravity model only became widely accepted in the 1990s (see Appendix to Chapter 5).

26. Sapir (2011, 1208) points out their absence in the influential survey of economic integration by Baldwin and Venables (1995). He also emphasizes that recognition of the location effect of integration was widely acknowledged only after the work by Krugman (1991) and Fujita et al. (2001) on economic geography.

3   DEEP INTEGRATION: CREATION OF THE EUROPEAN UNION (1982–1993)

1. In the late 1980s, the EU began levying a common percentage of members' gross national income, and by the 2000s, this had become the dominant revenue source. Meanwhile, the CAP's share of spending has fallen, and the shift toward solidarity payments for poorer regions became more important after 2004, highlighting that the redistribution is from rich to poor rather than to benefit a specific sector.

2. Italy's car quotas were an extreme example dating from the pre-1943 fascist era, grandfathered under the GATT, and apparently in the EEC. They had been even more extreme between 1952 and 1962 when "no Japanese vehicle was allowed to enter the Italian market" (Fauri 1996, 200). The UK and Spain also introduced VERs with Japan in the 1980s. A feature of such measures, which were, of course, not reported to the GATT secretariat, was the lack of transparency as they often went undocumented.

3. The new protectionism was not limited to cars. In November 1982, France required all imported videocassette recorders to be processed through the small customs post in the inland town of Poitiers. After the goods had piled up in the Poitiers parking lot over a few months, Japan agreed to a VER in videocassette recorders.

4. The importance of such nontariff barriers was recognized in the 1973–1979 Tokyo Round of multilateral trade negotiations resulting in the 1979 "Standards Code." This would be strengthened in the Uruguay Round as the Technical Barriers to Trade (TBT) Agreement. Under the agreement, the WTO aims to ensure that technical regulations, standards, and conformity assessment procedures are transparent and nondiscriminatory and do not create unnecessary obstacles to trade.

5. The success of the Single Market program is often ascribed to Delors and key commissioners, especially Lord Cockfield, who became Commissioner for the Single Market (on the roles of Delors and Cockfield, see Grant 1994 and Cockfield 1994). However, they were not alone. Before taking office, Delors toured the capitals of all members to find a central theme for his presidency and decided that strengthening the internal market was the only area in which he could anticipate general support. The June 1985 Milan vote indicated backing for deeper integration from seven of the ten members, which was also the position of the two countries about to join in 1986.

6. The most complete accessible source on the Single Market is the textbook by Jacques Pelkmans (2006 and earlier editions); the arguments are summarized and updated in Pelkmans (2016). More pessimistically, Mariniello et al. (2015) emphasize the length of the road toward a European single market.

7. In 1985, the Court of Justice censured the EU Council and Commission for failure to act in establishing a common transport policy.

8. This type of regulation is quite different to the economic regulation of the CAP or restrictions on car or textile and clothing imports, whose goal was to protect EU producers, or to sectoral management policies in areas characterized by market failure, such as the EU fisheries policy or energy policies. Protectionist economic regulations would diminish in importance after 1995. Meanwhile, risk assessment for food would be centralized in the European Food Safety Agency, which would adopt a value-chain approach "from farm to fork."

9. A separate track is provided by the European system for technical standardization—that is, CENELEC (Comité européen de normalisation électrotechnique, founded in 1973), which is responsible for electrical engineering, ETSI (European Telecommunications Standards Institute, founded in 1988), which is responsible for telecommunications, and CEN (Comité européen de normalisation, founded in 1961), which is responsible for other technical areas. These are not EU institutions, but their standards are national (voluntary) standards for all EEA members.

10. Prime Minister González in Spain and President Mitterrand in France were high-profile examples. Beyond Europe, the most dramatic changes were the liberalization of the New Zealand and Australian economies, which before the 1980s had been the most protectionist and regulated of all high-income countries.

11. Mariniello et al. (2015, 9–10) conclude that the Single Market program helped to maintain the productivity convergence, but its impact was short lived (especially as the EU failed to take as much advantage of the internet revolution after 1995 as the United States did)—that is, they found little evidence of the dynamic gains predicted by the new trade theories of the 1980s and by the heterogeneous-firms literature (e.g., realizing untapped scale economies). However, some researchers identify an impact on competitive behavior (Allen et al. 1998; Veugelers 2004) or on research and development investment (Griffith et al. 2010).

12. The June 1985 Milan summit, where the UK was outvoted, to the fury of the UK prime minister and the embarrassment of some of her senior ministers who recognized the role of her aggressive approach to the budget in creating UK isolation (Young 1998, 325–338; Grant 1994, 71), was the beginning of the end of Thatcher's undisputed leadership of her party, although it took until 1989/1990 before she was ousted. After her September 1988 Bruges speech, when Thatcher said, "We have not successfully rolled back the frontiers of the state in Britain, only to see them re-imposed at a European level," her opposition to European integration became more virulent. Thatcher's position was supported by sections of the tabloid press; on an occasion when she appeared to have resisted progress toward monetary integration, the *Sun* newspaper had the memorable headline, "Up Yours, Delors," which only resonates if the Frenchman's name is mispronounced.

13. The Schengen Information Service maintains a database in Strasbourg that allows police from any Schengen country to access information on whether a suspect has been involved in crimes committed anywhere in the EU.

14. The UK, by opting out of Schengen, placed national control of borders ahead of easier Single Market access. Ireland felt constrained to follow the UK because the open border between Northern Ireland and the Republic of Ireland that had been agreed as part of the Good Friday Agreement ending "the Troubles" was paramount. With the UK outside Schengen, the open border was inconsistent with Ireland being inside Schengen. The Irish border would become a major issue after the UK referendum on Brexit in 2016 (see Section 5.3).

15. The accession of Cyprus to the Schengen Area is complicated by the existence of British sovereign territories on the island (Akrotiri and Dhekelia) and the de facto separate Turkish Republic of Northern Cyprus.

16. Norway and Iceland had been members of the Nordic Passport Union, which predated the Treaty of Rome and provided free access to the Nordic EU members (Denmark, Sweden, and Finland); a formal Schengen cooperation agreement was signed in 1996. Switzerland acceded to the Schengen zone in 2008 and Liechtenstein in 2011. Monaco, San Marino, and Vatican City are de facto in the Schengen zone.

17. The 1994 Financial Instrument for Fisheries Guidance was replaced in 2006 by the European Fisheries Fund for the fiscal period 2007–2013. The fund was not considered successful (*The Effectiveness of European Fisheries Fund Support for Aquaculture,* European Court of Auditors Special Report N°10, Luxembourg, 2014), and it was replaced by the European Maritime and Fisheries Fund for 2014–2020. The general lack of growth in the EU aquaculture sector can be explained, at least partially, by strict environmental regulations, a high bureaucracy burden, and the widespread use of command and control instruments which are usually inflexible and do not incentivize producers to adapt and develop new technology (Guillen et al. 2019).

18. The conclusion and much of the content of this section are based on Pelkmans 2006, chapters 15 and 16. See also Bache 2015.

19. Norway ratified more United Nations Economic Commission for Europe environmental agreements than the EC, whose abstentions were often driven by individual member's objections—for example, UK opposition to an agreement restricting sulfur emissions (McNeill 2020, 42).

20. In soccer, application of EU law (notably in the 1995 Bosman ruling on labor contracts) and prohibition on state subsidies to individual firms (e.g., for stadium construction) have had a major economic impact. However, the monopoly power of the Union of European Football Associations (UEFA) and of national leagues and associations has not been challenged, presumably because fans' desire for a single acknowledged champion creates natural monopolies (Wilson and Pomfret 2014).

21. They were natural monopolies because of the large sunk costs in creating the electricity transmission, railway, or other network. Requirements to offer universal service in mail delivery, telephone connections, gas, or electricity reinforced the need for a monopoly to prevent entrants from skimming off more profitable services such as delivery to urban customers. The digital revolution and the internet undermined both the sunk costs and the universal provision justifications for state-owned monopolies.

22. From a public choice perspective, QMV in the Council reduced the influence of national vested interests as the Single Market was established after 1986, but those interests discovered an alternative route to influence through the Parliament, where logrolling (i.e., deals between parliamentarians to support one another's exemptions) was easier.

23. Findlay et al. (2019) found that some members' service exports became more focused on EU markets between 2002 and 2015 (Denmark, Estonia, France, Ireland, and the UK), but for the others, there was no change in focus or even increased focus on non-EU markets (e.g., Spain).

24. The 1999 Financial Services Action Plan acknowledged the weaknesses of EU financial markets, and some steps to promote integration and better regulation were undertaken in the 2004 directive on financial instruments. The principle, similar to mutual recognition, was that cross-border financial activities would be subject to home-country rules. Although some successes could be pointed out—for example, EU-wide regulations for pension funds—the overall impact in the first decade of the twenty-first century was piecemeal.

25. The harmful tax competition consisted of offering excessive incentives to FDI (Ireland and the Netherlands were the main targets). The fear was of a race to the bottom, which would undermine all EU countries' ability to tax corporations.

26. The Single Market program did include mutual recognition of higher education diplomas, and the Bologna Process, introduced in 1999, established a (voluntary)

common structure for tertiary education that facilitates student mobility and improves transparency in understanding the equivalence of qualifications.

27. Anticompetitive behavior by foreign firms exporting to the EU is covered by antidumping policy, although only a small share of such referrals (i.e., for predatory dumping) would be considered anticompetitive under EU competition policy.

28. The case and Commissioner Kroes's comments were widely reported—for example, "Heineken and Grolsch Fined for Price-Fixing," *Guardian*, 18 April 2007. Although the case illustrated the success of the leniency program in eliciting evidence, it also showed potential for gaming; as whistleblower InBev not only escaped punishment in 2007 but also triggered a large penalty on a major rival.

29. By contrast, after 9/11, the US Congress approved $5 billion in cash aid and up to $10 billion in loan guarantees to help US airlines survive the decline in air travel.

30. However, during the 2020 COVID-19 pandemic, a laxer response saw approval of (temporary?) state aid to Lufthansa, Air France, Austrian Airlines, airBaltic (Latvia), and other national airlines.

31. Although striking in saving taxpayers' money, the policy has loopholes when cities give nontransparent benefits to clubs (e.g., favorable zoning for redevelopment) or when stadiums are built for international events and then sold or leased to clubs (e.g., Manchester City and West Ham United in England); the market does not provide a good guide to a fair price or rent for a large stadium.

32. Bhagwati (1993) led an active debate over whether regional agreements were stepping-stones toward or stumbling blocks hampering multilateral trade liberalization. With hindsight, the debate shed more heat than light and faded as trade was liberalized by completion of the Uruguay Round and as global value chains triggered liberalization via trade facilitation.

33. In his book on global value chains, Baldwin (2016) identifies 1985 as a turning point. He contrasts the success of the Thai car industry with Malaysia's failure to establish an integrated car industry by an outdated import-substitution strategy.

34. A little later, in 1999, Renault took over the Romanian carmaker Dacia.

35. This was documented for the original customs union by Balassa (1966) and Grubel and Lloyd (1975) and confirmed for later enlargements by Sapir (1992) and by Brülhart (2009), who found that new members typically had low intraindustry trade and the measure increased after accession.

36. In large market economies, almost all goods, even at a fine level of disaggregation, are produced.

4 DEEPER AND WIDER: FROM MAASTRICHT TO LISBON (1993–2007)

1. EU law does not allow imprisonment of individuals for anticompetitive behavior (as happens in the United States), so fines are the only punishment beyond public shaming. The post-2000 fines can be compared to earlier fines on cartels such as

welded steel mesh in 1989 (9.5 million ecu), soda ash in 1990 (47 million ecu), steel beams in 1994 (104 million ecu), and the then-record of 280 million ecu in 1994 for the cement cartel (Pelkmans 2006, 252).

2. In their analysis of all decisions reached from 1966 to 2017, Ibáñez Colomo and Kalintiri (2020) find that the nature of the cases chosen by the Commission is consistent with a commitment since the 1990s to a "more economics-based approach," emphasizing that the legal status of a practice should not be based on its form but on its nature, objective purpose, and its actual or potential effects on competition. Especially since 2005, the Commission has focused on cases likely to cause greatest economic harm (e.g., against information technology companies) rather than on more legally clear-cut but less economically significant cases.

3. The European Monetary Institute was established in 1994 as a precursor to the ECB.

4. The debt ratio was over 100 percent in Belgium, Italy, and Greece and over 60 percent in the Netherlands, Spain, Austria, and Germany. The ratio was close to the 60 percent target in Germany, France, and Portugal, and only Finland and Ireland were clearly below the 60 percent threshold.

5. The impact of euro adoption by these smaller EU members depended on the previous exchange rate regime—for example, euro adoption had a strong pro-trade effect on Slovakia, which switched from a floating exchange rate to the euro, but almost no impact on Estonia, which had maintained a fixed exchange rate (Lalinsky and Meriküll 2019). Nguyen and Rondeau (2019) find that trade effects with the three largest eurozone economies (France, Germany, and Italy) were more positive for the three early euro adopters (Slovenia, Slovakia, and Estonia) than for the other new members from Eastern Europe, but Slovenia, Slovakia, and Estonia were also more exposed to spillover shocks from eurozone economics.

6. Roth et al. (2016) provide evidence of popular support for the euro in all EU countries using the euro and lack of support for the euro in other EU members. Trichet (2019), one of the euro's architects, highlights its success. Academic criticism has primarily come from US economists who argued in the 1990s that the common currency was a bad idea, that it would not be adopted, and if it were adopted, disaster would follow. Despite all of these predictions proving false, some continue to argue that the euro is a disaster, essentially on the grounds that countries need to pursue independent macro policies (e.g., Stiglitz 2016). Brunnermeier et al. (2016) argue that the euro is doomed due to conflicting ideologies between France and Germany, although this conflict seems similar to the ideological differences between blue and red US states and no US economist predicts demise of the dollar as the common currency of the United States.

7. For Norway and Iceland, fisheries are a particularly sensitive sector. In the first six months of 2019, Norwegian border guards seized eight tonnes of fish being smuggled out of the country in vehicles driven by fish tourists who exceeded the ten-kilogram catch limits permitted under *turistfisk* rules, some with over one

hundred kilograms of fish already filleted for sale. "Cod Awful: Norway Has Had Its Fillet of Fish-Smugglers," *Economist* (London), 10 August 2019.

8.   Monaco, San Marino, and the Vatican City maintain open or semi-open borders with Schengen member countries.

9.   The CARIFORUM states are Antigua and Barbuda, Bahamas, Barbados, Belize, Cuba, Dominica, Dominican Republic, Grenada, Guyana, Haiti, Jamaica, Saint Kitts and Nevis, Saint Lucia, Saint Vincent and the Grenadines, Suriname, and Trinidad and Tobago. All participating states in CARIFORUM, with the exception of Cuba, are signatories to the ACP-EU Partnership Agreement and the EPA.

10.   The southern group may have been a special case insofar as it is dominated by South Africa, and the smaller economies may have seen the EPA as a counterweight that would reduce their economic dependence on South Africa. In the other groups, the picture was of a few interim agreements provisionally implemented and, more commonly, of EPAs still under negotiation—for example, Nigeria had not signed an agreement by 2019 (Luke and Suominen 2019).

11.   Apart from excluding about one-third of tariff lines, the GSP scheme also has a graduation clause that excludes any partner that supplies over 15 percent of EU imports entering under a tariff line.

12.   Originally created in 1989 as the Poland and Hungary: Assistance for Restructuring their Economies (PHARE) program, PHARE expanded to provide pre-accession assistance to all ten Eastern European countries that joined the EU in 2004 and 2007. Albania, Macedonia, and Bosnia-Herzegovina were also beneficiaries of PHARE until 2000, but starting in 2001, they received financial assistance through the Community Assistance for Reconstruction, Development and Stability in the Balkans program. The Technical Assistance to the Commonwealth of Independent States (TACIS) program was launched in 1991 to help former Soviet republics and Mongolia in their transition to democratic market-oriented economies; TACIS projects were run down during the 2007–2013 EU Financial Perspective.

13.   Schumacher et al. (2018) provides a range of views on the ENP that generally challenge the original design for insufficiently differentiating between the two neighborhoods, for the EU's limited regard of the needs and aspirations of the partners, and for the inconsistent implementation and at best mixed results. The contributors also highlight the shift from economic to security objectives in the revised ENP.

14.   The fifteen non-EU members of the Union for the Mediterranean are Albania, Algeria, Bosnia and Herzegovina, Egypt, Israel, Jordan, Lebanon, Mauritania, Monaco, Montenegro, Morocco, Palestine, Syria (suspended in 2011), Tunisia, and Turkey. Libya is an observer.

15.   Decoupling involves designing subsidies so that they are unrelated to output or farm size and hence do not give farmers an incentive to increase their scale of operations.

16. The MFN tariff on white sugar remained at €419 per metric ton despite the fact that the 2006 sugar reform reduced the support price from €631.9 to €404.4 per ton (Swinbank and Daugbjerg 2017, 85).

17. The Commission uses allocation of the quota part of TRQs as a bargaining chip in negotiations with nonmember countries (https://ec.europa.eu/info/food -farming-fisheries/key-policies/common-agricultural-policy/market-measures /trqs_en).

18. After the recalibration and effective in 2015, direct payments include compulsory and voluntary schemes with a focus on environmental sustainability—for example, the greening payment accounts for 30 percent of decoupled direct aids to farmers and at least 30 percent of the rural development support must be reserved for environmental or climate-related actions.

19. The foreign policy disagreements of the early 1990s and difficulty establishing the positions of permanent president and of high representative for foreign affairs are described in Section 1.6.

20. However, integration into GVCs as car assembly locations provided a specific boost to all of the Visegrád countries. Ambroziak (2017b) provides evidence of differentiation between trade patterns of the Visegrád-Four and the other six Eastern European countries that joined the EU in 2004–2007 which is due to GVC participation. See also Chlopcik (2018) and, on Slovakia, Štofková et al. (2017) and Pavlinek (2016). An exception in the non-Visegrád countries is Romania's Dacia, which became a subsidiary of Renault in 1999 and twenty years later accounted for almost one-tenth of Romania's exports.

21. Some commentators placed these changes in the context of the Commission in 1988 seeking to direct more funding into cohesion policies and to work directly with subnational levels of government (Bache 2015, 252–254). National governments pushed back in 1993 to retain "gatekeeper" control over funds directed to their country. The fresh start after 2007 was related to the financial crises that began in that year and triggered concerns over fiscal stringency, as well as to the Lisbon treaty.

22. In another influential article, Obstfeld and Rogoff (2000) ascribed "The Six Major Puzzles in International Macroeconomics" to home bias in goods and financial markets.

23. Uncertainty has been less studied, but see Büge (2012) and Handley and Limão (2017).

24. Using US data to estimate how much traders are willing to pay for time, Hummels and Schaur (2013) draw the same conclusion that time is most important to participants in GVCs.

25. Pomfret (2014) and Baldwin (2016) review the emergence of GVCs and measurement issues. Inomata (2017) discusses the evolution of trade theory and other approaches to analyze the GVC phenomenon, and in the same volume, Ruta (2017)

assesses the two-way relationship between GVC formation and deep integration trade agreements.

26. Johnson and Noguera (2012, 2017) provide evidence and review the literature. Empirical work has also found that GVC activity has been concentrated in cars, electronics, and apparel, although this appears to be changing, and that even within the regions of concentration, most GVC activity is concentrated in a small number of countries (Pomfret and Sourdin 2018).

27. Andrew Rose (2000) highlighted the role of currency union in reducing trade costs and estimated that a common currency increased bilateral trade between a pair of countries by three times.

28. The Head-Mayer model is medium term because they accept the original distribution of production facilities and analyze only responses to parameter changes rather than fundamental revision of location decisions as will happen in the long term.

29. The other leading GVC sector globally, electronics, has differing structures to car GVCs. In mobile phones, despite early leadership of Nokia, Ericsson, and Apple, modularization has enabled changing leadership; Apple has fallen to fourth behind Samsung, Huawei, and BBK (with brands OPPO and vivo) and just ahead of Xiaomi, and the European brands are far behind. The Chinese firms use Android OS and import key inputs such as processing units from Qualcomm, with foreign firms accounting for about four-fifths of value-added (Xing 2019). Crucially, key modules are competitively provided (e.g., Apple shifted from Sony to Sunwada for its battery pack; Huawei's Kirin CPU is challenging Qualcomm's segment leadership; and Samsung, LG, and JDI dominate OLED displays) and entry into modules is fluid, so information here may be obsolete by the time the book is in print.

5 POST-LISBON CHALLENGES AND RESPONSES (2007–2019)

1. The Balassa–Samuelson effect explains the empirical observation that consumer prices tend to be higher in high-income countries due to greater variation in productivity in the traded goods' sectors than in the nontradable sectors. If productivity in a poor country's traded goods sector rises, then this will lead to increases in the prices of nontraded goods and appreciation of the real exchange rate that will accelerate the increase in real income (Mihaljek and Klau 2003).

2. Emter et al. (2019) argue that the large 2008–2015 decline in cross-border banking in the EU mainly consisted of deleveraging from cross-border loans to other banks, driven by fear of nonperforming loans in foreign EU jurisdictions.

3. How stress tests should be conducted remains a matter for debate. See European Banking Authority, *Discussion Paper on the future changes to the EU-wide stress test,* EBA/DP/2020/01 22 January 2020, available at https://eba.europa.eu/eba -consults-future-eu-wide-stress-test-framework.

4. The path to financial crises due to moral hazard was clear in Bangkok in 1998 and Almaty in 2007, and it is a partial explanation of the 2007–2008 financial crises in the United States, UK, and other countries (Pomfret 2010). In all of those cases, financial institutions made risky real estate loans that yielded high returns during the bubble but eventually led to a collapse of real estate markets and bankruptcy of financial institutions. Many owners and managers of the financial institutions made large incomes during the boom while the costs of the collapse were shared by other people, including the depositors and the taxpayers who underwrote bailouts.

5. In the United States, nontransparent real estate–based securities brought down major investment banks such as Lehman Brothers that went bankrupt in September 2008 and Merrill Lynch, which was absorbed by Bank of America. Gertler and Gilchrist (2018) review the US financial crisis and its impact on macroeconomic theory.

6. In Spain, the lending boom was exacerbated by the large number of local institutions, *cajas,* whose activities were often driven by the interest of local politicians (Santos 2017).

7. Roos (2019, 228) reports that "at the start of the crisis, some 80 percent of Greek bonds were held by only a handful of systemically important banks in the rich Eurozone countries, with the ten biggest bondholders alone accounting for more than half of the country's outstanding obligations in mid-2011, and the 30 biggest accounting for over two-thirds."

8. Between the first quarter of 2010 and the first quarter of 2011, German banks reduced their exposure to Greek debt by $9 billion and French banks by $13.9 billion (Roos 2019, 244).

9. Eurostat data on deficit / GDP ratios, as defined in the Maastricht Treaty, are available at http://ec.europa.eu/eurostat/tgm/table.do?tab=table&init=1&language =en&pcode=teco0127&plugin=1. Latvia had already experienced the largest fall in GDP in 2008, to which it responded with large public expenditure cuts and structural reforms, allowing labor costs to fall 25 percent by the end of 2009, with the result that GDP growth recovered by the third quarter of 2010 (Blanchard et al. 2013). Labor market adjustment costs via high unemployment and underemployment remained substantial until at least 2012 (Lehmann et al. 2020).

10. Lim et al. (2019) provide an account of the evolving balance of power between Greece and Germany in the bailout negotiations of 2010, 2012, and 2015, emphasizing the crucial role of the IMF in providing impartial inputs on the capacity of Greece to service its debt and on the technical feasibility of conditions placed on Greece.

11. "Let the Good Times Roll," *The Economist* (London), 3 August 2019.

12. Countries rarely have an insolvency crisis. Choices exist about the price of haircuts (Cruces and Trebesch 2013) and about enforcing a hard or soft default

(Trebesch and Zabel 2017). Roos (2019) argues that the power of creditors to prevent a hard default has increased substantially in recent years.

13. More detailed information on these procedures can be found on the EU Commission's website at https://ec.europa.eu/info/business-economy-euro/economic-and-fiscal-policy-coordination/eu-economic-governance-monitoring-prevention-correction/european-semester/framework/eus-economic-governance-explained_en.

14. Poland, Hungary, and Sweden opted out of the Fiscal Compact, and Croatia and the Czech Republic, which did not sign the TCSG until 2018, are not bound by the Fiscal Compact.

15. The treaty defines a balanced budget as a general budget deficit not exceeding 3.0 percent of GDP and a structural deficit not exceeding a country-specific medium-term budgetary objective that at most can be set to 0.5 percent of GDP for states with a debt / GDP ratio over 60 percent or at most 1.0 percent of GDP for states with debt levels under 60 percent of GDP. If a state suffers a significant recession, it will be exempted from the requirement to deliver a fiscal correction for as long as the recession lasts.

16. The ratio of nonperforming loans to total loans of "significant" banks declined substantially between 2014 and 2018, although it is difficult to separate the impact of better supervision and improved economic conditions. However, the ratios differed substantially between member countries, with Greece having over 30 percent of loans nonperforming in 2018, followed by Cyprus and Latvia with just under 10 percent (Angeloni 2020, 7–9). Smaller financial institutions are supervised by national authorities, although the ultimate authority of the ECB is acknowledged.

17. The maximum coverage has been agreed at €100,000, but introduction of the scheme has been delayed by concerns over mutualization. The deposit insurance scheme like the SRB will be funded by levies on all banks in order to reduce taxpayers' liability. This is inefficient because the costs of bailing out inefficient banks will be shared by efficient banks who will recoup these costs by increasing charges to their customers.

18. See "Why the Euro Zone Hasn't Seen More Cross-Border Bank Mergers," *The Economist,* 14 July 2018. Fears that removal of restrictions on capital mobility would allow EU citizens to shop around for retail banking services, exacerbating the moral hazard problem as the banks making the riskiest high-interest loans would be able to offer the biggest incentives to depositors in the Single Market, have not been realized.

19. Bankers will also resist pressure to hold a higher percentage of Tier 1 (i.e., least risky) assets because such assets will yield lower returns than riskier assets. Too great a focus on reducing risk can reduce economic dynamism (Table 5.1). The ECB appeared to require increases in Tier 1 capital ratios in 2014–2016, after it started conducting stress tests, and in 2017–2018 deemphasized the importance of further increases (Angeloni 2020, 4–6).

20. In a detailed account of the Spanish banking crisis of 2008–2012, Santos (2017) emphasizes the role of local financial institutions whose political connections inhibited focus on profitability. The crisis was only resolved, in July 2012, by obtaining EU bailout funds.

21. SBBS will enjoy the same regulatory treatment as national eurozone sovereign bonds in terms of capital requirements, the eligibility for liquidity coverage and collateral, and so forth. Further areas under discussion include strengthening banking regulation via the European Securities and Market Authority (ESMA) to oversee concentration of lending in government securities and a common approach to nonperforming loans.

22. Although Mundell was generally in favor of currency union, and specifically of European currency union, the optimum currency area literature has been dominated by macroeconomists who emphasize the costs of lost monetary policy independence (Pomfret 2005). Krugman (1993) was a prominent dissident in emphasizing the potentially large microeconomic benefits of a common currency.

23. For magnitudes of cross-border labor mobility within the enlarged EU, see Heinz and Ward-Warmedinger (2006). Evidence on increased labor mobility over time is provided by Dao et al. (2014), Beyer and Smets (2015), and Arpaia et al. (2016).

24. "The negative effect of skilled immigration on the hiring of natives in 'good job' sectors that we do find is small and therefore is not likely to be a major driver of social mobility. This paper has demonstrated theoretically that skilled immigration may have both negative and positive effects on native training and hiring. These may have broadly offset each other in the empirical estimation" (Mountford and Wadsworth 2019, 25). Altorjai (2013) provides evidence that the overqualification of migrants to the UK was especially pronounced among post-2004 Eastern Europeans, and it is explained by self-selection rather than policies (Longhi and Rokicka 2012).

25. With data on fourteen eurozone countries (excluding the three Baltic countries, Cyprus, and Malta due to data weaknesses) as migration destinations between 1999 and 2015, Huart and Tchakpalla (2019) find, after the start of crises in 2008, evidence of net inflows into the countries least affected by crises (Germany, Austria, and Luxembourg) and net outflows from Greece, Portugal, and Ireland; for Ireland, the flows were reversed in 2015, and Spain experienced no net outflow of citizens but net outflow of foreigners.

26. The European Agency for the Management of Operational Cooperation at the External Borders (commonly known by its French acronym, Frontex) was proposed in 2004 and established in 2005 with headquarters in Warsaw.

27. In a brief episode in 2015–2016, the Russia-Finland border became a crisis point as thousands of refugees from Afghanistan and the Middle East obtained Russian visas, flew to Russia, and then entered Finland. Russian authorities issued the visas, ignored the transients, and blocked their return until President Putin intervened to cut off the flow.

28. The Dublin Convention was signed in 1990 and came into force between September 1997 and January 1998 for the EU15. Norway and Iceland signed an agreement with the EU in 2001 to apply the provisions of the convention in their territories. The convention was revised in 2003 (Dublin II) and in 2013 (Dublin III) and extended to cover Switzerland in 2008 and Liechtenstein in 2011.

29. Such procedures have created the phenomenon of "invisible migrants" who avoid registering in the first country of entry into the Schengen zone because they prefer to be accepted elsewhere. Under the Dublin Convention, refugees registering in Italy can be sent back to Italy if they move to another EU member. In 2018, 6,351 *dublinati* were returned to Italy, although Italy was asked to take many more; after six months, the refugees become the responsibility of their new host state, which gave Italy an incentive to delay processing of requests. One consequence of such practices is that data on refugees are a poor proxy for reality ("Turning into a Trickle," *Economist* (London), 10 August 2019).

30. In 2019, the number had fallen to 123,663 informal migrants arriving by sea in Italy, Cyprus, and Malta and by land and sea in Greece and Spain.

31. Poland and Hungary opposed creation of the Border and Coast Guard with armed EU forces patrolling the external borders as an infringement on sovereignty.

32. Frontex resources were clearly inadequate to patrol the Mediterranean Sea and intercept immigrants. In November 2014, Frontex launched Operation Triton under Italian control and with voluntary contributions of equipment and staff from fifteen other EEA members (Croatia, Iceland, Finland, Norway, Sweden, Germany, the Netherlands, France, Spain, Portugal, Austria, Romania, Poland, Lithuania, and Malta) and Switzerland. In February 2018, Operation Triton was replaced by Operation Themis. Operation Themis also has a significant security component, including collection of intelligence and other steps aimed at detecting foreign fighters and other terrorist threats at the external borders. The EU estimated that over 528,653 lives had been saved between 2015 and 2020, and more than 12,677 people have died or went missing while trying to cross the Mediterranean (cited at https://www.consilium.europa.eu/en/policies/migratory-pressures/sea-criminal-networks/).

33. The antimigrant sentiment appears to have been directed against immigrants from outside the EU at least as much as against European migrants. However, this sentiment still justified an anti-EU vote because even outside Schengen, the UK's control over its borders may be limited by the EU Single Market in labor.

34. The UK also showed little regard for a common EU front when it actively supported the United States in the 2003 Iraq War, in contrast to France and Germany who opposed the use of force. Although other EU members supported the US position, only the UK, Australia, and Poland provided troops for the initial invasion of Iraq.

35. Citizens of OCTs are EU citizens, but their territories do not belong to the EU. All OCTs are dependencies or semiautonomous territories of France, the Neth-

erlands, the UK (until 2020), or Denmark enjoying association arrangements (special relations) with the EU.

36. *The United Kingdom's Exit from and New Partnership with the European Union White Paper,* available at https://www.gov.uk/government/publications/the-united -kingdoms-exit-from-and-new-partnership-with-the-european-union-white -paper.

37. Laffan (2019) emphasizes the vacuity of May's mantra "Brexit means Brexit" and the inability of UK leaders to accept that the *acquis communautaire* was nonnegotiable for countries leaving or joining the EU—that is, it was not possible to cherry-pick parts of the Single Market, which meant that May's red line left the UK as a third country with no special status in the EU market.

38. The bill was estimated at £39 billion. The number declined as the pre-Brexit period was extended and the UK remained an EU member into 2020. The present value of more distant obligations depended on interest rates.

39. Moreover, the UK missed out on further benefits of EU membership by failing to take advantage of deeper integration. Using a synthetic control, Saia (2017) estimated that if the UK had adopted the euro in 1999, aggregate trade flows between the UK and euro area countries would have been 17 percent higher and that euro adoption would also have led to a significant increase in British trade flows with non-euro countries—for example, UK trade with the United States would have been about 12 percent higher had the UK joined the euro, suggesting that trade diversion was less of a problem with deep integration than with a simpler customs union (see the Appendix to Chapter 6 for explanation of the synthetic control method; Saia's results are consistent with the GDP outcomes reported there).

40. Second best because Brexit will remove some distortions (e.g., tariffs on imports of some goods from third countries may fall) and introduce new distortions (e.g., trade costs with the EU27 will increase). First best would be the (unrealistic) world of distortion-free trade.

41. Only airlines majority owned by EU nationals can operate intra-EU flights.

42. The top five US investment banks accounted for a large part. In 2014, Goldman Sachs, JP Morgan, Citi, Morgan Stanley, and Bank of America Merrill Lynch held 92 percent of their EU assets and employed 89 percent of their EU labor force (26,697 out of 29,909) in London (Schoenmaker 2017, 127).

43. Drawing on the estimate by Born et al. (2019) of Brexit's impact on labor productivity, Crafts (2016) concluded that Brexit added to the UK's unprecedently bad productivity performance in the decade up to 2018, but its contribution to the negative performance was far smaller than that of the financial crisis and of the slowdown in ICT's contribution to productivity.

44. For more details and discussion of the synthetic control method, see the Appendix to Chapter 6. Synthetic Britain in Born et al. (2019) contains unsurprisingly high

weights to Canada and the United States but also, perhaps surprisingly, to Japan and Hungary. In the VoxEU update of their results, they estimate that in the first quarter of 2019, Brexit was costing the UK, relative to its synthetic counterfactual, £350 million a week.

45. Anderson and Wittwer (2018) analyze the impact of various post-Brexit trade regimes on wine trade, which is important because the UK is the largest wine importer and several EU27 countries are major wine exporters. However, the analysis is more significant for the consequence for nonmember countries such as Australia or Chile than for European consumers or producers, and changes in UK excise taxes are likely to have greater impact than trade policy.

46. This is consistent with the results in Bruno et al. (2017) who estimate with both synthetic counterfactuals and a gravity model that EU membership increases foreign direct investment by about 30 percent. Campos (2019a, 14–17) reviews the literature on foreign direct investment and Brexit.

47. Estimated effects also depend on the assumed post-Brexit trade relations. The pro-Brexit group Economists for Free Trade typically calculated the effects with the UK unilaterally cutting all trade barriers to zero, which leads to larger economic gains but was shown to be politically unrealistic when the UK published its new tariff schedule in May 2020.

48. Using the synthetic control method, Monastiriotis and Zilic (2019) found that the separation of Montenegro from Serbia had negative impact on the smaller country but no significant impact on the larger country.

49. The negotiated solution to the Irish border with a special customs regime for Northern Ireland seems fragile (O'Rourke 2019). Given the strong referendum vote for *remain* in Scotland, Brexit could also trigger Scottish independence and further disintegration of the UK.

50. As with any infrastructure investment, positive effects depend on the coexistence of other conditions favorable to growth (Crescenzi and Rodríguez-Pose 2012; Crescenzi et al. 2016). With respect to creating local and spillover benefits, road corridors compare favorably to high-speed rail lines that widen income differentials between nodes and locations that are passed by and to ICT that helps the region where investment is located but has few spillover effects.

51. The coalition's membership is fluid, but as of the December 2018 summit, it included Argentina, Canada, Colombia, Costa Rica, Denmark, Ethiopia, EU Commission, Fiji, Finland, France, Germany, Grenada, Italy, Jamaica, Luxembourg, Macedonia, Marshall Islands, Mexico, Monaco, the Netherlands, New Zealand, Norway, Portugal, Saint Lucia, Spain, Sweden, and the UK. The Marshall Islands are often credited with leadership of the group, but the EU and its largest member countries are clearly the largest economies in the group.

52. A particular problem for Kosovo is that five EU members (Spain, Slovakia, Cyprus, Romania, and Greece) do not recognize its independence from Serbia. At

the 2018 EU–Western Balkans summit, in order to preempt dispute, the Western Balkan participants were referred to as partners rather than countries.

53. Markovic Khaze (2018) analyzes enlargement fatigue and relates EU reluctance to expand to the rise of Russian and Chinese influence in southeast Europe, while Szolucha (2010) pointed out that enlargement fatigue was a feature of earlier enlargement episodes. Petrovic (2020) and Zhelyazkova et al. (2019) emphasize the combination of long-term consequences of rule in the 1990s by illiberal political leaders who were uninterested in post-Communist reform and lack of genuine interest in enlargement by some EU members in the 2010s, reinforced by continual tightening of the Copenhagen conditions for membership and lack of clarity in the revised conditions that made them difficult to meet.

54. The EU–Western Balkans summit is distinct from the Western Balkans summits that take place under the Berlin Process, a diplomatic initiative that Chancellor Merkel launched in 2014 and that brings together the six Western Balkans countries, like-minded EU partners, and representatives of the EU institutions to work together to support security, stability, and prosperity in the region. Following Berlin (2014), the Western Balkans summits have been held in Vienna (2015), Paris (2016) Trieste (2017), London (2018), and Poznan (2019).

55. Relations between Russia and EU members were positive under Boris Yeltsin's post–Cold War presidency, although a split among the Soviet successor states between the GUAM countries (Georgia, Ukraine, Azerbaijan, and Moldova) and those closer to Russia (Belarus, Kazakhstan, Kyrgyzstan, and Tajikistan) was soon apparent. President Vladimir Putin's position appeared to change around 2007 from viewing the North Atlantic Treaty Organization as bad and the EU as irrelevant to seeing both organizations as bad. The four CIS countries with warmest relations to the West (the GUAM countries) are the only post-Soviet states that have parts of their territory ruled by outlaw governments supported by Russia but recognized by few, if any, other countries. Shortly after Georgia ratified the DCFTA with the EU, Russia signed a Treaty on Alliance and Strategic Partnership with Abkhazia.

56. The Eurasian customs union was established by Belarus, Kazakhstan, and Russia in 2010. In 2014, the three countries signed a treaty establishing the EAEU, which took effect on 1 January 2015. Armenia and the Kyrgyz Republic joined in 2015. The core objective of the EAEU is free movement of goods, capital, services, and people within the single market. Sanctions imposed by the EU on Russia in July 2014 and strengthened in September 2014 undermined the EAEU's common external trade policy as sanctions did not apply to Belarus or Kazakhstan which could be used as entry points to the Russian market. Other EAEU members were not happy when Russia imposed countersanctions on the EU without discussion with fellow EAEU members. There were also discrepancies between the common external tariff and WTO commitments of Armenia and the Kyrgyz Republic.

57. These numbers are small compared to maritime freight. A single ship can carry twenty thousand containers. No more than 5 percent of all freight between Europe and Asia goes by rail. However, goods for which rail is preferred are higher value and more tech intensive than the bulk goods transported by sea.

58. The Commission's interest can be traced back to the 2007–2012 RETRACK project, which aimed to induce a modal shift of freight traffic to rail; RETRACK's focus was on developing a high-quality commercially sustainable rail freight corridor from the North Sea to the Black Sea (Rotterdam-Constanza), but it also considered prospects for establishing "Eurasian land bridges" to China.

59. European Union Global Strategy (2016), *Shared Vision, Common Action: A Stronger Europe—A Global Strategy for the European Union's Foreign and Security Policy*, available at http://eeas.europa.eu/archives/docs/top_stories/pdf/eugs_review _web.pdf. The 2018 Joint Communication on Connecting Europe and Asia recognized the significance of looking east and included specific proposals: European Commission, *Connecting Europe and Asia—Building Blocks for an EU Strategy*. Joint Communication to the European Parliament, the Council, the European Economic and Social Committee, the Committee of the Regions and the European Investment Bank JOIN(2018) 31 final, High Representative of the Union for Foreign Affairs and Security Policy, Brussels.

60. Diplomatic relations between the EU and the People's Republic of China were established in 1975. A trade agreement was signed in 1978 and replaced by a Trade and Economic Cooperation Agreement in 1985. An annual EU-China summit was initiated in 1998.

61. Reinhart (2019) argues that Chinese capital flowing to countries in financial difficulties is a reason why sovereign defaults were rare in the 2010s even though circumstances might have been conducive to default; Greece is a prime example.

62. In Warsaw (2012), Bucharest (2013), Belgrade (2014), Suzhou (2015), Riga (2016), Budapest (2017), Sofia (2018), and Dubrovnik (2019).

63. According to Premier Li Keqiang at the 2018 16 + 1 summit, China's cumulative investment in the sixteen Central and Eastern European countries is nearly $10 billion (mostly loans), whereas the Central and Eastern European countries have invested $1.4 billion in China.

64. There were also concerns that Chinese exports were displacing intra-EU trade. Stanojevic et al. (2020) find that Chinese exports of electronics and machinery products to Eastern Europe in 2006–2017 was complementary to EU15 exports to new members, but there was some crowding out of EU15 textiles and furniture.

65. Germany had been without pandas since 2012, when Bao Bao died in Berlin.

66. This episode is analyzed by Jakóbowski and Popławski (2018), who question whether China was seeking better relations with the EU or just with Germany— that is, continuing to play a divisive game with the EU.

67. China includes the Landbridge in its Belt and Road Initiative, although the Landbridge preceded the BRI by several years and has largely expanded through decentralized initiatives by individual Chinese and European cities and companies. The EU-China Connectivity Platform was established in 2015 to explore opportunities for cooperation in the area of transport with a view to enhance synergies between the EU's approach to connectivity, including TEN-T and China's BRI. Expert groups under the aegis of the Connectivity Platform have continued to meet through the ups and downs of diplomatic relations.

68. The investment issue arose in the context of the EU-Singapore trade agreement for which negotiations were completed in 2016 but whose ratification was delayed by appeals to the EU Court that investment articles in the agreement were outside the EU's jurisdiction. The EU-Singapore trade and investment protection agreements were eventually signed on 19 October 2018, and the European Parliament gave its consent on 13 February 2019. After the member states endorsed the trade agreement, it entered into force on 21 November 2019. However, the investment protection agreement will only enter into force after ratification by all member states according to their own national procedures.

69. It can be difficult to keep track, even on the regularly updated EU website (http://ec.europa.eu/trade/policy/countries-and-regions/negotiations-and -agreements/#_in-place), because of differences between the date when negotiations are completed and the dates when the agreement is signed, ratified, and implemented.

70. Venezuela joined Mercosur (Mercado Común del Sur or Southern Common Market) in 2012 but was suspended from membership in 2017. The protocol of accession of Bolivia to Mercosur was signed in 2012, but approval is pending in all Mercosur countries. After the October 2019 election in Argentina, the new president expressed doubts that he would ratify the EU-Mercosur agreement.

71. Falkenberg (2019) has a different perspective, viewing EU trade policy since the mid-1990s as a rush to bilateralism initially triggered by the North American Free Trade Agreement, after which EU exporters lost market share in the United States and Canada to Mexican exporters. The EU began negotiations with Latin American countries, the United States, and Canada, and each completed negotiation added complexity to trade rules, eroding the benefits of multilateralism. Agreements with Korea and Japan took bilateralism global.

72. Australia, for example, refuses to include human rights in trade agreements and is skeptical about climate change.

73. Use of environmental clauses as protection devices has worked both ways. The EU-Canada agreement excludes trade in used cars, intended to guard Canadians against pollution from imported cars incorporating laxer emissions standards but also reducing competition for the Canadian car industry.

74. The Armington assumption is that products traded internationally are differentiated by country of origin. Assuming that the elasticity of substitution between products from any pair of countries is finite generates smaller and more realistic responses of trade to price changes than would result from models assuming homogeneous products that are perfect substitutes (in contrast to Figure 2A1 in which *all* imports come from the world's least-cost suppliers or from the preferred trade partner). For a review of CGE modeling with focus on the use of the Armington assumption, see Dixon et al. (2016, 2018).

75. Arthi et al. (2020) illustrate the issue by applying a CGE model to the impact of Indian tariff increases during the 1920s and 1930s. Because the increased tariffs on imports from the UK were lower than India's tariffs on imports from Japan, the UK benefited from the increased trade barriers—that is, the positive trade diversion outweighed the negative trade destruction.

76. Escalating tensions between Malaysia and the EU over palm oil led to suspension in April 2020 of EU-Malaysia trade negotiations that would leave Malaysia behind other Association of Southeast Asian Nation countries such as Singapore and Vietnam who have already concluding EU agreements while Thailand and the Philippines move forward with negotiations (Varkkey 2020).

77. This result was criticized in part because the common currency countries in Rose's study tended to be either dependencies or microstates and hence atypical, but the positive relationship between common currency and bilateral trade is robust to other specifications even if the size of the effect is less than in Rose's initial study.

78. The same challenge arises in cross-country growth econometrics in, for example, explaining differences in growth rates in transition economies of Eastern Europe and the former Soviet Union during the 1990s. Differences may be due to history (length of time under Communism), geography (distance from Western Europe), or human capital (share of the population with university degrees, engineering qualifications, etc.) any of which may be established by including an appropriate variable. However, each variable is picking up the same phenomenon; Central and Eastern European countries outperformed Southeastern European countries that have done better than the western former Soviet Union and the Caucasus and the Central Asian countries ranked last (Pomfret 2002, chapter 4.2).

79. The six-digit level is popular because it often matches popular conceptions of a product or an industry, although many six-digit categories are heterogeneous. Some statistical authorities report even more detailed breakdown to the eight- or ten-digit level, as described in the next paragraph.

80. There is also a counting issue insofar as some preferential tariffs may be available in principle but in practice are underutilized due to the extra administrative costs of utilizing the preferential treatment.

6   THE EUROPEAN UNION IN THE 2020S

1. Other heads of the Commission have had a high profile in pushing specific goals—for example, Roy Jenkins on the European Monetary System in 1978 and, especially, Jacques Delors on the Single Market, but the Juncker Commission has acted as an EU government on a range of issues.

2. Tocci (2015) criticized Ashton for responding to events and praised Mogherini for working in 2014–2015 on the 2016 EU global strategy. However, events in the southern and eastern neighborhoods were already causing division, and Brexit and the outcome of the 2016 US election absorbed EU members' attention for the remainder of the decade.

3. In acknowledgment of failure to anticipate the Arab Spring or Russian annexation of Crimea, in 2014 the European External Action Service instituted an early warning system to identify countries at risk over a four-year time horizon. The difficulty of anticipation and prioritization can be seen in the International Crisis Group's December 2019 briefing, *Seven Priorities for the New EU High Representative,* at https://www.crisisgroup.org/europe-central-asia/sb003 -seven-priorities-new-eu-high-representative; the seven priority countries— Sudan, Libya, Iran, Venezuela, Bolivia, Syria, and Ethiopia—are different from the areas prioritized in this chapter.

4. Lagarde wanted governments to do more and urged eurozone members to consider issuing a jointly guaranteed, one-off "corona bond," but the response from the richer EU members was unenthusiastic.

5. However, there was considerable variation in national responses with Sweden, and to a lesser extent the Netherlands, adopting much lighter restrictions on movement or social distancing.

6. Reported in "Swiss Ventilator Company Inundated by Demand due to COVID-19," posted on 17 March 2020 at https://www.swissinfo.ch/eng/business/hamilton -medical-_swiss-ventilator-company-inundated-by-demand-due-to-covid-19 /45622132#.XnHSLbMfgVw.twitter.

7. Although generally underreported by the media, this happened to an admirable extent. The virus's genomic sequence was published on 12 January by Chinese researchers who created the first genetic test for COVID-19 a few days later; the results were immediately made public for the global research community. By 20 March, over six hundred papers on COVID-19 had been posted by researchers worldwide on the prepublication site medrxiv. Such sharing of preliminary research results helps evaluation of drugs or of other measures to address the pandemic before the normally lengthy approval processes. Research outcomes are intrinsically unknown and breakthroughs could occur anywhere, so result sharing trumps any boasts by national politicians that the best research is being done in their universities.

8. The frugal four insisted on national governments having a right to object to a recipient government's spending plans, delaying and complicating the grant, but this is a brake with a three-month limit rather than a veto.

9. Some of the RRF spending will be financed by cutting funding for other of the forty programs covered by the Multilateral Financial Framework. Reduced commitments to future-oriented EU programs—for example, on the environment and on research and development promotion—were agreed at the July summit, but the numbers were small relative to the size of the Next-Generation EU package and the larger budget areas of regional and rural assistance were left intact.

10. The carbon and digital taxes may be redesigned to fall primarily on foreigners, which could make them more attractive to member governments but unpopular with nonmembers. A carbon tariff on climate-unfriendly imports may be hard to enforce and would face challenges at the WTO. A levy on EU revenues of tech firms would face strong US opposition (as has happened to French proposals at the national level and in Organisation for Economic Co-operation and Development discussion of such a tax).

11. The Czech Republic, Slovakia, Hungary, and Romania voted against the original decision in September 2015, and they were joined by Poland after the Law and Justice Party won the October 2015 election.

12. In early 2020, according to the United Nations High Commissioner for Refugees, Turkey was hosting 3.5 million refugees from Syria and 300,000 from elsewhere. The Turkish government claimed that funding under the 2016 agreement with the EU was inadequate. An EU-Turkey accord was reached in March 2020, but the potential for future discord remained.

13. EEA members are part of the Single Market, accepting free movement of goods, services, capital and labor, and associated EU legislation. They also contribute to the EU budget—for example, Norway's payment per capita was estimated at 83 percent of the UK's current net payment to the EU in 2017. EEA countries set their own external tariffs, which requires border barriers with the EU, and higher trade costs for those countries within the Single Market.

14. A sign of spats to come arose when, following Brexit, the UK closed down the EU office in Belfast. The UK turned down the EU request to have a permanent office in Belfast in order to monitor whether the UK is keeping its commitments under the Irish protocol. The episode did not help the negotiations as EU leaders were left with a sense that the Johnson government signs agreements without serious intentions of following them through.

15. In the aftermath of the 2016 referendum, free-market Brexiteers saw an opportunity to remove EU regulations and tariffs. However, the new UK Global Tariff (UKGT) announced in May 2020 to take effect in 2021 (available at https://www .gov.uk/guidance/uk-tariffs-from-1-january-2021) clearly reflected the influence of myriad vested interests seeking to retain or even increase protection from imports. The government's claim that "the UKGT ensures that 60% of trade will come into the UK tariff free from January 2021" implicitly acknowledged that two-fifths of UK imports will be subject to tariffs, and many tariff lines differ from the EU's common external tariff.

16. Graziano et al. (2020) estimate substantial trade losses due to uncertainty about future relations between the UK and a large range of trade partners.

17. In July 2020, the UK government announced a £705 million funding package for border infrastructure, jobs, and technology to ensure border systems would be fully operational after the end of the transition period. The funding consists of £470 million to build port and inland infrastructure needed to ensure compliance with new customs procedures and controls and £235 million investment in staffing and IT systems, including £10 million to recruit around five hundred more Border Force personnel. Apart from spending on new facilities and customs officials, the UK government has provided £84 million in start-up assistance for the customs intermediary sector.

18. Pelkmans (2019, 13–15) notes that even with its shortcomings, EU service market integration goes well beyond the WTO's General Agreement on Trade in Services (GATS) or bilateral agreements such as CETA, because the core Single Market features include free movement of capital and labor and the right of establishment anywhere in the EU. Pelkmans (2019, 33–37) documents resistance to lowering the restrictiveness of laws on professional qualifications and conduct, and "the enormous regulatory discrepancies between the Member States."

19. In its 2018 report, *A European Retail Sector Fit for the 21st Century,* the Commission listed benefits from reduced regulatory barriers and showed by a Retail Restrictiveness Index that progress toward such reduction has been slow, with large variations across EU countries in restrictiveness of both establishment and operation of retail businesses. Zoning and other local planning rules are especially important for restricting operation of retail businesses.

20. Technological change has often moved faster than the EU response. After years of jurisdictional uncertainty, the European Court ruled in June 2019 that Skype is a telecommunications company and must comply with EU telecommunications regulations.

21. The Flixbus model proved to be more successful than the earlier Eurolines model of a cooperative arrangement among long-distance bus companies providing coordinated low-cost transport.

22. Barone and Cingano (2011) use sectoral data to show the connection between service regulation and growth. Nordås and Rouzet (2015) show that greater services trade restrictiveness harms both imports and exports of services. Lodefalk (2014, 2017) analyzes servicification.

23. Papi et al. (2018) use a different metric to show pre-2007 convergence. In 1995, the per capita income of Central, Eastern, and southeastern European countries was 29 percent that of Germany, and in 2007, it was 44 percent. However, after the crises, per capita income gaps converged very slowly, and some countries' income levels actually fell relative to Germany's.

24. Joint Communication to the European Parliament, the European Council, and the Council, *EU-China—A Strategic Outlook,* High Representative of the Union for Foreign Affairs and Security Policy, Strasbourg, 12 March 2019.

25. Similar internal divisions apply to relations with Russia. Although there was agreement on imposing sanctions after the annexation of Crimea in 2014, some countries or groups within EU countries seek improvement of EU-Russia bilateral relations without preconditions about Ukraine. As with China, some economic relations with Russia—for example, the rail Landbridge—continue to flourish despite dire political relations.

26. The first was Turkey, perhaps related to deteriorating bilateral relationships reflected also in the February 2020 refugee crisis described in Section 6.2. Youngs (2020) argues that the 2010s saw a steady shift toward a realpolitik of defending more narrowly defined EU economic interests through bilateral deals with emphasis on reciprocity, stricter screening of foreign investment, and questioning restrictions on state aid (which was activated during the COVID-19 crisis)—a shift from win-win liberalism to competitive interdependence.

27. Dubbed the Axis of Nice by Alan Beattie ("Canada and the EU Build the Transatlantic Axis of Nice," *Financial Times* [London], 26 July 2019). EU-Canada relations have been historically good (in stark contrast to EU-Australia relations in the last third of the twentieth century) but distant because Canada's economic and political relations are dominated by the United States. Dealing with the Trump presidency encouraged Canada to diversify relations after 2017.

28. According to Drysdale and Pangestu (2019), Indonesia and Australia have been considering similar options for some time. Japan is the obvious big candidate to join the Axis of Nice, but the official Japanese position has been to favor current-style investor-state dispute settlement processes.

29. In April 2020, the EU announced a package of €15.6 billion of emergency support for developing countries hit by the COVID-19 pandemic, including €3 billion of loans earmarked for macroeconomic assistance to ten neighbors (Ukraine, Georgia, Moldova, Jordan, Tunisia, and five Balkan states).

30. The principal consistent finding in the growth econometrics literature was of conditional convergence (Barro 2015), and there is evidence of this for the original Six (Ben-David 1993). After the enlargements of the 1980s and the 2000s, it is difficult to distinguish whether convergence was a consequence of integration or due to assistance from the EU budget (Sapir 2011, 1215).

31. Campos et al. perform a battery of robustness tests that reinforce the general conclusions but suggest that the 1973 cohort results may be most prone to inexactness. This could be because the donor countries entering into synthetic Denmark, Ireland, or UK may have had diverse experiences in the tumultuous economic conditions of the 1970s that would bias the results.

References

Adebahr, Cornelius. 2018. "Europe and Iran: The Economic and Commercial Dimensions of a Strained Relationship." IAI Papers 18/24, Istituto Affari Internazionali, Rome.

Ademmer, Esther, Toman Barsbai, Matthias Lücke, and Tobias Stöhr. 2015. "30 Years of Schengen: Internal Blessing, External Curse." Kiel Policy Brief 88, Institut für Weltwirtschaft, Kiel, Germany.

Aitken, Norman. 1973. "The Effect of the EEC and EFTA on European Trade: A Temporal Cross-Section Analysis." *American Economic Review* 63 (5): 881–892.

Allen, Chris, Michael Gasiorek, Alasdair Smith, Harry Flam, and Peter Birch Sørensen. 1998. "The Competition Effects of the Single Market in Europe." *Economic Policy* 27:441–486.

Altorjai, Szilvia. 2013. "Over-Qualification of Immigrants in the UK." ISER Working Paper 2013-11, Institute for Social and Economic Research, University of Essex, Colchester, UK.

Ambroziak, Łukasz. 2017a. "Gross versus Value Added Net Trade: The Case of the Central and Eastern European Countries (CEECs)." Poster presented at the 30th International Academic Conference, Venice International University, Venice, 27 April. https://www.researchgate.net/publication/325263762 _Gross_versus_value_added_net_trade_the_case_of_the_Central_and _Eastern_European_countries_CEECs.

Ambroziak, Łukasz. 2017b. "Trade in Value Added: The Case of the Central and Eastern European Countries." *World Academy of Science, Engineering and Technology International Journal of Economics and Management Engineering* 11 (4).

Anderson, James. 2010. "The Gravity Model." NBER Working Paper 16576, National Bureau of Economic Research, Cambridge, MA.

Anderson, James. 2011. "The Gravity Model." *Annual Review of Economics* 3:133–160.

Anderson, James, and Eric van Wincoop. 2003. "Gravity with Gravitas: A Solution to the Border Puzzle." *American Economic Review* 93 (1): 170–192.

Anderson, James, and Eric van Wincoop. 2004. "Trade Costs." *Journal of Economic Literature* 42 (3): 691–751.

Anderson, Kym, and Glyn Wittwer. 2018. "Cumulative Effects of Brexit and Other UK and EU-27 Bilateral Free-Trade Agreements on the World's Wine Markets." *World Economy* 41 (11): 2883–2894.

Angeloni, Ignazio. 2020. *Beyond the Pandemic: Reviving Europe's Banking Union*. London: CEPR Press.

Arpaia, Alfonso, Aron Kiss, Balazs Palvolgyi, and Alessandro Turrini. 2016. "Labour Mobility and Labour Market Adjustment in the EU." *IZA Journal of Migration* 5 (1): 1–21.

Arpaia, Alfonso, Aron Kiss, Balazs Palvolgyi, and Alessandro Turrini. 2018. "The Effects of European Integration and the Business Cycle on Migration Flows: A Gravity Analysis." *Review of World Economics* (*Weltwirtschaftliches Archiv*) 154 (4): 815–834.

Arthi, Vellore, Markus Lampe, Ashwin Nair, and Kevin O'Rourke. 2020. "The Impact of Interwar Protection: Evidence from India." NYU Abu Dhabi Working Paper #0043, New York University, Abu Dhabi, UAE.

Artis, Michael, and Mark Taylor. 1994. "The Stabilizing Effect of the ERM on Exchange Rates and Interest Rates." *IMF Staff Papers* 41 (1): 123–148.

Åslund, Anders. 2018. "What Happened to the Economic Convergence of Central and Eastern Europe after the Global Financial Crisis?" *Comparative Economic Studies* 60 (2): 254–270.

Bache, Ian. 2015. "Cohesion Policy: A New Direction for New Times." In *Policy-Making in the European Union*, 7th ed., edited by Helen Wallace, Mark Pollack, and Alasdair Young, 243–262. Oxford: Oxford University Press.

Badinger, Harald. 2005. "Growth Effects of Economic Integration: Evidence from the EU Member States." *Review of World Economics* (*Weltwirtschaftliches Archiv*) 141 (1): 50–78.

Baier, Scott, and Jeffrey Bergstrand. 2007. "Do Free Trade Agreements Actually Increase Members' International Trade?" *Journal of International Economics* 71:72–95.

Balassa, Bela. 1961. *The Theory of Economic Integration*. Homewood, IL: Richard Irwin.

Balassa, Bela. 1966. "Tariff Reductions and Trade in Manufactures among the Industrial Countries." *American Economic Review* 56:466–473.

Baldwin, Richard. 1989. "On the Growth Effects of 1992." NBER Working Paper 3119, National Bureau of Economic Research, Cambridge, MA.

Baldwin, Richard. 2016. *The Great Convergence*. Cambridge, MA: Harvard University Press.

Baldwin, Richard, and Daria Taglioni. 2006. "Gravity for Dummies and Dummies for Gravity Equations." NBER Working Paper 12516, National Bureau of Economic Research, Cambridge, MA.

Baldwin, Richard, and Anthony Venables. 1995. "Regional Economic Integration." In *Handbook of International Economics,* vol. 3, edited by Gene Grossman and Kenneth Rogoff, 1597–1644. Amsterdam: North Holland.

Baldwin, Richard, and Charles Wyplosz. 2015. *The Economics of European Integration,* 5th ed. London: McGraw-Hill Education.

Barbero, Javier, and Ernesto Rodriguez-Crespo. 2018. "The Effect of Broadband on European Union Trade: A Regional Spatial Approach." *World Economy* 41 (11): 2895–2913.

Barone, Guglielmo, and Federico Cingano. 2011. "Service Regulation and Growth: Evidence from OECD Countries." *Economic Journal* 121 (555): 931–957.

Barro, Robert. 2015. "Convergence and Modernisation." *Economic Journal* 125 (585): 911–942.

Basevi, Giorgio, and Silvia Grassi. 1993. "The Crisis of the European Monetary System and Its Consequences for Agricultural Trade." *Review of Economic Conditions in Italy* 47:81–104.

Ben-David, Dan. 1993. "Equalizing Exchange: Trade Liberalization and Income Convergence." *Quarterly Journal of Economics* 108 (3): 653–679.

Bernard, Andrew, and Bradford Jensen. 1995. "Exporters, Jobs, and Wages in U.S. Manufacturing: 1976–1987." *Brookings Papers on Economic Activity: Microeconomics* 1995:67–119.

Bernard, Andrew, Bradford Jensen, and Peter Schott. 2006. "Trade Costs, Firms and Productivity." *Journal of Monetary Economics* 53 (5): 917–937.

Beyer, Robert, and Frank Smets. 2015. "Labour Market Adjustments in Europe and the US: How Different?" *Economic Policy* 30 (84): 643–682.

Bhagwati, Jagdish. 1993. "Regionalism and Multilateralism: An Overview." In *New Dimensions in Regional Integration,* edited by Jaime de Melo and Arvind Panagariya, 22–51. Cambridge: Cambridge University Press.

Blanchard, Olivier, Mark Griffiths, and Bertrand Gruss. 2013. "Boom, Bust, Recovery: Forensics of the Latvian Crisis." *Brookings Papers on Economic Activity* 2013 (2): 325–388.

Blanchflower, David, and Chris Shadforth. 2009. "Fear, Unemployment and Migration." *Economic Journal* 119 (535): F136–F182.

Boltho, Andrea, and Barry Eichengreen. 2008. "The Economic Impact of European Integration." CEPR Discussion Paper No. 6820, Centre for Economic Policy Research, London.

Bonvicini, Gianni. 2020. "Orbán e il contagion delle democrazie." Affari Internazionali, IAI, 10 April.

Borjas, George. 2015. Immigration and Globalization: A Review Essay." *Journal of Economic Literature* 53 (4): 961–974.

Born, Benjamin, Gernot Müller, Moritz Schularick, and Petr Sedláček. 2019. "The Costs of Economic Nationalism: Evidence from the Brexit Experiment." *Economic Journal* 129 (623): 2722–2744.

Bown, Chad. 2018. "Trade Policy towards Supply Chains after the Great Recession." *IMF Economic Review* 66 (3): 602–616.

Bozo, Frédéric. 2005. *Mitterrand, la fin de la guerre froide et l'unification allemande: De Yalta à Maastricht.* Paris: Odile Jacob.

Bozo, Frédéric. 2009. *Mitterrand, the End of the Cold War, and German Unification.* New York: Berghahn.

Breidenbach, Philipp, Timo Mitze, and Christoph Schmidt. 2019. "EU Regional Policy and the Neighbour's Curse: Analyzing the Income Convergence Effects of ESIF Funding in the Presence of Spatial Spillovers." *Journal of Common Market Studies* 57 (2): 388–405.

Brülhart, Marius. 2009. "An Account of Global Intra-Industry Trade, 1962–2006." *World Economy* 32 (3): 401–459.

Brülhart, Marius. 2011. "The Spatial Effects of Trade Openness: A Survey." *Review of World Economics (Weltwirtschaftliches Archiv)* 147 (1): 59–83.

Brunnermeier, Markus, Harold James, and Jean-Pierre Landau. 2016. *The Euro and the Battle of Ideas.* Princeton, NJ: Princeton University Press.

Bruno, Randolph, Nauro Campos, Saul Estrin, and Meng Tian. 2017. "Foreign Direct Investment and the Relationship between the United Kingdom and the European Union." In *The Economics of UK-EU Relations: From the Treaty of Rome to the Vote for Brexit,* edited by Nauro Campos and Fabrizio Coricelli, 139–173. Cham, Switzerland: Palgrave Macmillan.

Büge, Max. 2012. "Three Essays on Institutions and International Economic Relations." PhD diss., Institut d'Etudes Politiques (SciencesPo), Paris.

Cadot, Olivier, Céline Carrère, Jaime de Melo, and Bolorma Tumurchudur. 2006. "Product Specific Rules of Origin in EU and US Preferential Trading Arrangements: An Assessment." *World Trade Review* 5 (2): 199–224.

Campos, Nauro. 2019a. "B for Brexit: A Survey of the Economics Academic Literature." IZA DP No. 12134, IZA Institute of Labor Economics, Bonn.

Campos, Nauro. 2019b. "The Economics of Brexit." In *New Palgrave Dictionary of Economics.* London: Palgrave Macmillan. https://link.springer.com /referenceworkentry/10.1057/978-1-349-95121-5_3079-1.

Campos, Nauro, and Fabrizio Coricelli. 2017a. "EU Membership, Mrs Thatcher's Reforms and Britain's Economic Decline." *Comparative Economic Studies* 59 (2): 169–193.

Campos, Nauro, and Fabrizio Coricelli, eds. 2017b. *The Economics of UK-EU Relations: From the Treaty of Rome to the Vote for Brexit.* Cham, Switzerland: Palgrave Macmillan.

Campos, Nauro, Fabrizio Coricelli, and Luigi Moretti. 2014. "Economic Growth and Political Integration Estimating the Benefits from Membership in the European Union Using the Synthetic Counterfactuals Method." IZA Discussion Paper 8162, Forschungsinstitut zur Zukunft der Arbeit / The Institute for the Study of Labor, Bonn.

Campos, Nauro, Fabrizio Coricelli, and Luigi Moretti. 2019. "Institutional Integration and Economic Growth in Europe." *Journal of Monetary Economics* 103:88–104.

Campos, Nauro, Paul De Grauwe, and Yuemei Ji, eds. 2018. *The Political Economy of Structural Reforms in Europe.* Oxford: Oxford University Press.

Cecchini, Paolo, Michel Catinat, and Alexis Jacquemin. 1988. *The European Challenge 1992: The Benefits of a Single Market.* Aldershot, UK: Wildwood House.

Cernat, Lucian. 2019. "Trade Policy and Global Uncertainties: How to Promote an Open Trade Agenda." *Australian Economic Review* 52 (4): 455–461.

Charlton, Michael. 1983. *The Price of Victory.* London: British Broadcasting Corporation.

Cherry, Judith. 2018. "The Hydra Revisited: Expectations and Perceptions of the Impact of the EU-Korea Free Trade Agreement." *Asia Europe Journal* 16 (1): 19–35.

Chlopcik, Tomas. 2018. "Automotive Industry in the Visegrád Group." Paper presented at the 7th Business and Management Conference, Budapest, 6–8 June. https://iises.net/proceedings/7th-business-management-conference -budapest/table-of-content/detail?article=automotive-industry-in-the -visegrad-group.

Cipollina, Maria, David Laborde Debucquet, and Luca Salvatici. 2017. "The Tide that does not raise all boats: An assessment of EU preferential trade policies." *Review of World Economics* 153(1): 199–231.

Claasen, Rutger, Anna Gerbrandy, Sebastiaan Princen, and Mathiei Segers. 2019. "Rethinking the European Social Market Economy: Introduction to the Special Issue." *Journal of Common Market Studies* 57 (1): 3–12.

Clapp, Alexander. 2020. "Europe Turns Its Back on Refugees—and Its Own Values: Clashes on the Greek Border with Turkey Reveal the EU's Failings." *Foreign Affairs*, 17 March. https://www.foreignaffairs.com/articles/greece/2020-03-17/europe-turns-its-back-refugees-and-its-own-values.

Cockfield, Arthur. 1994. *The European Union: Creating the Single Market.* Chichester, UK: Wiley Chancery Law.

Corden, W. Max. 1972. "Economies of Scale and Customs Union Theory." *Journal of Political Economy* 80 (3): 465–475.

Crafts, Nicholas. 2016. "West European Economic Integration since 1950." In *Routledge Handbook of Economics of European Integration*, edited by Harald Badinger and Volker Nitsch, 3–21. London: Routledge.

Crescenzi, Riccardo, Marco Di Cataldo, and Andrés Rodríguez-Pose. 2016. "Government Quality and the Economic Returns of Transport Infrastructure Investment in European Regions." *Journal of Regional Science* 56:555–582.

Crescenzi, Riccardo, and Andrés Rodríguez-Pose. 2012. "Infrastructure and Regional Growth in the European Union." *Papers in Regional Science* 91 (3): 487–513.

Cruces, Juan, and Christoph Trebesch. 2013. "Sovereign Defaults: The Price of Haircuts." *American Economic Journal: Macroeconomics* 5 (3): 85–117.

Dao, Mai, Davide Furceri, and Prakash Loungani. 2014. "Regional Labor Market Adjustments in the United States and Europe." IMF Working Paper No. 14/26, International Monetary Fund, Washington, DC.

De Grauwe, Paul. 2000. *The Economics of Monetary Union*, 4th rev. ed. Oxford: Oxford University Press.

De Sadeleer, Nicolas. 2014. *EU Environmental Law and the Internal Market.* Oxford: Oxford University Press.

Dhingra, Swati, Hanwei Huang, Gianmarco Ottaviano, João Paulo Pessoa, Thomas Sampson, and John Van Reenen. 2017. "The Costs and Benefits of Leaving the EU: Trade Effects." *Economic Policy* 32 (92): 651–705.

Djankov, Simeon. 2017. "The City of London after Brexit." Policy Brief 17–9, Peterson Institute for International Economics, Washington, DC.

Dixon, Peter, Michael Jerie, and Maureen Rimmer. 2016. "Modern Trade Theory for CGE Modelling: The Armington, Krugman and Melitz Models." *Journal of Global Economic Analysis* 1 (1): 1–110.

Dixon, Peter, Michael Jerie, and Maureen Rimmer. 2018. *Trade Theory in Computable General Equilibrium Models.* Singapore: Springer Nature.

Drysdale, Peter, and Mari Pangestu. 2019. "RCEP Is Now Vital in Defending the Global Trading Order." *East Asia Forum,* 4 August. https://www .eastasiaforum.org/?p=197289?utm_source=newsletter&utm_medium =email&utm_campaign=newsletter2019-08-04.

Duchêne, François. 1994. *Jean Monnet: The First Statesman of Interdependence.* New York: Norton.

Dür, Andreas, Jappe Eckhardt, and Arlo Poletti. 2020. "Global Value Chains, the Anti-Globalization Backlash, and EU Trade Policy: A Research Agenda." *Journal of European Public Policy* 27 (6): 944–956.

Dustmann, Christian, Francesco Fasani, Tommaso Frattini, Luigi Minale, and Uta Schonberg. 2017. "On the Economics and Politics of Refugee Migration." *Economic Policy* 32 (91): 497–535.

Dustmann, Christian, Tommaso Frattini, and Ian Preston. 2013. "The Effect of Immigration along the Distribution of Wages." *Review of Economic Studies* 80 (1): 145–173.

Eichengreen, Barry. 2007. *The European Economy since 1945: Coordinated Capitalism and Beyond.* Princeton, NJ: Princeton University Press.

Eichengreen, Barry. 2019. "The Euro after Meseberg." *Review of World Economics (Weltwirtschaftliches Archiv)* 155 (1): 15–22.

Eichengreen, Barry, and Andrea Boltho. 2010. "The Economic Impact of European Integration." In *The Cambridge Economic History of Modern Europe, volume 2 1870 to the Present,* edited by Stephen Broadberry and Kevin O'Rourke, 267–295. Cambridge: Cambridge University Press.

Emter, Lorenz, Martin Schmitz, and Marcel Tirpák. 2019. "Cross-Border Banking in the EU since the Crisis: What Is Driving the Great Retrenchment?" *Review of World Economics (Weltwirtschaftliches Archiv)* 155 (2): 287–326.

Erixon, Fredrik, and Hosuk Lee-Makiyama. 2010. "Stepping into Asia's Growth Markets: Dispelling Myths about the EU-Korea Free Trade Agreement." ECIPE Policy Brief No. 3/2010, European Centre for International Political Economy, Brussels.

Falkenberg, Karl. 2019. "Trade Policy: Is There a Way Back to Global Governance? A European View." In *Perspectives on the Soft Power of EU Trade Policy,* edited by San Bilal and Bernard Hoekman, 31–36. London: Centre for Economic Policy Research.

Farhi, Emmanuel, and Jean Tirole. 2018. "Deadly Embrace: Sovereign and Financial Balance Sheets Doom Loops." *Review of Economic Studies* 85 (3): 1781–1823.

Fauri, Francesca. 1996. "The Role of Fiat in the Development of the Italian Car Industry in the 1950's." *Business History Review* 70 (2): 167–206.

Fella, Stefano. 2018. "UK Adoption of the EU's External Agreements after Brexit." Briefing Paper No. 8370, House of Commons Library, London.

Fernández, Cristina, and Pilar García Perea. 2015. "The Impact of the Euro on Euro Area GDP per Capita." Working Paper No. 1530, Banco de España, Madrid.

Findlay, Christopher, Xianjia Ye, and Hein Roelfsma. 2019. "Documenting Three Trends in Commercial Services Trade." Paper presented at the Trade and Investment in Services Association Annual Conference, University of Bern, 20 September.

Fujita, Masahisa, Paul Krugman, and Anthony Venables. 2001. *The Spatial Economy: Cities, Regions, and International Trade.* Cambridge, MA: MIT Press.

Gertler, Mark, and Simon Gilchrist. 2018. "What Happened: Financial Factors in the Great Recession." *Journal of Economic Perspectives* 32 (3): 3–30.

Gilbert, Mark. 2012. *European Integration: A Concise History.* Lanham, MD: Rowman and Littlefield.

Gillingham, John. 1995. "The European Coal and Steel Community: An Object Lesson?" In *Europe's Postwar Recovery,* edited by Barry Eichengreen, 151–168. Cambridge: Cambridge University Press.

Glick, Reuven. 2017. "Currency Unions and Regional Trade Agreements: EMU and EU Effects on Trade." *Comparative Economic Studies* 59 (2): 194–209.

Glick, Reuven, and Andrew Rose. 2016. "Currency Unions and Trade: A Post-EMU Assessment." *European Economic Review* 87:78–91.

Goldmann, Kathrin, and Jan Wessel. 2020. "TEN-T Corridors—Stairway to Heaven or Highway to Hell?" Institute of Transport Economics Working Paper No.31, Westfälische Wilhelms-Universität, Münster, Germany.

González, Anabel. 2019. "The EU-Mercosur Trade Accord Sends a Signal to the World's Protectionists." *Peterson Institute for International Economics Trade and Investment Policy Watch,* 2 July. https://www.piie.com/blogs/trade-investment-policy-watch/eu-mercosur-trade-accord-sends-signal-worlds-protectionists.

González, Anabel, and Nicolas Véron. 2019. "EU Trade Policy amid the China-US Clash: Caught in the Cross-Fire?" Working Paper 19–13, Peterson Institute for International Economics, Washington, DC.

Grant, Charles. 1994. *Delors: Inside the House that Jacques Built*. London: Nicholas Brealey.

Graziano, Alejandro, Kyle Handley, and Nuno Limão. 2018. "Brexit Uncertainty and Trade Disintegration." NBER Working Paper No. 25334, National Bureau of Economic Research, Cambridge, MA.

Graziano, Alejandro, Kyle Handley, and Nuno Limão. 2020. "Brexit Uncertainty: Trade Externalities beyond Europe." *AEA Papers and Proceedings* 110:552–556. https://doi.org/10.1257/pandp.20201021.

Graziano, Paolo, and Miriam Hartlapp. 2019. "The End of Social Europe? Understanding EU social policy change." *Journal of European Public Policy*, 26: 1484–1501.

Grech, John. 1978. *Threads of Dependence*. Msida: University of Malta Press.

Grieveson, Richard, Julia Grübler, and Mario Holzner. 2018. "Western Balkans EU Accession: Is the 2025 Target Date Realistic?" Policy Notes and Reports 22, Vienna Institute for International Economic Studies (WIIW), Vienna.

Griffith, Rachel, Rupert Harrison, and Helen Simpson. 2010. "Product Market Reform and Innovation in the EU." *Scandinavian Journal of Economics* 112 (2): 389–415.

Gros, Daniel. 2012. *The Treaty on Stability, Coordination and Governance in the Economic and Monetary Union*. Brussels: Centre for European Policy Studies.

Grossman, Gene, and Elhanan Helpman. 1991. *Innovation and Growth in the Global Economy*. Cambridge, MA: MIT Press.

Grubel, Herbert, and Peter Lloyd. 1975. *Intra-Industry Trade: The Theory and Measurement of International Trade in Differentiated Products*. London: Macmillan.

Guillen, Jordi, Frank Asche, Natacha Carvalho, José Fernández Polanco, Ignacio Llorente, Rasmus Nielsen, Max Nielsen, and Sebastian Villasante. 2019. "Aquaculture Subsidies in the European Union: Evolution, Impact and Future Potential for Growth." *Marine Policy* 104:19–28.

Hamilton, Bob, and John Whalley. 1984. "Efficiency and Distributional Implications of Global Restrictions on Labour Mobility: Calculations and Policy Implications." *Journal of Development Economics* 14:61–75.

Handley, Kyle, and Nuno Limão. 2015. "Trade and Investment under Policy Uncertainty: Theory and Firm Evidence." *American Economic Journal: Economic Policy* 7 (4): 189–222.

Handley, Kyle, and Nuno Limão. 2017. "Policy Uncertainty, Trade, and Welfare: Theory and Evidence for China and the United States." *American Economic Review* 107 (9): 2731–2783.

Hantzsche, Arno, Amit Kara, and Garry Young. 2019. "The Economic Effects of the UK Government's Proposed Brexit Deal." *World Economy* 42 (1): 5–20.

Hare, Paul, and Richard Stoneman. 2017. "The Evolving Architecture of Europe: Functioning or Dysfunctional for the Twenty-First Century?" *Comparative Economic Studies* 59 (4): 433–471.

Hatton, Tim. 2017. "Refugees and Asylum Seekers, the Crisis in Europe and the Future of Policy." *Economic Policy* 32 (91): 447–487.

Head, Keith, and Thierry Mayer. 2015. "Gravity Equations: Workhorse, Toolkit, and Cookbook." In *Handbook of International Economics,* vol. 4, edited by Elhanan Helpman, Kenneth Rogoff, and Gita Gopinath, 131–195. Amsterdam: North-Holland.

Head, Keith, and Thierry Mayer. 2019. "Brands in Motion: How Frictions Shape Multinational Production." *American Economic Review* 109 (9): 3073–3124.

Heinz, Frigyes Ferdinand, and Melanie Ward-Warmedinger. 2006. "Cross-Border Labour Mobility within an Enlarged EU." ECB Occasional Paper No. 52, European Central Bank, Frankfurt.

Henrekson, Magnus, Johan Torstensson, and Rasha Torstensson. 1997. "Growth Effects of European Integration." *European Economic Review* 41 (8): 1537–1557.

Hu, Michael, Christine Jiang, and Christos Tsoukalas. 2004. "The Volatility Impact of the European Monetary System on Member and Non-Member Currencies." *Applied Financial Economics* 14:313–325.

Huart, Florence, and Médédé Tchakpalla. 2019. "Labor Market Conditions and Geographic Mobility in the Eurozone." *Comparative Economic Studies* 61 (2): 263–284.

Hummels, David. 2007. "Transportation Costs and International Trade in the Second Era of Globalization." *Journal of Economic Perspectives* 21:131–154.

Hummels, David, and Georg Schaur. 2013. "Time as a Trade Barrier." *American Economic Review* 103 (7): 2935–2959.

Hurley, John, Scott Morris, and Gailyn Portelance. 2018. "Examining the Debt Implications of the Belt and Road Initiative from a Policy Perspective." CGD Policy Paper No. 121, Center for Global Development, Washington, DC.

Ibáñez Colomo, Pablo, and Andriani Kalintiri. 2020. "The Evolution of EU Antitrust Policy: 1966–2017." *Modern Law Review* 83 (2): 321–372.

Ilzkovitz, Fabienne, Adrian Dierx, Viktoria Kovacs, and Nuno Sousa. 2007. "Steps towards a Deeper Economic Integration: The Internal Market in the 21st Century." European Economy—Economic Papers 271, Directorate General Economic and Financial Affairs, European Commission, Brussels.

Inomata, Satoshi. 2017. "Analytical Framework for Global Value Chains: An Overview." In *Global Value Chain Development Report 2017*, 15–35. Washington, DC: World Bank.

Jakóbowski, Jakub, and Konrad Popławski. 2018. "China's Offer to the EU: Tough Negotiations or a Coalition against Trump?" OSW Commentary 2018-08-23, Ośrodek Studiów Wschodnich (Centre for Eastern Studies), Warsaw.

Jensen, Mads Dagnis, and Peter Nedergaard. 2012. "From 'Frankenstein' to 'Toothless Vampire'? Explaining the Watering Down of the Services Directive." *Journal of European Public Policy* 19 (6): 844–862.

Johnson, Robert, and Guillermo Noguera. 2012. "Proximity and Production Fragmentation." *American Economic Review* 102 (3): 407–411.

Johnson, Robert, and Guillermo Noguera. 2017. "A Portrait of Trade in Value-Added over Four Decades." *Review of Economics and Statistics* 99 (5): 896–911.

Jones, Erik, Anand Menon, and Stephen Weatherill, eds. 2012. *Oxford Handbook of the European Union*. Oxford: Oxford University Press.

Krugman, Paul. 1979. "Increasing Returns, Monopolistic Competition and International Trade." *Journal of International Economics* 9:469–479.

Krugman, Paul. 1980. "Scale Economies, Product Differentiation and the Pattern of Trade." *American Economic Review* 70:950–959.

Krugman, Paul. 1991. *Geography and Trade*. Cambridge, MA: MIT Press.

Krugman, Paul. 1993. "What Do We Need to Know about the International Monetary System." Princeton Essays in International Finance No.190, International Finance Section, Princeton University, Princeton, NJ.

Laffan, Brigid. 2019. "How the EU27 Came to Be." *Journal of Common Market Studies* 57 (S1): 13–27.

Laffan, Brigid, and Johannes Lindner. 2015. "The Budget: Who Gets What, When and How?" In *Policy-Making in the European Union*, 7th ed., edited by Helen Wallace, Mark Pollack, and Alasdair Young, 220–242. Oxford: Oxford University Press.

Lalinsky, Tibor, and Jaanika Merik'll. 2019. "The Effect of the Single Currency on Exports: Comparative Firm-Level Evidence." NBS Working Paper 1/2019, Národná Banka Slovenska, Bratislava.

Lehmann, Hartmut, Tiziano Razzolini, and Anzelika Zaiceva. 2020. "The Great Recession and Labor Market Adjustment: Evidence from Latvia." *Comparative Economic Studies* 62 (1): 149–181.

Lehtimäki, Jonne, and David Sondermann. 2020. "Baldwin vs. Cecchini Revisited: The Growth Impact of the European Single Market." ECB Working Paper Series No. 2392, European Central Bank, Frankfurt.

Lewis, Michael. 2010. "Beware of Greeks Bearing Bonds." *Vanity Fair,* 1 October.

Lim, Darren, Michalis Moutselos, and Michael McKenna. 2019. "Puzzled Out? The Unsurprising Outcomes of the Greek Bailout Negotiations." *Journal of European Public Policy* 26 (3): 325–343.

Limão, Nuno, and Anthony Venables. 2001. "Infrastructure, Geographical Disadvantage, Transport Costs, and Trade." *World Bank Economic Review* 15 (3): 451–479.

Lodefalk, Magnus. 2014. "The Role of Services for Manufacturing Firm Exports." *Review of World Economics (Weltwirtschaftliches Archiv)* 150 (1): 59–82.

Lodefalk, Magnus. 2017. "Servicification of Firms and Trade Policy Implications." *World Trade Review* 16 (1): 59–83.

Longhi, Simonetta, and Magdalena Rokicka. 2012. "European Immigrants in the UK before and after the 2004 Enlargement: Is There a Change in Immigrant Self-Selection?" ISER Working Paper 2012–22, Institute for Social and Economic Research, University of Essex, Colchester, UK.

Lourie, Julia. 2004. "Employment Law and the Social Chapter." In *Britain in the European Union: Law, Policy and Parliament,* edited by Philip Giddings and Gavin Drewry, 121–144. London: Palgrave Macmillan.

Luke, David, and Heini Suominen. 2019. "Towards Rethinking the Economic Partnership Agreements." In *Perspectives on the Soft Power of EU Trade Policy,* edited by San Bilal and Bernard Hoekman, 143–150. London: Centre for Economic Policy Research.

Macmillan, Margaret. 2001. *Peacemakers: The Paris Conference of 1919 and Its Attempt to End War.* London: J. Murray.

Macmillan, Margaret. 2002. *Paris 1919: Six Months that Changed the World.* New York: Random House.

Mariniello, Mario, André Sapir, and Alessio Terzi. 2015. "The Long Road towards the European Single Market." Bruegel Working Paper 2015 / 01, Brussels.

Markovic Khaze, Nina. 2018. "European Union's Enlargement Fatigue: Russia's and China's Rise in Southeast Europe?" *Australian and New Zealand Journal of European Studies* 10 (1): 48–63.

Mayes, David. 1978. "The Effects of Economic Integration on Trade." *Journal of Common Market Studies* 17:1–25.

McCallum, John. 1995. "National Borders Matter: Canada-US Regional Trade Patterns." *American Economic Review* 85 (3): 615–623.

McKinnon, Ronald. 1963. "Optimum Currency Areas." *American Economic Review* 53:717–725.

McNeill, Jeffrey. 2020. "Exporting Environmental Objectives or Erecting Trade Barriers in Recent EU Trade Agreements." *Australian and New Zealand Journal of European Studies* 12 (1): 40–53.

Melitz, Marc. 2003. "The Impact of Trade on Intra-Industry Reallocations and Aggregate Industry Productivity." *Econometrica* 71 (6): 1695–1725.

Mihaljek, Dubravko, and Marc Klau. 2003. "The Balassa-Samuelson Effect in Central Europe: A Disaggregated Analysis." BIS Working Papers No 143, Monetary and Economic Department, Bank for International Settlements, Basel.

Minford, Patrick. 2019. "The Effects of Brexit on the UK Economy." *World Economy* 42 (1): 57–67.

Monastiriotis, Vassilis, and Ivan Zilic. 2019. "The Economic Effects of Political Disintegration: Lessons from Serbia and Montenegro." ETZ Working Paper EZ-WP-1903, Ekonomiski Institut, Zagreb.

Monteagudo, Josefina, Aleksander Rutkowski, and Dimitri Lorenzani. 2012. "The Economic Impact of the Services Directive: A First Assessment Following Implementation." European Economy Economic Papers 456, European Commission, Brussels.

Mountford, Andrew, and Jonathan Wadsworth. 2019. "Trainspotting: 'Good Jobs,' Training and Skilled Immigration." CReAM Discussion Paper Series 1907, Centre for Research and Analysis of Migration, Department of Economics, University College London, London.

Mulabdic, Alen, Alberto Osnago, and Michele Ruta. 2017. "Deep Integration and UK-EU Trade Relations." Policy Research Working Paper 7947, World Bank, Washington, DC.

Mundell, Robert. 1961. "Theory of Optimum Currency Areas." *American Economic Review* 51:657–665.

Mundell, Robert. 1964. "Tariff Preferences and the Terms of Trade." *Manchester School of Economic and Social Studies* 32:1–13.

Murray, Philomena. 2019. "From Friction to Free Trade Negotiations: Australia's Engagement with the European Union." *Australian Economic Review* 52 (4): 448–454.

Nelli Feroci, Ferdinando. 2020. "EU–UK Relations after the High Level Conference." IAI Commentary 20 / 45, Istituto Affari Internazionali, Rome.

Nguyen, Hoang Sang, and Fabien Rondeau. 2019. "The Transmission of Business Cycles: Lessons from the 2004 Enlargement of the EU and the Adoption of the Euro." *Economics of Transition and Institutional Change* 27 (3): 729–743.

Nordås, Hildegunn Kyvik, and Dorothée Rouzet. 2015. "The Impact of Services Trade Restrictiveness on Trade Flows." OECD Trade Policy Paper No. 178, Organisation for Economic Co-operation and Development, Paris.

Obstfeld, Maurice, and Kenneth Rogoff. 2000. "'The Six Major Puzzles' in International Macroeconomics: Is There a Common Cause?" In *NBER Macroeconomics Annual 2000*, 339–390. Cambridge, MA: MIT Press.

Oehler-Sincai, Iulia Monica. 2018. "16 + 1, a New Issue in China-EU Relations?" China-CEE Institute Working Paper 2018 No. 1, China-CEE Institute, Budapest.

Ordóñez-De-Haro, José Manuel, Joan-Ramon Borrell, and Juan Luis Jiménez. 2018. "The European Commission's Fight against Cartels (1962–2014): A Retrospective and Forensic Analysis." *Journal of Common Market Studies* 56 (5): 1087–1107.

O'Rourke, Kevin. 2018. *Une brève histoire du Brexit.* Paris: Odile Jacob.

O'Rourke, Kevin. 2019. *A Short History of Brexit from Brentry to Backstop.* London: Pelican.Papi, Laura, Emil Stavrev, and Volodymyr Tulin. 2018. "Central, Eastern, and Southeastern European Countries' Convergence: A Look at the Past and Considerations for the Future." *Comparative Economic Studies* 60 (2): 271–290.

Pavlinek, Petr. 2016. "Whose Success? The State–Foreign Capital Nexus and the Development of the Automotive Industry in Slovakia." *European Urban and Regional Studies* 23 (4): 571–593.

Pelkmans, Jacques. 2006. *Economic Integration, Methods and Economic Analysis,* 3rd ed. Harlow, UK: Financial Times.

Pelkmans, Jacques. 2016. "Why the Single Market Remains the EU's Core Business." *West European Politics* 39 (5): 1095–1113.

Pelkmans, Jacques. 2019. *Contribution to Growth: The Single Market for Services. Delivering Economic Benefits for Citizens and Businesses.* Brussels: Policy Department for Economic, Scientific and Quality of Life Policies, European Parliament.

Pelkmans, Jacques, and Anabela Correia De Brito. 2012. *Enforcement in the EU Single Market.* Brussels: Centre for European Policy Studies.

Petith, Howard. 1977. "European Integration and the Terms of Trade." *Economic Journal* 87:262–272.

Petroni, Nadia. 2020. "EU Integration and Policy (In)coherence towards Irregular Migration." In *The Future of the European Union: Demisting the Debate,* edited by Mark Harwood, Stefano Moncada, and Roderick Pace, 230–241. Msida: University of Malta Press.

Petrovic, Milenko. 2020. "The Post-Communist Transition of the Western Balkans: Europeanisation with a Small Enlargement Carrot." In *30 Years since the Fall of the Berlin Wall: Turns and Twists in Economies, Politics, and Societies in the Post-Communist Countries,* edited by Alexandr Akimov and Gennadi Kazakevitch, 57–82. Singapore: Palgrave Macmillan.

Plummer, Michael. 1991a. "Ex-Post Empirical Estimates of the Second Enlargement: The Case of Greece." *Weltwirtschaftliches Archiv* 127 (1): 171–182.

Plummer, Michael. 1991b. "Efficiency Effects of the Accessions of Spain and Portugal to the EC." *Journal of Common Market Studies* 29 (3): 317–325.

Pomfret, Richard. 1981. "The Impact of EEC Enlargement on Non-Member Countries' Exports to the EEC." *Economic Journal* 91:726–729.

Pomfret, Richard. 1986. *Mediterranean Policy of the European Community: A Study of Discrimination in Trade.* London: Macmillan.

Pomfret, Richard. 1991. "The Secret of the EMS's Longevity." *Journal of Common Market Studies* 29:623–633.

Pomfret, Richard. 2001. *The Economics of Regional Trading Arrangements.* Oxford: Oxford University Press.

Pomfret, Richard. 2002. *Constructing a Market Economy: Diverse Paths from Central Planning in Asia and Europe.* Cheltenham, UK: Edward Elgar.

Pomfret, Richard. 2005. "Currency Areas in Theory and Practice." *Economic Record* 81 (253): 166–176.

Pomfret, Richard. 2010. "The Financial Sector and the Future of Capitalism." *Economic Systems* 34 (1): 22–37.

Pomfret, Richard. 2011. *The Age of Equality: The Twentieth Century in Economic Perspective.* Cambridge, MA: Harvard University Press.

Pomfret, Richard. 2014. "Expanding the Division of Labour: Trade Costs and Supply Chains in the Global Economy." *Australian Economic History Review* 54 (3): 220–241.

Pomfret, Richard. 2016a. *International Trade: Theory, Evidence and Policy.* Singapore: World Scientific.

Pomfret, Richard. 2016b. "Currency Union and Disunion in Europe and the Former Soviet Union." *CESifo Forum* 17 (4): 43–47.

Pomfret, Richard. 2019a. "The Eurasian Land Bridge: Linking Regional Value Chains along the New Silk Road." *Cambridge Journal of Regions, Economy and Society* 12 (1): 45–56.

Pomfret, Richard. 2019b. "The Eurasian Landbridge and China's Belt and Road Initiative: Demand, Supply of Services, and Public Policy." *World Economy* 42(6): 1642–1693.

Pomfret, Richard, and Patricia Sourdin. 2011. "Why Do Trade Costs Vary?" *Review of World Economics (Weltwirtschaftliches Archiv)* 146 (4): 709–730.

Pomfret, Richard, and Patricia Sourdin. 2017. "Where Will Your Next Holden Come From? The 2004 EU Enlargement and Trade with Australia." *Australian Economic Review* 50 (2): 181–194.

Pomfret, Richard, and Patricia Sourdin. 2018. "Value Chains in Europe and Asia: Which Countries Participate?" *International Economics* 153:34–41.

Puzzello, Laura, and Pedro Gomis-Porqueras. 2018. "Winners and Losers from the Euro." *European Economic Review* 108):129–152.

Reinhart, Carmen. 2019. "The Curious Case of the Missing Defaults." AEI Economics Working Paper 2019-05, American Enterprise Institute, Washington, DC.

Ricardo, David. 1817. *On the Principles of Political Economy and Taxation.* London: John Murray.

Rivera-Batiz, Luis, and Paul Romer. 1991. "Economic Integration and Endogenous Growth." *Quarterly Journal of Economics* 106 (2): 531–555.

Roederer-Rynning, Christilla. 2015. "The Common Agricultural Policy: The Fortress Challenged." In *Policy-Making in the European Union*, 7th ed., edited by Helen Wallace, Mark Pollack, and Alasdair Young, 196–219. Oxford: Oxford University Press.

Roos, Jerome. 2019. *Why Not Default? The Political Economy of Sovereign Debt.* Princeton, NJ: Princeton University Press.

Rose, Andrew. 2000. "One Money, One Market: The Effect of Common Currencies on Trade." *Economic Policy* 30:9–45.

Rose, Andrew, and Eric van Wincoop. 2001. "National Money as a Barrier to Trade: The Real Case for Monetary Union." *American Economic Review* 91 (2): 386–390.

Roth, Felix, Lars Jonung, and Felicitas Nowak-Lehmann. 2016. "Crisis and Public Support for the Euro, 1990–2014." *Journal of Common Market Studies* 54 (4): 944–960.

Ruta, Michele. 2017. "Preferential Trade Agreements and Global Value Chains: Theory, Evidence, and Open Questions." In *Global Value Chain Development Report 2017*, 175–185. Washington, DC: World Bank.

Saia, Alessandro. 2017. "Choosing the Open Sea: The Cost to the UK of Staying Out of the Euro." *Journal of International Economics* 108 (3): 82–98.

Sampson, Thomas. 2017. "Brexit: The Economics of International Disintegration." *Journal of Economic Perspectives* 31 (4): 163–184.

Santos, Tano. 2017. "El Diluvio: The Spanish Banking Crisis, 2008–12." Columbia Research Archive. https//www8.gsb.columbia.edu/researcharchive/articles/25448.

Sapir, André. 1992. "Regional Integration in Europe." *Economic Journal* 102: 1491–1506.

Sapir, André. 2011. "European Integration at the Crossroads: A Review Essay on the 50th Anniversary of Bela Balassa's 'Theory of Economic Integration.'" *Journal of Economic Literature* 49 (4): 1200–1229.

Schoenmaker, Dirk. 2017. "The UK Financial Sector and EU Integration after Brexit: The Issue of Passporting." In *The Economics of UK-EU Relations: From the Treaty of Rome to the Vote for Brexit*, edited by Nauro Campos and Fabrizio Coricelli, 119–138. Cham, Switzerland: Palgrave Macmillan.

Schumacher, Tobias, Andreas Marchetti, and Thomas Demmelhuber, eds. 2018. *Routledge Handbook on the European Neighbourhood Policy*. London: Routledge.

Serwicka, Ilona, and Nicolò Tamberi. 2018. "Not Backing Britain: FDI Inflows since the Brexit Referendum." Briefing Paper 23, UK Trade Policy Observer, University of Sussex, Brighton, UK.

Smith, Adam. 1776. *An Inquiry into the Nature and Causes of the Wealth of Nations*. London: Strahan and Cadell.

Solow, Robert. 1956. "A Contribution to the Theory of Economic Growth." *Quarterly Journal of Economics* 65:65–94.

Sourdin, Patricia, and Richard Pomfret. 2012. *Trade Facilitation: Defining, Measuring, Explaining and Reducing the Cost of International Trade.* Cheltenham, UK: Edward Elgar.

Stanojevic, Savo, Qiu Bin, and Chen Jian. 2020. "Sino-EU15 Export Competition in Central and Eastern Europe: Is China Crowding Out Exports from the EU15?" *Eastern European Economics* 58 (3): 264–282.

Stiglitz, Joseph. 2016. *The Euro: How a Common Currency Threatens the Future of Europe.* New York: Norton.

Štofková, Jana, Stanislav Štofko, and Katarína Gašová. 2017. "Some Aspects of Industrial Policy in Slovakia." Paper presented at the 30th International Academic Conference, Venice, 24–27 April. https://iises.net/proceedings/30th -international-academic-conference-venice/table-of-content/detail?article =some-aspects-of-industrial-policy-in-slovakia.

Swinbank, Alan, and Carsten Daugbjerg. 2017. "The Changed Architecture of the EU's Agricultural Policy over Four Decades." In *Australia, the European Union and the New Trade Agenda,* edited by Annmarie Elijah, Don Kenyon, Karen Hussey, and Pierre van der Eng, 77–95. Canberra: Australian National University Press.

Szolucha, Anna. 2010. "The EU and 'Enlargement Fatigue': Why Has the European Union Not Been Able to Counter 'Enlargement Fatigue'?" *Journal of Contemporary European Research* 6 (1): 107–122.

Tinbergen, Jan. 1965. *International Economic Integration,* 2nd ed. Amsterdam: Elsevier.

Tocci, Nathalie. 2015. "Towards an EU Global Strategy." In *Towards an EU Global Strategy: Background, Process, References,* edited by Antonio Missiroli, 115–120. Paris: EU Institute for Security Studies.

Trebesch, Christoph, and Michael Zabel. 2017. "The Output Costs of Hard and Soft Sovereign Default." *European Economic Review* 92:416–432.

Trefler, Daniel. 1995. "The Case of the Missing Trade and Other Mysteries." *American Economic Review* 85 (6): 1029–1046.

Trichet, Jean-Claude. 2019. "The Euro after Twenty Years Is a Historic Success." *Review of World Economics (Weltwirtschaftliches Archiv)* 155 (1): 5–14.

Usherwood, Simon, and John Pinder. 2018. *The European Union: A Very Short Introduction,* 4th ed. Oxford: Oxford University Press.

Utton, Michael. 2006. *International Competition Policy: Maintaining Open Markets in the Global Economy.* Cheltenham, UK: Edward Elgar.

Vandenbussche, Hylke, William Connell, and Wouter Simons. 2017. "Global Value Chains, Trade Shocks and Jobs: An Application to Brexit." CEPR Discussion Paper 1230, Centre for Economic Policy Research, London.

Vanhoudt, Patrick. 1999. "Did the European Integration Induce Economic Growth? In Search of Scale Effects and Persistent Changes." *Review of World Economics (Weltwirtschaftliches Archiv)* 135 (2): 193–220.

Varkkey, Helena. 2020. "Palm Oil Politics Still Threaten EU-Malaysia Ties." *East Asia Forum,* 2 April.

Versan, Patrik, and Francesco Corti. 2019. "New Tensions over Social Europe? The European Pillar of Social Rights and the Debate within the European Parliament." *Journal of Common Market Studies* 57 (5): 977–994.

Veugelers, Reinhilde. 2004. "Industrial Concentration, Market Integration and Efficiency in the European Union." In *European Integration and the Functioning of Product Markets,* edited by Adriaan Dierx, Fabienne Ilzkovitz, and Khalid Sekkat, 84–112. Cheltenham, UK: Edward Elgar.

Viner, Jacob. 1950. *The Customs Union Issue.* New York: Carnegie Endowment for International Peace.

VoxEU. 2019. "£350 Million a Week: The Output Cost of the Brexit Vote." VoxEU, 29 May. https://voxeu.org/article/300-million-week-output-cost -brexit-vote.

Wadsworth, Jonathan. 2018. "Off EU Go? Brexit, the UK Labour Market and Immigration." *Fiscal Studies* 39 (4): 625–649.

Wallace, Helen, Mark Pollack, and Alasdair Young. 2015. *Policy-Making in the European Union,* 7th ed. Oxford: Oxford University Press.

Walton, Simon. 2019. "TEN-T and New Silk Road Integration—Top Priority in 2020." RailFreight.com, 27 December. https://www.railfreight.com /beltandroad/2019/12/27/ten-t-and-new-silk-road-integration-top-priority -in-2020/.

Wilks, Stephen. 2015. "Competition Policy: Defending the Economic Constitution." In *Policy-Making in the European Union,* 7th ed., edited by Helen Wallace, Mark Pollack, and Alasdair Young, 141–165. Oxford: Oxford University Press.

Wilson, John K., and Richard Pomfret. 2014. *Public Policy and Professional Sports.* Cheltenham, UK: Edward Elgar.

Winters, L. Alan. 1987. "Britain in Europe: A Survey of Quantitative Trade Studies." *Journal of Common Market Studies* 25:315–335.

Xing Yuqing. 2019. "Global Value Chains and the Innovation of the Chinese Mobile Phone Industry." GRIPS Discussion Paper 19–14, National Graduate Institute for Policy Studies, Tokyo.

Yannopoulos, George. 1990. "Foreign Direct Investment and European Integration: The Evidence from the Formative Years of the European Community." *Journal of Common Market Studies* 28 (3): 235–259.

Yotov, Yoto, Roberta Piermartini, José-Antonio Monteiro, and Mario Larch. 2016. *An Advanced Guide to Trade Policy Analysis: The Structural Gravity Model.* Geneva: World Trade Organization.

Young, Hugo. 1998. *This Blessed Plot: Britain and Europe from Churchill to Blair.* London: Macmillan.

Youngs, Richard. 2020. "Geopolitics and the COVID-19 Pandemic: A Distorted Turn in EU External Relations." European Policy Analysis, Swedish Institute for European Policy Studies (SIEPS), Stockholm.

Zhelyazkova, Asya, Ivan Damjanovski, Zoran Nechev, and Frank Schimmelfennig. 2019. "European Union Conditionality in the Western Balkans: External Incentives and Europeanisation." In *The Europeanisation of the Western Balkans: A Failure of EU Conditionality?*, edited by Jelena Džankić, Soeren Keil, and Marko Kmezić, 15–37. Cham, Switzerland: Palgrave Macmillan.

Index

Recurring words like the names of EU member countries, Europe or euro are excluded.
t refers to Table, f to Figure, n refers to endnote.